BAKING BREAD

Old and New Traditions

By Beth Hensperger

Photography by
Joyce Oudkerk Pool

Chronicle Books • San Francisco

ACKNOWLEDGMENTS

Thank you to DL and Martha Casselman for technical and moral support; to Sue White for her stylistic flair; and to Gibson Sheid for lending a hand.

Thank you to Daniel Bowe and Sandra Griswold for props from their personal collections; to Missy Hamilton for her beautiful handmade surfaces; to Sue Fisher King for her amber platter; and especially to Lynn and Arnold Scher of Beaver Bros. Antiques for wonderful furniture and many antiques.

Printed in Hong Kong.

LIBRARY OF CONGRESS CATALOGING-IN-PUBLICATION DATA

Hensperger, Beth.
   Baking bread : old and new traditions / by Beth Hensperger ; photography by Joyce Oudkerk Pool.
      p.   cm.
   ISBN 0-8118-0228-0 (hb). —
   ISBN 0-8118-0078-4 (pb).
   1. Bread.   I. Title.
TX769.H43   1992
641.8′15 — dc20   92-2899
                                       CIP

Book and Cover Design:
Ingalls + Associates
Designer: Tracy Dean
Photography: Joyce Oudkerk Pool
Assistant to photography:
Elizabeth Graham
Props: Gibson Scheid
Food Stylist: Sue White
Backgrounds: Missy Hamilton
Support: Beth and Martha
Editing: Carolyn Miller

Distributed in Canada by Raincoast Books, 112 East Third Ave., Vancouver B.C. V5T 1C8

10 9 8 7 6 5 4 3 2

Chronicle Books
275 Fifth Street
San Francisco, CA 94103

Contents

Introduction

Hail the Grain

How many types of grain have you tasted? If you are like most people in America today, the answer is probably wheat, corn, rice, oats, and rye.

The world of grain goes way beyond these basics to comprise a large, robust family. Although the natural flavors of grains are difficult to describe because of their neutral quality, they complement a wide variety of foods, adding texture and profound nourishment. Grains can be chewy, nutty, crunchy, fluffy, woodsy, earthy, or hearty. To the tongue they have a creamy quality that is usually described as "starchy."

Grains make us feel satisfied and well fed. High in valuable water-soluble fiber and a major source of complex carbohydrates, they are a gold mine of minerals. During the digestion process, they provide an even flow of energy and stamina as well as balancing body chemistry. Cholesterol free and low in fat, they contain *pacifarins,* an antibiotic element that helps to protect the body against disease. Grains have the lowest percentage of chemical and inorganic residues found in foods today. The natural substance *auxone* helps rejuvenate cells, playing a part in preventing premature aging. Grains also contain phytic acid, which is thought to neutralize radioactive and chemical toxins.

The *germ* of a single grain, which is protected by an inedible hard outer shell called the *hull,* is also called the *embryo,* and is the part capable of producing a new organism. It is rich in vitamins E, A, B-complex (B6 is known for removing toxins from the body), protein, calcium, and iron. Surrounding the germ is the *endosperm,* rich in the starch and protein needed to nourish a seedling. The seed's husk is called *bran,* and is composed of cellulose, a complex sugar and a kind of fiber.

Grains have supported entire civilizations throughout history, yet they are the rediscovered favorites of gourmet food enthusiasts. As primary staples, grain foods are essential to life. They are food as well as fodder, building, fuel, and clothing materials. Grains such as barley, bulgur, buckwheat, grits, wild rice, and millet have found their way out of health food stores and into supermarkets. Ethnic dishes such as couscous, risotto, polenta, and kasha are becoming common American foods. The New World's "lost" sacred grains, amaranth and quinoa, known for their high percentage of lysine, an essential amino acid, are now successfully grown for the United States market.

The rich soil of the United States grows mostly commercial wheat and corn. But this country also grows many other grains, most of them transplanted from other countries. Wheat originally hailed from the Eurasian continent and has been cultivated since prehistoric times. Buckwheat was grown on the poor, rocky steppes of Russia; rye thrives in cold, windswept Scandinavia; oats and barley like the dampness of Scotland; millet is a staple of dry, harsh Indian and African lands; barley grows in the rugged mountains of Afghanistan and Tibet; corn is native to Mexico; and in the desert climates of the Middle East wheat is parcooked and cracked for quick cooking in a land with limited fuel sources. For all the varieties of grain in the world, corn, wild rice, quinoa, and amaranth are the only native New World grains.

Hulled whole grains dominated cooking worldwide until processed grains, such as white rice and white flour, eventually became a status symbol for the upper classes. An affluent diet was one high in processed foods, dairy products, and meat. People wanted food that looked "pure." A new habit was born, and the demand for processed grains increased.

The wheat flour we buy in the supermarket is made by commercial steel-milling processes. Flour may also be made by stone grinding, an ancient method, and home grinding by hand or electric mills. Small family-owned mills grind fresh flour, and if you happen to have one in your area, that is the place to buy a superior product; you can also order fresh-ground flour by mail (see Source Directory). These small mills run at a slower speed than commercial mills, generating less heat in the process. Hence, stone-ground flour retains all its nutrients and flavor and even stays fresh longer when stored correctly. It is very rare for any flours from large commercial steel mills to be ground at such low speeds.

This book calls exclusively for unbleached all-purpose or unbleached bread flour when white flour is required. Unbleached flour is allowed to age and whiten naturally, although the bran and germ have been removed, a process known as "bolting." It contains a bit more protein than bleached flour, which is whitened by a chemical bleaching and maturing process that destroys vitamins, especially vitamin E. Unbleached flour and whole-wheat flour surprisingly contain the same amount of vitamin E, while bleached flour contains none. The flavor and rising ability of unbleached flour is superior to bleached flour, as the aging process intensifies the gluten, making for a springier dough. It is available in the flour section of your local supermarket. Reputable nationwide brands are Gold Medal, Pillsbury, and the organically grown Arrowhead Mills. East of the Mississippi, look for Robin Hood, Hodgson Mill, and King Arthur brands. Naturally aged Stone-Buhr flours are distributed west of the Rocky Mountains, and White Lily and Martha White are Southern brands. Look for locally ground grains in specialty and natural foods stores.

An increasing number of avid home gardeners are growing, reaping (cutting stalks and binding into sheaves), threshing (shaking the grain from heads), and winnowing (separating the grain from chaff and straw bits) their own grains. Amaranth, corn, rye, and wheat are the easiest grains to process at home because they are hull-less. Home grano-culture uses strains of hard and soft red wheat, such as Early Stone Age and Roughrider, available through seed houses. The ever-available Sears catalog still carries tools, such as the sickle, for hand harvesting. Rosalind Creasy's exceptional book *Cooking from the Home Garden* (Sierra Club Books, 1988) devotes an entire chapter to home grain cultivation and is a worthwhile reference if this stirs your interest.

Wheat flour contains proteins, called gluten, that create strong, elastic doughs when inflated by the leavening gases produced by yeast, baking into the light honeycomb structure we associate with bread. The only other grain to contain gluten is rye, which has a relatively small amount.

The imaginative addition of other whole grains or flours to wheat flour loaves creates bread with a fascinating variety of new flavors, aromas, and textures. If you tried to create a yeasted loaf from all or a large percentage of specialty flour, you would produce a dense, flat loaf. It's necessary to use only a small percentage of low-starch and low-gluten grains and flours in order to create a light-textured, yet hearty loaf.

Most people have become well acquainted with the virtues of whole grains through the highly advertised need for more fiber in today's modern diet. *Insoluble fiber* is the rough, stringy part of a plant that provides bulk as an aid to a healthy gastrointestinal tract. Grains such as wheat bran, whole-wheat flour, corn, rye, millet, oats, barley, nuts, and seeds are in this category. *Soluble fiber* helps regulate blood sugar, fat, and cholesterol levels. You can tell when a food has soluble fiber, because, like oatmeal or apples, it thickens after being cooked. The best sources of soluble fiber are oats, wheat, corn, rice brans, and legumes. Unbleached flour contains about 75 percent of the fiber contained in whole-wheat flour.

Low-fat, low-sugar, low-sodium, and high-fiber diets are nutritionally sensible. A diet high in complex carbohydrates includes grains, seeds, nuts, beans, pasta, potatoes, fruits, and vegetables. A good guideline for adequate nutritional balance is to consume 60 percent of daily calories from carbohydrates, 15 percent from protein, and 25 percent from fats. This means eating as many unrefined, unprocessed, unhulled whole grains, cereals, and flours as possible. Baking your own bread is the perfect way to incorporate more fiber and nutrition into your diet.

Each new recipe in this book is designed to stimulate renewed interest in the art of baking. The world of the bread baker has a sense of innocence; it is peaceful, creative, and life-giving. It utilizes the power of observation, scientific techniques, and a flair for combining precious flavors with earthy elements, all infused with a traditional concern for quality.

In this book, the baker will find extravagantly embellished celebration breads; savory main-dish breads; the stalwart dinner roll; irresistible breakfast rolls; luscious spreads and butters; and flavorful, yet health-giving daily loaves. There are lots of American-style country breads, baked in their comforting rectangular-loaf shape and tending to be a bit sweeter and richer than their free-formed, crusty European ancestors.

Intertwined in the text is mythology, cultural cross-references, a dash of whimsical taxonomy, herbal traditions, and historical anecdotes to give the reader a sense of the rich heritage of bread making. All the recipes were written in the hope that they would inspire the reader to innovate new breads. Yet no matter how exotic or humble the ingredients, all the recipes rely on traditional bread-making techniques, allowing even beginning bakers to create masterpieces of sustenance.

INGREDIENTS

A Guide to the "New" Grains

AMARANTH *(Amaranthus hypochondriacus):* Higher in calcium and phosphorus than any other grain except millet, amaranth contains around 16 percent protein and is about the size of a poppy seed. It also boasts a high proportion of lysine, an essential amino acid rarely found in vegetable matter. Related to the common pigweed, amaranth has large seed heads, and its leaves and stems vary in color from purple to orange to white. Known as the Aztec grain for its use in early Mexican and Central American cultures, it has a strong, wild flavor and a rather gelatinous texture. Amaranth may be popped into tiny puffs, like popcorn. Adding the cooked grain to batters helps baked goods to retain moisture and lightness.

BARLEY *(Hordeum vulgare):* A hardy grain that grows well in northern climates because of its short growing season, barley is larger and plumper than all other grains except corn, and is rich in protein, niacin, thiamine, and potassium. The most common variety in the United States has a triple hull, which clings tightly to the kernel. After milling, only a small white pearl is left, called "pearl barley." Barley was used as currency by the Sumerians around 4000 B.C.; it may well be the oldest of all cultivated cereal grains. It has a chewy texture and a mild, sweet flavor. Pearl barley can be toasted and rolled into barley flakes, which are used like rolled oats. Barley flour is low in gluten. Barley malt, a sweet syrup made from the whole grain, is similar to molasses and a wonderful sweetener for breads.

BUCKWHEAT *(Fagopyrum esculentum):* Usually eaten in its robust roasted form, called "kasha," buckwheat is technically not a grain, but the seed of a red-stemmed plant related to rhubarb. It was introduced to Europe in the Middle Ages by the Crusaders, who brought it back to Venice from Asia Minor. It is still known in France as *blé noir,* "black wheat," or *sarrasin,* "Saracen corn." A very hardy plant native to Siberia, buckwheat grows rapidly even in poor, rocky soil and in extreme climates. Containing all eight essential amino acids, including lysine, it is a good source of calcium, with up to twice as much as other grains. It is particularly rich in both vitamin E and the B-complex vitamins. Buckwheat flour is low in protein, which makes for a tender baked product with an assertive, musky, slightly bitter flavor. The buckwheat grown in Europe has a rather mild taste, distinctly different from the buckwheat grown in the United States, which can be quite strong and musky. Small amounts of buckwheat flour combined with wheat flour make delicious bread.

BULGUR: Bulgur is wheat berries which have been pearled (which means the bran is removed), steamed, dried, and then cracked into a variety of textures. It originated in the Middle East, where cooks needed to cook grains quickly in order to conserve fuel. Large quantities of wheat berries were processed into bulgur, then cooked quickly in small batches for daily consumption. Bulgur is different from plain cracked wheat, which needs long cooking to soften the grains and still contains the bran and germ. Bulgur wheat is uniform in color, making it easy to distinguish from regular cracked wheat. High in protein, phosphorus, and potassium, bulgur also contains calcium, iron, thiamine, and riboflavin. Tabooli salads are made with the fine grind, and the most commonly available grind for baking is medium, found in most supermarkets and natural foods stores. Ethnic markets may carry as many as four different grinds.

CORN *(Zea mays):* Corn, a long-standing staple in Southwest cuisine and North America's most common indigenous grain, comes in a rainbow of colors, including pink, maroon, and speckled. **White and yellow cornmeals** come in a variety of grinds, from fine to coarse, and are used for corn breads, spoon breads, and tamales. Degerminated cornmeal has had the germ removed for longer shelf-life. For best flavor, search out fresh stone-ground meals. **Blue cornmeal,** *maiz azul,* is slightly grainier and sweeter than yellow corn, making a purple-pink, blue-green, or lavender-tinged baked product depending on the type of ingredients it is combined with. It needs a bit more fat when used to make muffins, biscuits, and tortillas, and is available in a variety of grinds. Also known as "Hopi corn," blue cornmeal is grown exclusively in the Southwest and is a favored ingredient in breads of that region. *Harina de maiz azul* is a coarse grind especially for tortilla making, and *harinilla* is a fine grade of corn flour, good in yeast breads and pancakes. **Hominy,** or *nixtamal,* is whole hulled white or yellow field corn that has had the germ removed and has then been soaked in a lime bath. It is available canned or dried. When dried and coarsely ground into hominy grits, it can be used to make excellent pancakes, breakfast cereal, and soufflés. Quick-cooking grits are the finest grind. **Masa harina** is finely ground golden cornmeal made from *nixtamal.* When made into a paste with water, it is called *masa,* the main ingredient for tortillas and tamales. **Harina de arepas** is a Latin and South American yellow corn flour for rolls, with a flavor similar to *masa.* **Corn bran** is a good source of soluble fiber and is used like oat or wheat bran.

All types of cornmeal and corn flour can be used in bread making. Baked goods made with cornmeal are crumbly in texture and a bit gritty. Because cornmeal is unique in flavor and texture, there is no substitute for it. The kind of corn used to make meal and flour is flint, or field, corn, not sweet table corn, which is eaten when immature. Store cornmeals, tightly covered, in a cool, dry place or refrigerate for up to six or eight months.

MILLET (*Panicum miliaceum*): Tiny round yellow millet grains resemble mustard seeds. A staple in India and much of Africa, millet is rich in B vitamins, phosphorus, iron, calcium, riboflavin, and niacin, and has the most complete protein of any of the true cereal grains. Millet is particularly well suited to poor soil and adverse climates, managing to lie dormant through periods of drought, then sprouting with the first rainfalls. It has a slightly bitter taste, a fluffy texture, and is very easy to digest. It may be used interchangeably with teff flour and is often used to prepare *injera* flatbreads.

OATS (*Avena satira*): Oat bran is the outer covering of the hulled oat. Although not the universal panacea for health problems that was originally claimed, oat bran does contain plenty of fiber and is a delicious addition in baking. Studies show that the consumption of oat bran lowers blood cholesterol levels, as do rice, corn, and wheat brans. Since it is the oil in the bran that contains the nutrients, all brans need to be stored in the refrigerator to prevent rancidity. **Rolled oats** are hulled, steamed, and flattened into flakes. They may be ground into a coarse meal suitable for bread making. Oats grow in cold climates, and are a staple food crop in Norway, the British Isles, and Switzerland.

QUINOA (*Chenopodium*): Quinoa (KEEN-wah) has the highest protein content of any grain (about 17 percent), is high in the amino acid lysine, and contains abundant vitamin E, calcium, iron, assorted B vitamins, and very high amounts of phosphorus. Best grown at altitudes above 10,000 feet, it positively flourishes under extreme conditions including thin air, hot sun, frost, and drought. Before it can be used, quinoa must be thoroughly rinsed, because it is coated with saponin, a resin-like substance with a bitter, soapy taste that protects the grains from insects. Rinse and drain it about five times with cold running water. The more rinsing, the milder the flavor of the cooked grain will be. When cooked, the disc-shaped sesame-like grains are translucent. Quinoa's 5-foot-tall stalks bear large, varigated seed heads that vary in color — red,

orange, yellow, lavender, green, and white. An annual herb, quinoa is related to lamb's quarters and is sometimes called "vegetarian caviar" because of its soft, crunchy consistency.

RICE (*Oryza sativa*): There are thousands of varieties of rice, each with its own distinct flavor, texture, aroma, color, length of grain, and degree of translucency. Descended from wild grasses found in Asia and Indochina, it is the staple grain for over half the world's population. Rice is a good source of fiber and vitamins B and E. Long-grain white rice is fluffy and light, containing less fiber and vitamins than the heartier short-grain rices. When the long-grain *indica* was introduced into the United States in the 1700s by English colonists aided by African slaves, South Carolina's swampy terrain was found to be perfect for its cultivation. Rice is also grown in Arkansas, Louisiana, Mississippi, Texas, and California.

Indian and Texas basmati rices have long, slender grains that remain separate during cooking and have a very fragrant aroma. **American long-grain white rice** has larger, fluffier grains and a woodier flavor than the delicate Indian variety. White rice is polished, a process in which the brown bran is removed by rubbing. This helps the rice cook faster, but it also results in the loss of important vitamins and fiber. Della Gourmet White Rice is a cross between American long-grain and Asian basmati, grown exclusively in Arkansas. **Jasmine rice** is a very white, fragrant rice. It has a slightly sticky, but firm quality, and is popular in Southeast Asian cuisine. **Arborio rice** has slightly translucent, fat grains. This favorite of Italian cuisine is a short-grain rice with lots of flavor; it has a firm and creamy consistency when cooked, and is used to make risotto. **Glutinous white rice** is short-grained, very sticky, and chewy. This favorite Asian rice can be formed, without added ingredients, into balls or used in the preparation of sushi. **Long-grain brown (Texmati) rice** is beige in color and nutty in flavor. Fluffy, light, and very popular in cooking, it takes twice as long to cook as white rice. **Wild pecan rice** is exotic sounding, but is really a rather sticky, long-grain dark brown rice, developed by Louisiana State University, which tastes woody rather than nutty and is grown only in the Acadian bayou country of South Louisiana. It is a cross between Louisiana long-grain rice and several species of Indochina aromatic rices. **Wehani rice** is a long-grain red-brown rice with a chewy texture and earthy aroma, very much like a slightly stronger-flavored, sticky, short-grain brown rice. The water it cooks in turns quite brown. **Japonica,** or **black rice,** is a long-grain deep-purple grain from Thailand, sticky and grass-like in flavor. **Short-grain brown rice** is nutty, sweet, dense, and chewy. It is unpolished, so it retains a layer of bran, which adds fiber and flavor. It takes twice as long to cook as white rice. **Rizcous** is a cracked rice that may be used interchangeably with bulgur wheat or couscous. **Rice bran** is ground and is said to be as effective as oat bran as a soluble fiber. **Rice flour** may be ground from brown or white rice. It is an excellent thickener and is good for dusting, as it absorbs moisture slowly. All cooked rice is an excellent addition to bread doughs.

RYE *(Secale cerale):* Rye, a newcomer to the world of cultivated grains, was once regarded as a weed in wheat fields. The Romans first planted fields of rye and carried it on their journeys throughout Europe. It took hold in countries with cold climates and poor soil, such as Russia, Scandinavia, and the British Isles, where it became a staple flour for bread making. Similar to wheat, it has a characteristically strong, earthy flavor and contains a small amount of gluten. Whole-grain rye (known as *groats* or *berries),* cracked rye, light to medium rye flours, and pumpernickel, the coarsest rye meal, may all be used to make full-flavored breads.

SEMOLINA: The finest white flours are ground exclusively from the endosperm of whole-grain wheat. Cream-colored semolina flour is the finely ground endosperm of durum wheat and used exclusively in pasta making. It makes a delicious, high-protein addition to Italian-style breads. Semolina flour is not the same as semolina meal, which is a coarse-ground cereal like farina (which is the ground endosperm of spring or winter wheat) or wheatina (which is ground whole-grain wheat) and is used in a manner similar to coarse cornmeal.

TEFF *(Eragrostis teff):* The smallest of all grains, teff is only about twice the size of the period at the end of this sentence, and 150 grains are equal in weight to one kernel of wheat. Perhaps this explains why the name of the staple cereal of Ethiopia literally translates from the Amharic language as "lost." It has been made for thousands of years into an ancient flatbread with a spongy texture called *injera.* Teff is now grown commercially in the high-desert volcanic fields of Idaho and distributed through natural foods stores. The overall nutrition of the grain is high in relation to other true cereal grains, and it is especially high in calcium and iron. It has an excellent flavor and is good used in combination with other grains. Teff flour is better used in quick rather than yeasted breads.

Substitute for half the total wheat flour in pancakes, waffles, scones, muffins, and quick loaves.

TRITICALE *(Triticum secale):* Triticale, the first human-engineered grain, is a hybrid offspring of durum wheat and rye. Hardier than wheat, it has a higher protein content and a better amino acid balance than either of its parent grains. It tastes rather sour, much like rye, though less flavorful. Low in gluten, it should be used in combination with wheat flours for the best texture and can be substituted in recipes developed for whole-wheat flour. Unfortunately, early crop yields were not as high as projected, and triticale has enjoyed limited acceptance among farmers. Developed in Sweden in the late 1800s, most triticale currently is grown in small quantities in Nebraska, Minnesota, and the Dakotas.

WILD RICE *(Zizania aquatica):* Delicious by itself or in combination with other rices, wild rice has a strong woodsy flavor and a chewy texture. It has a higher protein content than wheat and contains high levels of B vitamins and potassium. It is not really a rice, but the seed of an aquatic grass native to the Great Lakes region. Known as the "gourmet grain," it has actually been a staple in the Chippewa and Sioux Indian diets for centuries. Some wild rice is still harvested by hand in lakes by Native Americans in traditional canoes, but most is cultivated in man-made paddies, with California the biggest producer. There are three grades of wild rice: (1) "Select," which contains short broken grains; (2) "Extra-fancy," which has uniform ½-inch-long grains and is the most common variety available; and (3) "Giant," the most expensive, with grains that are uniformly about 1 inch long. All grades can be used interchangeably in recipes. Paddy rice is cultivated in seeded ponds and machine harvested. It is left to cure out in the weather, causing the characteristic shiny, dark kernels. Hand-harvested rice is parched immediately over open fires, giving it a variety of distinctly matte colors from a ruddy red-brown to a subtle gray-green. Labels usually note if the rice is hand harvested or cultivated, but the color will tell you immediately how it was grown. If you find the husky flavor of wild rice too strong, use it in combination with other rices for a milder taste, or use hand-harvested varieties, which are known for their delicate flavor. Note: Each brand of wild rice has its own particular taste, so if you have experienced some very strong or bitter rices, experiment with other brands. Wild rice is an excellent addition to yeast breads, muffins, and pancakes.

COOKING WHOLE GRAINS *(Per 1 cup uncooked grain)*

Grain	Water	Cooking Time	Yield
Amaranth	1-1/2 cups	20 minutes	2 cups
Pearl barley	2-1/2 cups	40 minutes	3-1/2 cups
Bulgur wheat	2 cups	15 minutes	2-1/2 cups
Cornmeal	3 to 4 cups	25 minutes	4 cups
Kasha (buckwheat)	2 cups	10 minutes	3-1/2 cups
Millet	1-3/4 cups	30 minutes	2-1/2 cups
Oat groats	2 cups	60 minutes	2-1/2 cups
Rolled oats	2-1/4 cups	8 minutes	1-1/2 cups
Quinoa	2 cups	15 minutes	3-1/2 cups
Rice (white)	2 cups	20 minutes	3 cups
Rice (brown)	2 cups	60 minutes	3 cups
Rye berries	2-1/4 cups	2 hours	3 cups
Teff	3 cups	15 minutes	3 cups
Tritical berries	2-1/4 cups	1 hour	2-1/2 cups
Wheat berries	2-1/4 cups	1 hour	3 cups
Wild rice	2-1/2 cups	55 minutes	3-3/4 cups

• Add 1/2 teaspoon salt per cup of uncooked grain after cooking •

TIPS FOR BAKING WHOLE-GRAIN AND OTHER YEAST DOUGHS

- Purchase whole grains from a reliable store: They will have been cleaned and picked over before packaging. If buying in bulk, inspect the bin for insects.

- To prevent rancidity, store whole grains and flours in tightly covered containers in a cool, dry place for a maximum of about a month. For longer storage, keep grains and flour in the refrigerator or freezer, as they absorb moisture readily and mold quickly.

- Rinsing whole grains to remove dust and debris is optional. Use a strainer under running water. Cracked, rolled, and processed grains do not need rinsing.

- Cook whole grains al dente, or slightly chewy.

- Some uncooked grains, such as millet and quinoa, may be added to raw dough. Others must be soaked or cooked before adding, such as bulgur. Each recipe has specific instructions. Leftover cooked grains, such as rice, are perfect additions to bread dough.

- Salt whole grains after cooking. Each grain reacts differently to salt, and some, like wehani rice, do not absorb salted liquid well.

- For traditional high-domed loaves of bread, keep the ratio of specialty grains and flours, which have little or no gluten, small in proportion to wheat flour, which is high in gluten. The general rule is about 1 cup whole grains or whole-grain flour per 5 cups whole-wheat or unbleached all-purpose or bread flour.

- Egg whites are low in calories and free of cholesterol. You can substitute two egg whites or an equivalent amount of commercial egg substitute for one whole egg in traditional bread recipes.

- While mixing and kneading, leave whole-grain dough more moist than dough using all white flour. Whole grains and flours tend to soak up lots of moisture as they rest and rise. Look for a "tacky" and "springy" feel, rather than a "smooth" and "stiff" quality. Always keep a reserve of ¼ to ½ cup of the required amount of flour. During kneading, add the remaining flour 1 tablespoon at a time as necessary to prevent sticking, and knead until it is completely absorbed. This ensures a moist loaf rather than a dry, crumbly-textured one. Heavy whole-grain doughs benefit from the use of a sponge, or from being mixed in a heavy-duty electric mixer to develop a light texture.

- Allow dough to rise only until just doubled in bulk for the best-formed baked loaves and the richest grain flavor. Over-rising creates a sour, yeasty flavor.

- Yeast doughs may be refrigerated at any point in their rising phase to slow down the process if you are busy and cannot complete the recipe at the time. Cover with a double thickness of plastic wrap, with room for expansion, to prevent a crust from forming. Plastic wrap is best for retaining moisture in doughs, but a moist, clean tea towel may also be used. Plan on triple the rising time for doughs to come completely back to room temperature.

- Whole-grain breads are best when they are cooled completely after baking, then reheated. This gives excess moisture a chance to evaporate, and "sets the crumb"; otherwise, bread will easily collapse when cut.

- *To cook whole grains:* Bring the water to a full boil; stir in the grain; wait for the water to return to a boil; cover tightly and reduce heat to a simmer. Set the timer and do not peek. Grains are done when all liquid is absorbed. Remove from heat and let stand 15 minutes.

Other Basics

LIQUIDS

Yeast needs a warm liquid in which to be dissolved and activated. Flour needs to absorb liquid in order for its gluten to be activated during the kneading process. Liquids should be about 105° to 115°F, or feel comfortably warm on the inside of your wrist.

A loaf made with **water** has a heavy, crisp crust and a chewy texture, as in French breads. **Milk** is very popular for breads, giving a light, even texture and a thin brown crust, and adding fat to keep bread fresh longer. Instant nonfat dried milk is also excellent. Milk no longer needs to be scalded and cooled for making bread, unless it is raw, as pasteurization and homogenization eliminate any enzymes that would slacken the gluten. **Buttermilk,** either fresh or dried, **sour cream,** and **yogurt** make fine-textured breads with a sour tang. Yeast thrives in the starch of **potato water** and makes a moist, dense loaf. Other liquids for making breads are **beer, wine, broth,** and fruit and vegetable **juices.**

SWEETENING

Granulated sugar, brown sugar, honey, maple sugar and syrup, molasses, barley malt, and sorghum feed yeast, give color to crusts, and sweeten doughs. Although they are used in small amounts, different sweetenings can change the flavor of a loaf. To substitute honey and other liquid-based sweeteners for granulated sugar, use ¾ cup honey per each cup of sugar and reduce the total liquid used in the recipe by ¼ cup. For recipes in which no liquid is required, compensate by adding an extra ¼ cup flour.

FAT

Butter, vegetable shortening, oil, and lard give a moist, rich-tasting, soft-textured quality to a loaf along with acting as natural preservatives. Lean doughs with no fat, such as French breads, will begin to stale within a few hours of baking. For good flavor and cholesterol-free diets, substitute cold-pressed vegetable oils such as soy, sesame, sunflower, and corn. Grease pans with butter, margarine, or liquid lecithin, as oils tend to be absorbed into the dough and can make bread stick to the pan. Spray products, such as Pam, are a combination of lecithin and corn oil.

EGGS

Eggs add a wonderful, golden color and a tender cake-like texture to bread. One whole egg may be substituted for two egg yolks and vice versa in baking recipes. One large egg equals ¼ cup liquid measure; the white equals 3 tablespoons and the yolk is equal to 1 tablespoon. Substitute three small eggs for two large eggs in recipes. Use duck or quail eggs, if you should have an abundance, to vary color and flavor. All eggs should be at room temperature when added to yeast doughs.

SALT

Salt is a flavor enhancer. It is optional in bread, but a lack of salt is very noticeable in the finished flavor. Too much salt leaves a bitter quality and can inhibit yeast activity. Too little salt leaves bread tasting flat and can cause dough to feel slightly slack during kneading (although some ethnic breads, such as Tuscan bread, contain no salt and are used to complement salty foods). Iodized and fine sea salt can be used interchangeably. Coarse salt must be ground before being used in dough; it may be sprinkled on top of breads such as focaccia and bagels before baking.

The Leavener

YEAST

The soul of bread is a one-celled natural living microorganism scientifically known as *Saccharomyces cerevisiae*. To be activated and multiply, yeast needs the combination of sugar, moisture, warmth, and air. It is important to remember that yeast can be killed by too much heat, about 140° or above. Below 50°, it goes into a suspended state, allowing dough to be refrigerated or frozen for periods of time. Maximum fermentation occurs at 80° to 90°. Yeast eats the sugars and complex carbohydrates in the flour, and, instantly, the yeast begins to reproduce at a rapid rate. The mixture will appear foamy. The by-products of all this activity are alcohol, the beer-like or yeasty smell in a raw dough, and carbon dioxide, which becomes trapped within the stretchy mesh-like gluten structure of the dough in the process known as rising. The heat of the oven kills the yeast, burns off the alcohol, and sets the porous pattern, creating the familiar texture of bread.

Yeast is sold to the consumer in four different forms: active dry yeast, compressed fresh cake yeast, quick-rise yeast, and instant dried yeast. Nutritional yeasts, such as brewer's and torula, are not leavening agents. As with all culinary choices, let your palate, availability, and the final product be a guide to which yeasts you use.

Active dry yeast is sold in a dated ¼-ounce flat foil-wrapped packet, in a three-packet strip, 4-ounce jars, or in bulk from your local natural foods store. One scant tablespoon of dry yeast is equal to a ¼-ounce premeasured package or a .06-ounce cube of fresh cake yeast. Dry yeast is not activated until first dissolved in warm (about 105° to 115°) liquid. It is advisable to invest in a good yeast or candy thermometer to be certain of your liquid temperatures until you can recognize the exact warmth by feel. Without a thermometer, test the water by dripping a few drops on the inside of your wrist. It should feel warm without being uncomfortably hot, as for baby formula. If the water is too cool, the yeast will be slow to activate. If the water is too hot, the yeast may be killed, in which case it will fail to produce the characteristic foamy effect, and the dough will not rise. Keep dry yeast in the refrigerator in a tightly covered container. If properly stored, dry yeast can remain fresh for up to about one year. But, to be certain, always proof your yeast if there are long lapses between your baking sprees, and do not buy packages after their pull date.

Compressed fresh cake yeast is known for its dependability, excellent rising ability, and, some claim, superior flavor when compared to dry yeast strains. It is sold in .06-ounce and 2-ounce cakes and 1-pound blocks, sometimes available from your local bakery. The 1-pound professional size is absolutely the best yeast available. The smaller cakes sold in the deli case of your grocery are stabilized with starch to prolong shelf life, which also tends to decrease potency. Fresh yeast is highly perishable, must be refrigerated, and will keep for about 2 weeks. When fresh, it is an even tan-gray with no discoloration and breaks with a clean edge. Compressed yeast should be dissolved in lukewarm liquids (about 95°) before being added to the dry ingredients. Compressed yeast may be successfully frozen for several months, but its potency seems to decrease.

Quick-rise yeast is a new development in yeast technology, and there are numerous American brands on the market. It is a new strain of low-moisture yeast that raises dough 50 percent faster than regular yeast. It works best when added directly to the dry ingredients and when the liquid added is about 120° to 125°. Follow the manufacturer's instructions, as dough temperature and rising times are different than for general bread making. I find there is a small loss of flavor and keeping quality in the finished loaves, due to the very fast fermentation. Use a bit less quick-rise yeast in a recipe where a slower, more normal rising time is desired. It is available in ¼-ounce packages, sold in a three-package strip.

Instant dried yeast from Europe, another relative newcomer to the yeast family, is dried to a very low percentage of moisture. A different strain of yeast cells than our domestic brands, it is combined with an emulsifier and a form of sugar, enabling the yeast to activate immediately on contact with warm liquid. With three times as many yeast cells as active dry yeast, this strain cannot tolerate a lot of sugar, as in sweet dough recipes, or long, slow proofing temperatures, because it is constantly rising. This yeast enables a dough to be baked without any rising period.

EQUIPMENT

The Pans

Different sizes and shapes of molds give yeasted loaves a unique character. It is important to note that there is an ideal amount of dough appropriate for each mold. While the bread actually may taste the same, a pleasing appearance is certainly as important as its flavor. As much care needs to be taken in forming the loaves as in the assembly of dough from pure, fresh ingredients.

No matter what size pan is used, after forming the loaf, the dough should fill a full half to two thirds of the pan. Any less and you will have a flat loaf; any more and you will have an overflowing top-heavy loaf that looks awkward. You can use trial and error, or you can weigh dough portions, which is called "scaling," and is the method used in professional bakeries. As your guide, a small 5-pound postal or kitchen scale will do nicely in your home kitchen.

Department, hardware, and specialty stores offer an astonishingly large variety of loaf-style pans from which to choose. These pans mold the traditional rectangular loaf shape. The standard, or large loaf, is 9 by 5 inches or 10 by 4½ inches, which is nice for sandwich breads. Recipes using a total of 6 cups of flour comfortably yield two loaves of this size. The raw dough is weighed out, or "scaled," at 2 pounds each for these pans. When the dough has risen to double in bulk, it will be approximately 1 inch above the pan rim and delicately domed. It is important not to let the dough rise much beyond this point, or the loaf may collapse during the initial "oven spring" time in the oven and have an over-yeasty taste. Unless noted in a specific recipe, bread is usually baked at 375°, and this size loaf should bake for 35 to 40 minutes.

Medium loaf sizes are 8½ by 4½ inches and 7½ by 3½ inches. The raw dough for this size pan weighs 1½ pounds and 1 pound, respectively. Recipes calling for a total of 4½ to 5 cups of flour yield two loaves of this size. Baking times are 30 to 40 minutes. These loaves are the size I find most visually appealing and easiest to work with.

Small loaf pans are usually welded together in a "strap" form for easiest handling, with 4 to 12 loaf sections per strap. If you have individual pans, place them on a large baking sheet during the rising and baking. This eliminates lots of awkward juggling of small hot pans on and off the oven rack. Small pans are usually 5¾ by 3¾ inches or 4½ by 2½ inches, one of my favorite sizes. The raw dough weighs 8 ounces and 5 ounces, respectively. These loaves bake in approximately 20 to 30 minutes.

In general, a recipe using 5 to 6 cups of flour will produce two 9-by-5-inch standard loaves, two 9-inch round pans, two or more free-form loaves, two 9-inch fluted tube pans, four 7½-by-3½-inch loaves, four 1-pound coffee cans, seven to eight 5¾-by-3¾-inch loaves, or fourteen to sixteen 4½-by-2½-inch loaves. Please remember that the choices of shape and how many loaves to make are your decisions alone. A recipe yield is meant to be used as a guide rather than law, but you should substitute a pan that has a similar dimension or volume for best results. Keep a handy tape measure in the kitchen for measuring pans and loaf lengths. Measure a pan straight across the top and note the width from the two inside edges. Height is measured from bottom to top. To determine a pan's volume, count the number of liquid cup measures it takes to fill it to the top.

Other commonly used baking pans include smooth-sided or fluted tube pans, usually available in 10-inch and 6-inch diameters. These may be called tube pans, springform tubes, bundts, or kugelhopf molds. They may be used interchangeably as long as the sizes correspond. They sometimes are made of beautiful copper, but unless they are lined with tin, these are best left for decoration. Fluted earthenware molds, which are heavier than metal, are excellent for baking, and often can be found in antiques stores. To form tall cylindrical shapes, look for smooth-sided panettone molds 7½ by 6½ inches in diameter, and black-tinned 5½-by-4½-inch fluted monkey bread pans. The tube shape is designed to conduct heat to the center of the dough, allowing it to rise and bake evenly throughout. It also gives a large amount of dough more surface to cling to during rising.

I keep a set of traditional 2½-inch-deep aluminum springform pans, ranging in size from 6 to 12 inches in diameter, for forming round loaves and coffee cakes. I find a 14-inch deep-dish pizza pan perfect for large flat savory or sweet breads. I have also baked loaves in heart-shaped pans, soufflé dishes, charlotte molds, clean coffee cans, and different-sized muffin cups on occasion. I especially like Silverstone nonstick coatings, which make molds easy to care for.

Baking pans come in a variety of materials, each with its own qualities. There must be as many differing opinions about which pan to use as there are bakers. Please also consider which pans work best in your oven to produce the type of loaf you like best. Aluminum is lightweight, inexpensive, easy to clean, and the best conductor of heat for baking, as it responds quickly to changes in heat. The gauge, or thickness, of pans determines their efficiency in reflecting heat: The thicker the gauge, the less likely a pan is to warp or develop hot spots. Many pans are coated or lined with a nonstick surface. The best grade is for professional use and is readily available to the home baker from a restaurant supply or reputable cookware shop.

Glass and black-tinned pans brown loaves faster, as they are good conductors of heat. Lower your oven temperature by 25° when using these pans, as they absorb heat quickly. Glass may be conveniently washed in a dishwasher. Black-tinned pans need to have the loaf removed immediately, otherwise the trapped moisture will begin the rust process. Wipe the pan with a clean, dry cloth and store in a dry cupboard. I often layer my pans with a section of paper toweling to prevent scratching during storage. Clay loaf pans, once rare, are becoming more available nowadays (see Source Directory). Whether glazed or unglazed on the inside surfaces, they are the heaviest pans (next to cast iron) and are slow, steady conductors of heat. Always bake clay loaves on the lowest oven rack for the bottom to brown properly, and avoid sugary doughs, which will stick to the porous clay. These pans produce a very thick, crisp crust on both white and whole-grain loaves. Scrub with soap and water to clean, and dry completely before storing.

Stainless steel is iron combined with carbon and chronium. It is durable, easy to clean, and nonreactive to acid foods. Unfortunately, it is the least efficient conductor of heat and therefore not good for baking purposes. Cast iron was the early American all-purpose baking pan. Heat diffuses evenly through cast iron, but it is slow to heat up and cool down. Cast iron needs proper seasoning before using, and it is important to maintain that protective coating to keep the iron from rusting.

European tin is a nonstick alloy that should not be washed with soap or in the dishwasher. Lots of pâté and pizza pans are made of this material. Follow the manufacturer's instructions for seasoning before baking. Rinse with hot water and dry immediately. They also dry nicely in the oven with a pilot light. Disposable aluminum pans come in a wide variety of sizes, bake a beautiful loaf of bread, and can even be washed on the top rack of a dishwasher for reuse. Keep a stock on hand for emergencies. They are great for messy breads such as Orange Cinnamon Swirls (page 119).

A wide variety of square, oblong, and rectangular pans (known as sheet or jelly-roll pans) are available to the home baker. Look for well-constructed pans of the heaviest-gauge aluminum or tin-plated steel. Black steel is fine, but be aware that the dark finish causes a dark, heavy crust. The sizes of baking sheets range from the classic jelly-roll pan at 10 by 15 inches, to the classic all-purpose baking sheet at 12 by 15½ inches. The raised edge will be about 1 inch high.

Since greasing or not greasing a pan makes a big difference, note the specific instructions for each recipe. Alternatively, pans may be lined with baking parchment or aluminum foil to prevent sticking and to facilitate the easy removal of loaves. Baking parchment is a very strong, stiff paper that has been treated with sulphuric acid to bond the fibers, making a heat- and grease-resistant paper perfect for baking needs. Look for it in the supermarket or cookware shops. It is not the same as the parchment used for writing purposes.

When baking at high temperatures, stack two baking sheets together (which is known as "double panning") to protect the bottoms of the baked goods from overbrowning. As with all baking pans, be certain to have at least 2 inches of space all the way around the pan in the oven for air circulation.

The Bread Machine

I have to admit I never thought I would bake bread in an automatic machine and say I enjoyed it. I have a high level of expectation about the foods I prepare and eat, and I never expected to have an automatic bread machine in my kitchen. Bread making by hand or food processor was always efficient enough for me. But I found that a bread machine creates fresh, satisfying, full-flavored yeast breads with no compromise of standards when time is an important consideration. Cleanup is also minimal.

Automatic bread-bakers produce bread the "painless" or "no work" way. Often described as looking like a leftover robot from *Star Wars,* the appliance is a Japanese invention (small Japanese kitchens typically have no Western-style baking ovens). They are a revolutionizing innovation in the age-old art of yeast baking. In a machine the size of an old-fashioned bread box is an internal motor that turns a kneading blade, a nonstick-coated mixing and baking cannister, an electric coil to bake the loaf, and a microcomputer. Sophisticated electronics control the motor, temperature, humidity, all timing, and often even store a recipe file in the bread machine's memory bank. The machine can weigh anywhere from 15 to 20 pounds and definitely commands your visual attention when it sits on the kitchen counter.

The process is nothing short of magical. The machine mixes, kneads, punches down, allows for the proper rising time, bakes, and often cools the loaf, all automatically. The electronic process differs from hand bread making because the rising and baking times are fixed, rather than being variable. With a bread machine, a high, light loaf comes from the precise, carefully measured liquid-flour ratio measured into the cannister, rather than a series of risings. To set the process in motion, all you do is assemble and combine the ingredients into the mixing cannister, then push a button to specify your choice of recipe and program the timing. A special signal also alerts the baker when to add embellishments such as raisins or nuts, so that the kneading of the dough is not inhibited. The result is very tasty homemade bread with a nice crust and an even, soft-textured crumb. A loaf made in this manner is superior in nutrition, texture, and taste to its commercially packaged store-bought cousin.

Most bread machines have the capacity for 1 cup of liquid and 3 cups of flour, which means dividing most traditional yeast bread recipes in half. The loaf will be approximately 1½ pounds when baked, serving about 12 slices. This total amount of flour includes any other dry ingredients such as bran, whole-wheat flour, oatmeal, and other specialty flours. Some larger machines on the market use 1½ cups liquid to 4 total cups of flour, making close to a 2-pound loaf. The smallest machines use ½ cup liquid to 2 total cups of flour, making a 1-pound loaf serving about 8 slices.

The loaves are shaped according to the mixing cylinder: oval, cubed, or a high rectangle reminiscent of English cottage pan loaves. Every loaf has the distinctive mark of the automatic bakery: the bottom hole created by the kneading paddle. The entire process takes about 3 to 4 hours, unless programmed otherwise. The timer may be set on a delayed cycle for up to 13 hours, which will give you fresh bread for breakfast or an evening meal after a long day.

The attractions of an automatic bread machine are its perfect ease in preparation and full control of ingredients, the latter especially nice for special or restricted diets, and for people who like whole-grain and specialty breads that are not readily available commercially. The machine is also a lifesaver for people who can't make bread by hand for some reason, but love the unique homemade aroma, taste, and texture of homemade bread. The controls may also be set to "manual," so the machine can be used for just the mixing-kneading process. The dough then may be shaped by hand and baked in a conventional oven to make such breads as whimsically shaped dinner rolls.

The bread machine's drawbacks include a high noise level; some uneven baking; the necessity for caution in handling any parts during the bake cycle, when the machine may radiate heat; the odd, rather small shapes of the loaves as compared to handmade; and sometimes a depression on the top of the loaf caused by over-rising in the warm machine. Some machines do not have a removable cannister, so when measuring, you should take care not to spill ingredients onto the heating element. To ensure proper rising, it's important to use cold rather than warm water when assembling the ingredients. In warm climates or during the summer, place the cannister in the refrigerator to cool the ingredients. The ingredients must be measured precisely to keep them from spilling over into the heating element, as the workbowl has a limited capacity. Once the machine is set, leave it alone. Do not attempt to change settings while the machine is running. Some models have a setting to produce the "crisp" crust and airy texture characteristic of bakery-style baguettes.

If the model does not have a cool cycle to remove the warm, moist air at the end of the baking cycle, the loaf may have a gummy and soggy interior. To avoid this, remove the loaf from the pan as soon as possible and cool on a rack. The best loaves are made with a high proportion of high-gluten bread flour, rather than all whole-wheat flour or all-purpose flour; this helps to ensure a loaf that is not too dense. Many people add a few tablespoons of gluten flour to offset heavier flours called for in some recipes. Loaves with some whole-grain flours or meals will always be more compact in texture than all-white-flour loaves.

All bread machine models require the use of active dry yeast, which does not need preliminary fermentation. The amounts of yeast in recipes will vary, so you will have to experiment to get your own desirable shape and taste. Remember that yeast is a living organism and responds to seasonal changes in humidity and texture. To prevent rancidity, use water and dried milk, instead of fresh milk, especially if you plan to set the computer for a longer cycle time. Experiment with other liquids such as fruit and vegetable juices, applesauce, potato water, etc. Fat brings out the flavor and makes the texture of the bread softer. Use butter or margarine for delicate, rich breads; vegetable oils such as sunflower, walnut, corn, or canola for hearty, whole-grain breads; and good olive oil for Italian or low-cholesterol breads.

Brands on the market to date are Panasonic and National (both made by Matsushita Electric and distributed by Williams-Sonoma), Zojirushi, Hitachi, Regal, Sanyo, Magic Mill, and Welbilt (the last named is listed under the Dak Industries label; see Source Directory). These models all produce the large, 1½-pound loaf, as well as a smaller one. The retailers I interviewed stated that consumers are very satisfied with these appliances, and usually the only reason they are returned is to upgrade to a larger model.

It is important to follow *exactly* the manufacturer's instructions and recipe guidelines for your model. The recipe booklets accompanying most models include a wide variety of very good plain and specialty bread recipes that will appeal to a wide range of home-baking needs. Once the basic recipe has been mastered, feel free to substitute and experiment, with the original recipe serving as your guide. In adapting your own recipes, allow for some trial-and-error time to adapt the timing techniques to your particular machine, especially when monitoring the rising and baking cycles.

Each baker has his or her own individual *batterie de cuisine* of traditional as well as time-saving equipment, and you'll be seeing more of these machines in the kitchens of your friends as time goes on, especially as the price goes down.

Hints for Using Bread Machines

- Layer the ingredients so that the yeast and dry milk are in the bottom of the baking cylinder. It is important that they do not touch the liquid, especially during delayed cycles.

- Measure the ingredients exactly as specified in recipes to avoid the overflowing of the dough onto the heating element or having the top portion of the loaf underbaked. If the dough does overflow, clean the container and element with warm soapy water. Dry thoroughly. If there is still a burnt smell, lay a clean towel in the bottom of the container and cover it with a layer of baking soda. Close the lid and let stand for about 2 days to clean the system.

- Humidity affects the exact volume content of flour. If the dough is too moist, add an additional 1 to 2 tablespoons of flour.

- Eggs and milk are extremely perishable and should not be used in delayed cycles.

- If the dough rises too high, then collapses back into the mixing cylinder, check your rising time. Either the dough has risen too long, or the total amount of dough yielded by the recipe was too large for your model. You might also try cutting back liquid by 2 tablespoons and yeast by ½ teaspoon.

- Use distilled, bottled, or purified water, as the hardness or softness of tap water can affect the final loaf.

- Substituting honey, molasses, malt, or maple syrup for sugar can make a crust exceptionally dark or even burn it. Turn down the crust-crisp control for these breads.

- For regular servings, cut loaves into wedges. For sandwiches, cut off the domed top portion and slice the loaf into rounds and then into halves.

TECHNIQUES

Three time-honored methods are used to create yeast breads. The first and most traditional method involves mixing the yeast with a bit of sugar and a small amount of warm water and allowing it to stand a few minutes until it activates, or "proofs." It is then mixed with the remaining liquid and dry ingredients to form a dough. Most of the recipes in this book use this procedure, known as the **direct method.** Some recipes use the **sponge method,** which involves making an initial batter with the yeast, some liquid, and a small amount of flour to start fermentation. This batter is allowed to proof for an hour up to a day before the remaining ingredients are added to form the bread dough. This ancient method creates a full-flavored and even-textured baked bread. The final method is called **rapid mix method** and is used a few times in the book: Yeast and a portion of the dry ingredients are mixed with hot liquid, then the remaining flour is added to form the dough. Any yeasted bread recipe can be made by hand or in an electric mixer with any of these interchangeable methods.

PROOFING THE YEAST

"Proofing" is a term used by professional bakers to describe the initial process of activating yeast. Sprinkle active dry yeast, with a dash of sugar for food (compressed yeast may be crumbled with the fingers), over lukewarm liquid. Within about 10 minutes, the yeast will become foamy and creamy if it is active. The ideal range for activating active dry yeast is between 100° and 120°. If no yeast or other kitchen thermometer is available when you are learning, test a drop of the warm liquid on the inside of your wrist as for baby formula; it should be comfortably warm. If the liquid is too hot, the living yeast organisms will be killed and the bread will not rise to maximum capacity. If it is too cold, the rise will be slowed considerably. Yeast cells go dormant at 50° or below and are brought back to life at 80° to 90°. The only way to completely inactivate good yeast is with too much heat, 140° and over. One scant tablespoon or one commercial package of active dry yeast is sufficient to raise about 6 cups of flour. Use 2 tablespoons of yeast per that amount for heavy whole-grain flours, or with the addition of embellishments such as fruit and nuts. More than that amount can produce a strong yeast flavor.

SPONGE METHOD

Yeast, a pinch of sugar, a portion of the total liquid, and some flour are beaten with a whisk until creamy and batter-like, covered loosely, and allowed to rise at room temperature until bubbly, usually 1 hour to overnight, depending on the kind of bread. A sponge, or starter, allows for an initial period of fermentation that begins to develop the gluten and gives the bread a fine texture and flavorful tang similar to a mellow sourdough. Any salt and fat required by the recipe are added with the remaining ingredients in the later stages when the dough is formed. The dough is mixed, risen, formed, and baked as in any other bread recipe. This is the oldest method for fermenting European-style doughs and gives a distinctive flavor to the bread.

RAPID-MIX METHOD

This technique was developed by the Fleischmann Yeast Test Kitchens during the 1960s, using their strain of active dry yeast. It is a fast method of mixing a dough, as proofing the yeast in liquid first is not necessary. A portion of the flour and all the other dry ingredients, including the yeast, are combined. Hot liquid (120° to 130°) is added, and the dough is mixed vigorously to form a creamy batter. The yeast is dissolved instantly. The dough is then mixed, kneaded, risen, formed, and baked as in any bread recipe.

MIXING THE DOUGH

It is important for the beginning baker to know how bread dough should feel during all stages of mixing. You may choose to make bread by hand, electric mixer, automatic bread machine, or food processor. Mixing by hand takes about 10 minutes by the clock, the electric mixer takes about 5 minutes total, and the food processor about 1 minute. Automated bread machines are programmed. There seems to be no great difference in the texture or flavor of bread made by these different methods, but it is nice to use a mixer or processor to knead sticky and very soft doughs that require lots of arm work, such as whole grains or brioches.

Most of the recipes in this book give instructions for mixing the dough both by hand and by heavy-duty electric mixer. The latter method is advised for developing tricky whole-grain doughs. Any traditional bread recipe can be adapted easily to being mixed in a heavy-duty electric mixer.

By hand: Place the ingredients for the initial stage of mixing in a large bowl and beat vigorously with a large whisk for about 3 minutes to create a smooth and creamy batter. Add flour slowly, *1/4 to 1/2* *cup at a time,* for the most thorough and controlled incorporation, switching to a wooden spoon when the dough becomes too stiff to beat with the whisk. When ready to knead, the dough will just clear the sides of the bowl. Turn the dough out onto a lightly floured work surface to knead.

By heavy-duty electric mixer: Place the ingredients specified by the recipe to be mixed by a whisk in the workbowl of a heavy-duty mixer fitted with the paddle attachment. Beat at low speed for about 1½ minutes to create a smooth, creamy batter. The whisk attachment can also be used at this stage, if you prefer. Add the flour slowly on low speed, ½ cup at a time, until a soft dough is formed. When ready to knead, the dough will just clear the sides of the bowl and begin to work itself up the paddle. With a plastic dough scraper, remove the dough from the paddle and bowl onto a lightly floured surface for kneading. The dough will consist of dry bits collected on the bottom of the bowl and wet dough on the top. Knead by hand on a lightly floured surface to even the dough out. The dough hook may be used at the very end of mixing, but is not recommended in the early stages of mixing as it cannot blend thoroughly and the batter will remain lumpy.

By food processor: This fast method of mixing dough is completely different from the two previous methods. There are many excellent publications entirely devoted to recipes developed specifically for the processor available. Check your manufacturer's instructions for specifics on your machine, as some processors have a motor too weak for bread dough. Small processors can handle about 3 cups total of flour and 1½ cups of liquid. The standard, or larger, processor can handle 6 to 8 cups total of flour and 2½ cups of liquid.

In the workbowl, dissolve the yeast and sugar in half the total amount of liquid called for in the recipe. Add the remaining amount of cool (80° to 90°) liquid and half the total flour, as the processor itself will heat up the dough. Using the plastic yeast blade or steel blade, process for the time directed and then add the remaining flour; the batter should just form a ball of dough. Adjust the dough consistency now, if necessary, by adding more flour or liquid. I always give a few kneads by hand to "feel" and even out dough consistency.

Making brioche doughs by hand: Traditional brioches are quickly and easily made in a heavy-duty electric mixer, but for those readers who do not have such machines, this unique dough may be made by hand by the traditional French method. For first attempts, please note that a cool day is best for making brioche.

Place all but ½ cup of the flour in a pile on a clean work surface, preferably marble. Make a well in the center. Place the yeast, a tablespoon of the sugar, and warm (105° to 115°) water into the well. Stir to dissolve. Let stand until bubbly, about 10 minutes. Sprinkle the rim of the well with the remaining sugar and salt. Add all the eggs into the yeast mixture and blend thoroughly with fingers. Using your fingertips to beat the egg mixture, gradually bring the dry ingredients into the center of the well. The dough will be very sticky, yet elastic. Alternately lift the dough with your fingers and slap it onto the work surface to develop the dough. Knead in this manner vigorously for 8 to 10 minutes, gradually adding the last ½ cup flour as necessary to keep the dough from sticking. The dough will be smooth, satiny, and able to be lifted in one mass easily.

To incorporate the butter in small amounts, divide the room temperature butter into 4 equal portions. Position each at one of the 4 corners of the dough. Slapping the butter until malleable with the 4 fingers of your working hand held stiff, quickly smear the butter into the mass of dough, alternating from all 4 directions. The goal is to incorporate the butter quickly and evenly into the dough with a slapping action without allowing it to melt from the friction of your hand. The total working time should be no more than about 5 minutes. Knead the dough gently a few times by hand to finish incorporating the butter, but do not crash or slap the dough anymore at this point. Form the dough into a ball and let rise, form, and bake as for Brioche, page 51.

KNEADING

Kneading is a logical and practical set of physical motions that transform a dough from a rough, shaggy mass to a soft and smoothly pliable dough. The proteins in wheat flour, called gluten, become stretchy when worked, creating a structure strong enough to contain the expanding carbon dioxide gases, by-products of the yeast's reproduction. Techniques for kneading are unique to each baker: Some push, some press, some squeeze or slam. Some are gentle, others vigorous. If you are happy with the consistency of your dough and satisfied with the finished loaves, then you are doing a good job.

Mechanical action in the form of beating by hand, an electric mixer, or a food processor forms the initial batter. The barely stiff and sticky dough will just clear the sides of the workbowl when the dough has absorbed close to its limit of flour; it is then ready for kneading. Be certain your work surface is at a height that allows your arms easy movement at the elbows. A table that is too high will constrict your movements, while one too low will strain the muscles.

Sprinkle the smooth marble, wood, or plastic work surface with a light dusting of flour, about 1 to 2 tablespoons, just enough to prevent sticking. If the dough sticks to the work surface, it will inhibit the smooth, easy kneading motions. A light dusting of the palms is also helpful, but some patches of dough almost always stick to the hands. Scrape the shaggy dough mass out of the bowl with a spatula or plastic scraper onto the floured surface. This first step of incorporating small amounts of flour may also be done by manipulating the dough with a plastic scraper, a universal baker's tool that acts as a hand extension, until the dough automatically picks up enough flour to eliminate very sticky patches and you can take over with your hands.

Place your feet slightly apart, keep your knees flexed, and bend a bit at the waist toward the work surface. Place one hand gently on the dough surface. Using large, fluid movements, slowly push the dough away from your body with the heel of the hand. Remember to breathe with the pushing motion. This motion, which uses the whole body rather than just the arms and shoulders, has been likened to tai chi exercises. As you pull back, use the fingers to lift the farthest edge of the dough and give it a quarter turn, then fold the dough in half towards you and push away again. The dough will

slide across the surface, absorbing the small amount of flour it requires.

Repeat the sequence: push, turn, and fold rhythmically, rather like following a mantra. Use a pressure equal to the resistance felt. The dough will at first be quite soft, needing gentle motions. There are schools of hard kneaders and soft kneaders—your own nature will indicate your particular style. Neither one seems to make a difference in the texture of the finished loaf. The kneading process can take anywhere from 2 to 10 minutes, with hand-mixed dough taking more time and machine-mixed dough taking less. If too much dough sticks to your hands, simply rub them together to flake off the excess. On the work surface, scrape up any large dry slabs of sticky dough with a dough scraper and discard. They will stay dry patches if added to the dough.

As you work, add additional flour only 1 tablespoon at a time as necessary to prevent sticking by sprinkling it on the work surface. Wait until the flour has been absorbed before adding more. This helps you maintain the maximum amount of control so that the dough will end up the exact consistency required by the recipe. Kneading the dough strengthens the gluten fibers, and will eventually create a soft, firm honeycomb pattern in cut slices of baked bread. Whole-wheat and rye doughs tend to be denser, wetter, and stickier to the touch than white doughs. The amount of flour to be incorporated at this point will vary, but it is important not to add too much. The level of humidity, the amount of moisture in the flour, and the amount of initial beating are all variables. Every batch of dough is unique in the exact amount of flour used.

As you learn from experience in kneading dough, the rhythm of your motions will begin to adjust automatically to the requirements of the dough. At this point in the kneading process, the dough will quickly evolve into a smooth ball with tiny blisters forming just under the skin. It will have two surfaces: a smooth one that is in contact with the work surface, and a creased, folded top. The smooth surface will pick up and absorb the flour while the top is being worked.

When to stop kneading depends on what type of bread you are making. Adding too much flour creates a stiff dough and a dry baked loaf. This is by far the most common mistake for beginning bakers. If the dough is wet and slack, add more flour. The amount of flour used in a recipe is meant to be a *guide,* rather than a constant. Because of atmospheric, emotional, and technical variables, each loaf of bread is unique. This is where experience eventually comes in as a guide. Doughs made with all high-gluten bread flour will require a bit more kneading than doughs made of all-purpose flour. Under-kneading will give any dough a slack appearance and feel. Generally, you want a mass that can just hold its own shape, especially if it will not be baked in a pan. Remember, more flour will be absorbed into the body of the dough during the rising process.

If the dough is cut at this point, you will notice a very sticky section often called the "wound." Enclose that area by pinching it closed, rather than adding more flour. You will now have a dough ready to be "fermented," or "proofed," during the rising period.

A **soft dough,** such as that for batter breads, yeast coffee cakes, brioches, or other breads containing a large proportion of fat, requires an exact measure of flour, tends to be sticky, and may not be able to retain its shape. Chilling the dough is required for handling.

A **medium dough** will just hold its shape yet be smooth, such as that for sweet doughs and whole-grain breads. The moisture in these doughs contributes to a moist, tender, light-textured baked bread. While being kneaded, whole-grain doughs will have a definite tacky, even grainy or nubby quality. It is important that dough not be worked beyond this point. Refer to the sections devoted specifically to sweet breads and whole-grain breads for specific pointers for perfect loaves.

A **stiff dough** will be firm, smooth, and begin to have a slightly unyielding, yet resilient tension. All-white-flour doughs are in this category. Whole-grain doughs kneaded to this point will be dry and crumbly. White doughs with eggs will tend to have a translucent quality.

Most of the breads in this book are **kneaded breads.** Enough flour must be used to form a dough stiff enough to be kneaded. Lean doughs, such as those for French and country breads, have little or no fat added. Rich doughs have fat added and are used to make sweet doughs and exotic batter breads such as Crescia al Fromaggio, page 142.

A **rolled bread** undergoes a double leavening process: once with yeast in the initial mixing and again with the dough being folded or layered (usually with butter), as in Whole-Wheat Croissants (page 129), Almond Butter Coffee Cake (page 120), and Danish pastry. The moisture in the butter evaporates during baking, creating steam and raising the delicate layers of dough.

In **batter breads,** the ingredients are combined and beaten with a wooden spoon or an electric mixer to make a soft, sticky dough that is not kneaded. Brioches, savarins, and "casserole" loaves are batter breads. Batter breads always need to be baked in a container, such as a loaf pan, as they cannot hold their own shape.

RISING

I use deep 3- and 4-quart plastic containers with lids for raising dough, although almost any large bowl will do. Avoid metal bowls, as they conduct heat easily and can "cook" the dough if it rises in too warm a spot, such as over a pilot light. Dough tends to do best in a deep container rather than in a wide shallow bowl where it will rise horizontally and form a big puddle. Grease the container and place the ball of dough in it, turning it once to grease the top to prevent drying. Plastic wrap is good as a cover, helping to retain the precious moisture and to inhibit the formation of a thick skin. A moist, clean tea towel may be substituted. Mentally note or mark on the container for reference where the dough will be when risen to double.

It is difficult to predict exact rising times, as they depend on the temperature of the finished dough, the amount of yeast used, and the general atmospheric conditions. Drafts will cause a dough to rise slowly and unevenly. Whole-grain breads and doughs high in fats and fruits take longer than lean white-flour doughs. Generally, a dough will take 1 to 2 hours to rise to the classic "doubled in bulk" stage at a warm room temperature, about 75° to 80°. Test a risen dough by poking two fingers into it. If the indentations remain, the dough is adequately risen. If the marks fill in, re-cover the bowl and let the dough sit 15 minutes longer before testing it again.

Most of the recipes in this book specify letting the dough rise in a warm place. Some of the choices are:
- Turn the oven to 150° for 3 minutes. Turn off the heat and allow the dough to sit in the oven with the door ajar.
- Allow the dough to rise over a gas pilot on the stovetop, or inside the oven with the door ajar, or on top of the dryer while drying clothes.
- Place the bowl in or over a pan of warm water away from drafts.
- Take it for a nice ride around town in the back of a car. Dough loves the gentle motion and warmth.

If you have the time, a longer rise always makes for a tastier loaf. I either raise my dough at a cool to warm room temperature for however long it takes to rise, or I leave it overnight, as dough activity at room temperature decreases by over half at night in an unheated house. To slow a dough further, I let it rise in the refrigerator for 8 hours to overnight, covered tightly with plastic wrap to retain moisture. Dough that has been refrigerated must come back to room temperature to complete its rising process, so count on about 4 extra hours for the dough to return to room temperature.

COOL-RISE METHOD

Many recipes use the "cool rise" or "refrigerator" method. Developed by the midwestern Robin Hood Consumer Test Kitchen, this method allows the baker to prepare dough one day and bake it the next. Mix and knead the dough per recipe instructions. Let the dough rest, loosely covered with plastic wrap, for about 30 minutes. Divide and shape the dough as stated in the recipe. Cover the prepared pans loosely with plastic wrap to allow for dough expansion. Refrigerate for 2 to 24 hours. The dough will continue to rise as the internal temperature drops, to about 1 inch above the rim of the pan. Remove it from the refrigerator to bake at any time. Let the pans stand at room temperature while preheating the oven to the specified temperature for 20 minutes. The dough will still be cold as it goes into the oven. Note that bread pans for the cool-rise method must be able to take fast changes in temperature and should be made of metal, rather than Pyrex or clay. This method can be used with any bread recipe, and is especially nice for sweet rolls.

DEFLATING THE DOUGH

After rising, the dough will be light and delicately domed. Turn it out onto a lightly floured work surface. The act of turning out the dough will naturally deflate it, alleviating the need for a specific "punching down," although this is a gratifying old ritual. No more kneading is required at this point, as it will activate the gluten and give the dough a springy tension that can make it difficult to sculpt. Divide the dough into equal portions and shape into the desired loaves. If the dough resists forming, cover it and let it rest for 10 minutes on the work surface before continuing. Add any embellishments at this time by patting the dough into a large rectangle, sprinkling it with fruits and nuts as directed in your recipe, and folding the dough into thirds. Knead the dough gently to distribute. This technique quickly and efficiently adds any heavy ingredients not added to the dough during mixing.

FORMING A LOAF

Pat the dough portion into a rough rectangle with the heel of your hand and your fingertips. Tightly roll the dough towards you, rotating it to make a rectangle, oval, or round shape. The shaping of loaves is a highly individual technique and takes some practice. Many bread experts have complicated instructions for forming a loaf, but the main objective is to produce a tight surface tension and a smooth top. Pinch all seams together to close. Once the loaf is formed and the gluten is activated, it will have to sit about 15 minutes for the dough to relax before it can be reshaped. Place the loaves on greased or parchment-lined baking sheets or in well-greased pans, seam side down. The dough should fill a full half to two thirds of the pan. Any less and you will have a flat loaf; any more and you will have an overflowing loaf that looks top-heavy.

SECOND RISE

Let the dough rise, with plastic wrap loosely draped over it, in a warm area. The dough is ready when doubled in bulk, or about 1 inch above the pan rim. This takes half the amount of time of the initial rise, usually about 30 to 45 minutes. Twenty minutes before baking, preheat the oven to the specified temperature.

Before being placed in the oven, most loaves are slashed decoratively, which allows the dough to expand during baking. The slashes should be no deeper than ¼ inch, and are made with a quick motion with a very sharp edge, such as a serrated knife. The patterns you choose can become your trademark. A glaze is then applied to protect the crust during baking and to give a finished look (see page 155 for glaze recipes).

BAKING

Place the pans into the preheated oven, on the center to lowest shelf unless the recipe states otherwise, with at least 2 inches of space between the pans for best heat circulation. Breads on baking sheets are best baked in the center of the oven, one sheet at a time. Baking stops the fermentation of the yeast by raising the internal temperature past 140° and evaporating the alcohol. Within the first 10 minutes, the rapidly expanding gas reaches its maximum, a stage known as "oven spring," and the shape of your finished loaf will be set. After that time, except for allowing heat to escape, you can open the oven door without affecting the finished shape. Check the bread at least 10 minutes earlier than the recipe specifies for doneness, to look for signs of early or uneven browning.

If the dough didn't rise long enough before baking, the loaf will be small and compact. If it rose too much, the loaf may collapse in the oven. Every baker I know has seen both of these classic mistakes at least once.

Generally, lean doughs such as French and Vienna are baked at high temperatures of 400° to 425°, and rich, more cake-like doughs with a high percentage of butter and other embellishments are baked at 350°. Each recipe specifies baking times.

Practice using all of your senses to determine when a loaf is done: Your sense of smell will determine whether all the alcohol is evaporated; your sight will tell you if a crust is browned enough; your hearing will verify the hollow sound a finished loaf makes when it is tapped. And remember to appreciate irregularities! Homemade bread is supposed to look homemade.

COOLING AND SLICING

Remove the bread immediately from the pans, unless otherwise directed, and cool completely on racks before slicing. Technically bread has not finished baking until it is cool and the excess moisture has evaporated. French breads and rolls are best eaten when cooled to room temperature, but richer whole-grain and cake-like breads should be cooled completely and then reheated.

A serrated bread knife is designed for slicing bread without squashing or tearing it. Slice the loaves on a bread board with a sawing motion. Bread should be cool when it is sliced; if you must cut warm bread, turn it on its side to prevent squashing. Store bread in the refrigerator or at room temperature in a plastic bag.

REHEATING

Bread may be reheated in a 350° oven. Place the unsliced loaf, au naturel or wrapped in aluminum foil, into a preheated oven for 15 to 20 minutes to crisp the crust and just heat through. Sliced breads and rolls reheat best wrapped. To reheat bread in a microwave oven, place an unwrapped loaf or slice on a paper towel. Microwave on high only until slightly warm, about 15 seconds. If bread or rolls are overheated, they will become hard and tough as they cool.

Home Freezing

High-Altitude Guide

Home freezing is a simple and safe method of preserving food. Although fresh is best when it comes to yeast and quick breads, frozen baked goods are good to have on hand. Please remember that the freezer compartment of a refrigerator is not a true deep freeze, but is intended for short storage. It will keep foods for a few months, but for long-term safe storage, you should freeze at 0° or below. To freeze yeast breads and dinner rolls, completely bake according to the recipe. Let cool to room temperature on a rack. Wrap whole or presliced loaves first in good-quality plastic wrap, then aluminum foil or polyethylene freezer bags. Label and date loaves, if possible. The maximum storage time is about three months.

To thaw, let the loaf stand at room temperature for about 3 hours completely wrapped. Bread may be refreshed, or thawed, in a 350° oven. Place an unsliced loaf, au naturel or wrapped in aluminum foil, in a preheated oven for 15 to 30 minutes to crisp the crust and heat it through. Sliced breads may be refreshed in a toaster. Rolls reheat best wrapped, as they dry out quickly.

To freeze yeasted coffee cakes and sweet rolls, completely bake according to the recipe. Cool to room temperature, wrap, and store as for yeast breads. After the bread is thawed and heated, glaze, ice, or dust with powdered sugar just before serving.

To freeze biscuits, coffee cakes, muffins, waffles, and nut breads, completely bake according to the recipe. Cool to room temperature, wrap, and store as for yeast breads. Stack waffles, separating them with plastic wrap or parchment. Waffles are best reheated in a toaster directly from the freezer. The maximum storage time for all frozen quick breads is two months.

It is important to note that altitudes over 3,000 feet affect baking procedures. Because the atmosphere is drier, due to lower air pressure, flours will dry out. Bread recipes will require a little more liquid to produce a soft, silky yeast dough. Water usually takes longer to boil. Sugar and chocolate tend to become more concentrated in batters, and liquid evaporates quickly. The scientist in you will need to closely observe results and experiment to get the proper dough consistencies for quick and yeast breads. Asking a neighbor or coworker for first-hand information is the best guide. There are special reference books devoted to the art of high-altitude baking.

Fermentation is faster the higher you go: The leavening carbon dioxide gases are able to expand faster due to the thinner air, and rising times will be decreased by up to one half. For bread baking there is really only one technique to remember: *To avoid over-rising, reduce yeast by ½ teaspoon for every tablespoon or package called for in the recipe.* A second rise is recommended for the best flavor and texture. No temperature adjustment of liquids is necessary.

Please note that oven temperatures should be increased by 25° to compensate for faster rising in the oven and slower heating. The same rules apply to sourdough and quick-bread baking. The lower boiling point for water also affects deep-frying methods for fritters, sopaipillas, and doughnuts. The following is a general guide in case you find yourself baking in Yosemite, Denver, or an Adirondack Mountains cabin:

Liquids: For each cup, increase the amount by 1 tablespoon at more than 3,000 feet; 2 to 3 tablespoons at 5,000 feet; and 3 to 4 tablespoons at 7,000 to 8,000 feet.

Sugar: For each cup, decrease the amount by 1 tablespoon at more than 3,000 feet; 2 tablespoons at 5,000 feet; and 3 tablespoons at 7,000 to 8,000 feet.

Flour: For each cup, increase flour by 1 tablespoon at more than 3,000 feet; 2 tablespoons at 5,000 feet; and 3 tablespoons at more than 6,500 feet. Store in airtight containers.

Baking Soda and Powder: For each teaspoon, decrease by ⅛ teaspoon at more than 3,000 feet, and ¼ teaspoon at more than 5,000 feet.

Deep-frying: Lower the cooking heat of oil by 3° for every 1,000 feet above 3,000 feet.

RECIPES

EUROPEAN COUNTRY BREADS

On my first visit to France so long ago, I was invited to dine in a very old country house of hand-cut stone in a truffle-oak orchard south of Albi. Nestled in the west part of Languedoc near the Gascony border, this is the land of fois gras, Toulouse-Lautrec, Gallo-Roman masonry, and Perrier mineral water. I was seated at the end of a long, rough-hewn plank table for a hearty family-style Sunday midday meal. I sat in outright amazement at the makings of a true country feast and certainly one of the most memorable meals I have ever eaten.

A gigantic rump of Auvergne beef encrusted with coarse sea salt and Dijon mustard was roasting over an open hearth fire in an even more gigantic lidded cast-iron kettle. In the far corner stood a small four-burner gas range with two ancient cast-iron frying pans pushed to the rear of the stove; both contained vegetables waiting to be sautéed in sweet butter. One was heaped with the ubiquitous French-cut green beans, and the other held a mound of the fresh mushrooms known as *cèpes,* a member of the Boletus family gathered locally under the oaks. My mind's eye can still see the handles of these huge black pans at parallel angles in the dark corner.

In the center of the table was coarse homemade *pâté de campagne* in a glass spring-top jar, crisp sticks of baguette, and a salad glistening with a pungent Dijon mustard and Mediterranean olive oil vinaigrette to follow the roast. An immense cut-crystal bowl was filled to the rim with the legendary tiny *fraises des bois* to accompany the cheese course. Pastries from the town bake shop were last, along with small, acrid cups of the strong coffee the French hold so dear to finishing their meal. Strangely enough, that crystal bowl of berries is the main visual element that sparkles in my memory of that afternoon. The hinged wooden shutters opened to let in the only light, which reflected through the crystal and sent fragments of rainbows onto the clay walls while we ate. That, and the conversation, was the entertainment.

But what I remember most clearly from that midsummer repast is the larger-than-life dominating presence of a round loaf of peasant bread. A locally produced loaf weighing over ten pounds and a full foot in diameter, hearty with whole grains and deeply browned almost to black, this bread was hacked, not cut or sliced, into asymmetrical pieces. The crust was 2 to 3 inches thick, bordering on the inedible, but the interior was soft and porous from the hot wood-fired oven, and was easily pulled out with the fingers to eat. The slightly acid taste of the bread was a perfect foil to the oily vinaigrette and the rich cheeses: a very young Brie, a little Cabecou, and a local Roquefort.

What was this bread? Where was it made, and by whom? Could I reproduce it at home? The memory of this experience continues to fuel my interest in the rough, sustaining country loaves so dear to Europeans. For a while, it seemed these breads would be lost to mass production and mechanization. But they have resurfaced with the trend to *retro cuisine,* created by the demand for wholesome and chemically untreated food. The alchemistic artisans who create these loaves regard bread making more as a craft than a business. They tend a collection of Gothic fieldstone and brick ovens throughout Europe, many on the sites of medieval monasteries. These breads are one of the oldest forms of sustenance, the foundation of a diet based on simple indigenous ingredients and influenced by local traditions.

Known simply as "daily bread," "country bread," *pain de campagne, pain paysan,* or *pane bianco,* these impressive loaves are usually over-sized, hand-molded into uneven shapes, dusted heavily with flour, and baked until bordering on black. They are encased in a thick, rugged crust that is at times hard to break, protecting a soft- to dense-textured moist interior. Ranging in size from a small roll to a very large family loaf, one loaf can weigh as much as 14 pounds. There is no one definition of country bread, since they may be made from all-white flour or a combination of locally available hearty whole grains such as rye, barley, oats, and, of course, whole wheat. Country breads are not only astoundingly delicious, but, due to good fresh-milled flour, they are nutritionly superior. Low in fats, these wholesome loaves fit in well with modern health consciousness.

For country breads, the longer and slower the rise, the better the flavor and texture of the baked loaf. This is achieved by letting the breads rise at a cool room temperature rather than in a warm place. The formed rounds of raw dough rest in *bannetons,* canvas-lined wicker rising baskets. They are turned out onto a *pelle,* a long-handled wooden paddle used to thrust dough onto the hot oven floor. There are no thermometers or timers needed, as the baker's senses are fine-tuned by experience.

Many of these breads utilize a starter, also known as a "sponge." A starter, known as *levain* in France, "chef" or *desum* in Flemish, and *biga* in Italy, is simply flour, water, and sometimes a small amount of yeast combined and allowed to sit for a designated period of initial fermentation before being incorporated into the actual bread dough. Starters give strength to weak flours and produce a wonderful aroma and the light texture under a characteristically thick crust. A starter can produce a loaf with a tang ranging from a slightly sour taste to the sharp bite of true San Francisco sourdough, depending on the length of time it ferments. A good, fresh starter should smell very much like ripe apples or pears.

The secret to re-creating crusty hearth baking in a home oven is to use an unglazed clay baking stone on the lowest rack in an electric oven or on the oven floor in a gas range. Some bakers also place a second stone on the topmost shelf to further imitate brick ovens. Breads may be baked directly on the stone, or on baking sheets placed on the stone. Avoid placing doughs that drip butter or sugar on the stone's porous surface, as drips burn quickly and will produce a bitter-smelling smoke-filled oven and stains that cannot be cleaned.

Use commercial pizza stones sold in gourmet shops, kiln shelves from a pottery supply, or unglazed 6-inch-square quarry tiles. The commercial pizza stones are available in two round sizes, 12 inches or 16 inches in diameter, or as a 12-by-14-inch rectangle. Always leave 2 inches of air space between the tiles and the oven walls for heat to circulate. The clay will produce a steady, moderately radiating heat and bake breads in a fashion similar to the ancient *querns* of Egypt, the *hornos* of the American Southwest, the rural village *fournos* of the Greek countryside, and the Italian domed brick ovens with their oak and birch fires.

A Note on Bannetons
To season a new basket in which bread dough is to rise:
Choose a closely woven, natural, unglazed basket from 6 to 10 inches in diameter, as desired. Brush the basket with olive oil and lay it upside down in the sun for a few hours. The heat will help the basket absorb the oil. Dust heavily with flour to cover all moist areas, then tap out the excess. Store the basket in a dry, protected area. Add flour as needed. The basket pattern will be imprinted on the dough, which is inverted and turned out before baking.

HOW TO BAKE COUNTRY BREADS IN A DUTCH OVEN

Any country bread baked in a Dutch oven is a real taste treat. The crust is exceptionally thin and crisp and the interior sweetly fragrant. This bread is reminiscent of that baked by early-American mountain sheepherders in outdoor kitchens. Whether you are rafting the Colorado, camping in the Sierra or the Alleghenys, or picnicking in the backyard, the combination of hot cast iron radiating heat from all sides, glowing coals, and fresh air contributes to a loaf similar in consistency to one baked in an enclosed outdoor oven.

Grease with butter the inside of the lid and the inside of a 12-inch (6-quart) seasoned cast-iron Dutch oven cooking pot. Line the bottom with parchment, if desired. Add a ball of dough at any point in its rising cycle. Cover the pot with the lid and let the dough rise at room temperature until doubled in bulk, about 1½ hours. Burn a wood, charcoal, or combination fire until you have a good supply of coals. Sweep the coals into a shallow depression in the ground dug next to the fire, saving some larger coals. Set the pot on a grill or balance it on three stones ½ inch above a ring of 6 to 8 evenly spaced hot coals. Set 12 to 16 larger coals directly on the pot lid around the edges and in the middle for even heat distribution from the top as well as the bottom of the pot. Check the bread after 35 minutes; please note that the handle will be very hot. Use a pair of pliers to lift the lid, and wear leather gloves to avoid burns. Bake for 45 to 50 minutes, fanning the coals periodically, until the bread is golden brown, crisp, and hollow sounding when tapped. Remove the loaf with care from the hot pan using oven mitts, and serve immediately.

Italian Country Bread

(Italian-style White Bread)

This is a classic rustic bread, sometimes known as *pane bianco* or *pane casalinga*, made into one large round and baked on a hot stone to produce a crusty, domed outer crust and a moist interior full of irregular holes. It is perfect with food and wonderful to have on hand to serve with wine before a meal. Note that the technique varies from traditional American bread recipes: cool liquid, a small amount of yeast, an initial rising with a sponge, a long resting time to develop taste, moist dough, and a high baking temperature. It appeals to the purist since nothing is added to detract from the developed fragrance and flavor of grain. Note that unbleached all-purpose flour is used, as it has a protein content similar to that of 00 grade flour in Italy (12 percent) and creates a fine, white loaf.

For a winter picnic serve with Red Pepper Cream Cheese (page 161), fresh cracked crab or cold smoked chicken, and a good dry white wine.

Yield: 1 large or 2 small round loaves

Sponge
1 teaspoon active dry yeast
1/3 cup lukewarm water (90° to 100°)
2/3 cup milk at room temperature
1 teaspoon honey, maple syrup, or malt syrup
2 cups unbleached all-purpose flour

Dough
1 teaspoon active dry yeast
2 cups water at room temperature
1 tablespoon salt
About 5 to 5 1/2 cups unbleached all-purpose flour

1. To prepare the sponge: In a large bowl, sprinkle the yeast over warm water and milk. Stir to dissolve. Add the honey or syrup and flour. Beat with a whisk until smooth. Cover loosely with plastic wrap and let stand at room temperature at least 4 hours to overnight. This sponge can be stored up to 1 week in the refrigerator before using, if necessary. It will be bubbly.

2. To make the dough: Add the yeast, water, salt, and 1 cup of the flour to the sponge. Beat hard with a whisk for 3 minutes, or for 1 minute in a heavy-duty electric mixer fitted with the paddle attachment on medium speed. Add the remaining flour 1 cup at a time, switching to a wooden spoon when necessary if making by hand. The dough will be smooth, yet not pull away from the sides of the bowl.

3. Turn the dough out onto a lightly floured surface and knead vigorously until very elastic, yet still moist and tacky, about 5 minutes. This is important for a good, light texture. Slam the dough hard against the work surface to develop the gluten. Set aside uncovered for 5 to 10 minutes. Knead again, and the sticky dough will smooth out without any extra flour.

4. Place in an ungreased deep container (plastic is good), cover with plastic wrap, and let rise at room temperature for 3 hours to overnight. The dough should triple in volume.

5. Remove the dough from the container. Place on the work surface, knead lightly into 1 large or 2 small rounds, and flatten slightly. Dust lightly with flour and place in 1 or 2 dusted cloth-lined baskets, or bannetons, or on a greased or parchment-lined baking sheet, smooth side down. Let rise uncovered at room temperature until soft and springy, 1 to 3 hours. Twenty minutes before baking, preheat the oven to 400° with a baking stone in it, if desired.

6. Slash a criss-cross design into the top of the free-form loaves no deeper than 1/4 inch, using a serrated knife. Slide the baking sheet into the hot oven (or carefully invert the loaves directly onto the baking stone from the baskets), and bake until very dark and crusty, about 55 to 60 minutes. Cool on a rack. This bread is best completely cooled and reheated.

Italian Whole-Wheat Country Bread
(Pane Bigio)
In Step 2, substitute 1 1/2 cups stone-ground whole-wheat flour and 1/3 cup barley flour for an equal amount of unbleached flour. The total amount of unbleached flour used will be 3 1/2 to 4 cups. Proceed to mix, let rise, shape, and bake as for Country Bread.

Italian Whole-Wheat and Rye Bread
(Pane Integrale con Segale)
In Step 2, substitute 1/3 cup each coarse stone-ground whole-wheat flour and rye meal (pumpernickel flour) for an equal amount of unbleached flour. The total amount of unbleached flour used will be about 4 to 4 1/2 cups. Proceed to mix, let rise, shape, and bake as for Country Bread.

Rosemary-Raisin Bread
(Pane di Rosmarino all'Uva)
In Step 2, add 1/4 cup sugar, 3 eggs, 1/3 cup good olive oil, and 1 tablespoon dried rosemary or 3 tablespoons chopped fresh rosemary leaves during the mixing. Add about 1/2 cup more flour. Proceed to mix and let rise as for Country Bread.

In Step 5, sprinkle 1⅓ cups dark raisins, which have been plumped in hot water for 10 minutes and drained, over the dough before kneading lightly to evenly distribute the raisins. Proceed to shape, let rise, and bake as for Country Bread.

Country Bread with Bran and Olive Oil
(Campagnolo)
In Step 2, add 3 tablespoons good olive oil and 1⅓ cups wheat bran during the mixing. Proceed to mix, let rise, shape, and bake as for Country Bread.

Country Raisin and Walnut Bread
(Pane di Uva con Noci)
In Step 2, add 2 tablespoons each room temperature unsalted butter and sugar during mixing. In Step 5, pat the dough into a large rectangle and sprinkle with 2 cups each golden raisins and chopped walnuts. Fold over the dough and knead lightly to evenly distribute the fruit and nuts. Form into 2 round loaves or 10 rolls. Let rise and bake as for Country Bread.

Pain de Campagne

(French-style Whole-Wheat Country Bread)

This loaf is the home-style version of *boule de Poilâne*. The Boulangerie de Poilâne is the most famous bakery in Paris, located at no. 8, rue du Cherche-Midi, on the site of Presmontres, a twelfth-century convent. Steep winding stairs descend to the archaic vaulted cellar where the bread is mixed, risen, and baked around the clock in brick ovens. This big round loaf has been made in Paris since the Middle Ages, and is known

as *le vrai pain*, "real bread." It is the flavor of France, utilizing the age-old baking wisdom of *la technique*, which brings out the best flavors in bread.

This whole-grain country bread is baked to a deep brown and decorated with a traditional grape pattern made of dough. A healthful, earthy bread with no fat, it is baked on the third day after it is first mixed. It has a chewy, whole-grain texture and complements both elegant and rustic meals. Because it uses a starter, this loaf will stay moist for 2 to 3 days at room temperature. This recipe also makes 2 medium loaves or wonderful small rolls for individual servings (spread them with Chèvre Coeur à la Crème with Thyme and Walnuts, page 163). Pain de Campagne is excellent served with all types of cheese.

Yield: 1 large round loaf

Starter
1 tablespoon (1 package) active dry yeast
½ cup whole-wheat flour
½ cup lukewarm water (90° to 100°)

Sponge
2 cups lukewarm water (90° to 100°)
Starter, above
1½ cups unbleached all-purpose or bread flour
1½ cups whole-wheat flour

Dough
Sponge, above
3½ to 4 cups unbleached all-purpose or bread flour
4 teaspoons salt

Glaze
1 egg
2 teaspoons water

1. Day one: To make the starter: Place the yeast and whole-wheat flour in a deep bowl or a plastic 4-quart bucket with a lid. Add the water and whisk hard until a smooth batter is formed. Cover and let stand at room temperature for about 24 hours. The starter will bubble and begin to ferment.

2. Day two: Make the sponge by adding the water to the starter. Whisk to combine. Add the unbleached and whole-wheat flours alternately 1 cup at a time, changing to a wooden spoon when necessary, until a smooth batter is formed. The sponge will be very wet. Scrape down the sides of the bowl, cover, and let rise again at room temperature for about 24 hours.

3. Day three: To make the bread dough: Stir down the sponge with a wooden spoon. Add 1 cup of the unbleached flour and the salt. Gradually add most of the remaining flour ½ cup at a time to make a firm and resilient dough.

4. Knead the dough on a lightly floured work surface until smooth, slightly tacky, and springy, about 3 to 5 minutes, adding 1 tablespoon of flour at a time as necessary to prevent sticking. The dough will form little blisters under the surface when ready to rise. Place the dough in a greased deep container, cover tightly, and let rise at room temperature until fully doubled in bulk, about 1½ to 2 hours.

5. Turn the dough out onto the work surface. Reserve a small amount of the dough to use as decoration, if desired. Shape the remaining dough into a tight round and place on a greased or parchment-lined baking sheet. (Or shape to fit a long or round cloth-lined basket lightly dusted with flour; let rise before

turning out onto a prepared baking sheet or onto a hot baking stone.)

6. Cover the dough loosely with plastic wrap and let rise about 1 hour at room temperature. Twenty minutes before baking, preheat the oven to 425°, with a baking stone placed on the lowest rack, if desired. (To form a crisp crust: Fifteen minutes before baking, pour hot water into a broiler pan and place the pan on the bottom rack to steam the oven for the initial baking period. This is an optional step.) Slash the loaf decoratively with a serrated knife. In a small bowl, whisk together the egg and water to make a glaze, and brush the entire surface of the loaf. If you have reserved dough for decoration, form it into a pile of round grapes and a few leaves and tendrils. It is important that any decoration made from reserved dough be applied after the loaf has had its final rise and glazing. Glaze the decoration after applying.

7. Bake in the preheated oven for 40 to 45 minutes, or until the loaves are browned, crisp, and hollow sounding when tapped. Remove from the oven and place on a rack to cool completely before slicing.

Vienna Bread

Vienna Bread is a crusty French-style loaf with the flavorful qualities of milk and a bit of butter. This is a versatile daily bread, good for sandwiches, French toast, or soaking up meat juices. It stays fresh for 2 to 3 days at room temperature.

Yield: 3 oval loaves

Sponge
1½ tablespoons (1½ packages) active
dry yeast
1 tablespoon sugar
1 cup warm water (105° to 115°)
1 cup warm milk (105° to 115°)
2 cups unbleached all-purpose or bread flour

Dough
1 tablespoon salt
3 tablespoons unsalted butter, melted and
cooled
3½ to 4 cups unbleached all-purpose or
bread flour
Sponge, above

Rich Egg Glaze, page 155
3 tablespoons sesame seeds

1. To make the sponge: In a large bowl, whisk together the yeast, sugar, water, milk, and flour. Beat hard until smooth and creamy. Cover loosely with plastic wrap and let the sponge rise at room temperature about 1 hour, or until bubbly and doubled in bulk.

2. To make the dough: Add the salt, butter, and 1 cup of the flour to the sponge. Beat with a whisk for 1 minute. With a wooden spoon, add the remaining flour ½ cup at a time to form a soft dough that just clears the sides of the bowl.

3. Turn the dough out onto a lightly floured work surface and knead for about 3 minutes to form a smooth, springy dough, adding flour 1 tablespoon at a time as necessary to prevent sticking. The dough should be firm enough to hold its own shape. Place in a greased deep container, turning once to coat the top, and cover with plastic wrap. Let rise at room temperature until the dough is doubled to tripled in bulk, about 2 hours.

4. Turn the dough out onto the work surface and divide into 3 equal portions. Form each into a fat oval loaf. Taper the ends by pinching them firmly. Place seam side down on a greased or parchment-lined baking sheet. Cover loosely with plastic wrap and let rise at room temperature until almost doubled in bulk, about 1 hour. Twenty minutes before baking, preheat the oven to 425°, with a baking stone if desired.

5. With a serrated knife, slash the top of the loaves with 3 parallel gashes. Pinch the ends gently to redefine the tapering. Brush the dough gently with the egg glaze and sprinkle with the sesame seeds. Bake in the preheated oven for 10 minutes, then reduce heat to 375° and bake another 25 to 30 minutes, or until brown and crusty. Let cool on a rack before serving.

Five-Grain Country Bread

(Pane ai Cinque Cereali)

Whole grains add a dense, nubby texture and sweet flavor to homemade bread. The noble grains are prepared as for old-fashioned porridge and combined with a bubbling sponge to create a moist, fine texture. Barley flakes (available in natural foods stores) add a nice sweetness to the bread, but if you have trouble finding them, add an equal amount more of rolled oats. Slash the top in a loose diamond pattern before baking and serve with Huntsman cheese (layers of English Double Gloucester and Stilton) and tossed seasonal greens.

Yield: 2 round loaves

Sponge
1½ tablespoons (1½ packages) active dry yeast
2 cups warm water (105° to 115°)
2 tablespoons brown sugar
⅓ cup rye flour
1½ cups whole-wheat flour

¼ cup bran flakes
⅓ cup yellow cornmeal or polenta
⅓ cup barley flakes
⅓ cups rolled oats
1 tablespoon salt
2 cups boiling water
3 tablespoons unsalted butter or walnut oil
3¾ to 4¼ cups unbleached all-purpose flour

1. To make the sponge: In a large bowl or plastic bucket, whisk together the yeast, water, sugar, rye flour, and whole-wheat flour until very smooth, about 1 minute.

Scrape down the sides with a spatula and cover with plastic wrap. Let stand at room temperature for 1 hour, or until bubbly.

2. Meanwhile, place the bran, cornmeal or polenta, barley, oats, and salt in another large bowl. Add the boiling water and butter or oil. Stir until evenly moistened. The mixture will be mealy. Cover with plastic wrap and let stand at room temperature for at least 15 to 20 minutes for the grains to soften and absorb the water.

3. Combine the sponge and grains. Beat with a whisk until thoroughly blended. Add the remaining unbleached flour ½ cup at a time with a wooden spoon, mixing well after each addition to make a sticky, yet springy dough. This may be done in a heavy-duty mixer.

4. When the dough clears the sides of the bowl, turn it out onto a lightly floured work surface and knead for 3 minutes, adding 1 tablespoon of flour at a time as necessary to prevent sticking. Do not add too much flour or bread will be dry. This dough will be quite tacky, but should just hold its own shape. Place the dough in a greased deep container, turn once to coat the top, and cover with plastic wrap. Let rise at room temperature until doubled in bulk, about 2 to 2½ hours.

5. Turn the dough out onto the work surface and divide it into 2 equal portions. Shape into tight round loaves. Place on a greased or parchment-lined baking sheet and cover loosely with plastic wrap. Let rise at room temperature until doubled in bulk, 1 to 1½ hours. Twenty minutes before baking, preheat the oven to 450° with a baking stone, if desired.

6. Slash the loaves gently and place the baking sheet directly on the hot stone. Immediately reduce the heat to 375°. Bake until crusty and brown, about 45 to 50 minutes. The loaves will sound hollow when tapped. Place on a rack and cool completely before slicing.

Peasant Bread with Figs and Pine Nuts

White bread has always been a status symbol, but coarse, dark breads of wheat and rye are more healthful and flavorful. Bread with dried figs and pine nuts dates back well into the Middle Ages, when bakers transformed daily breads into sweet and succulent celebration breads for Sundays and feast days. Serve with Gorgonzola Butter (page 161), slices of fresh ham, and a good Italian wine such as a Soave.

Yield: 1 large or 2 medium round loaves

1½ tablespoons (1½ packages) active dry yeast
Pinch brown sugar or honey
2½ cups warm water (105° to 115°)
3 tablespoons olive oil
1 tablespoon salt
¼ cup oat or wheat bran
¼ cup rye flour
½ cup graham flour
4 to 4½ cups unbleached all-purpose or bread flour
⅔ cup pine nuts
1 cup dried figs, such as Calimyrna, each cut into 12 thin strips and tossed in 2 tablespoons flour
Cornmeal for sprinkling

1. In a small bowl, sprinkle the yeast and sugar over ½ cup of the warm water. Stir until dissolved and let stand until foamy, about 10 minutes.

2. In a large bowl, whisk together the remaining 2 cups water, olive oil, salt, bran, rye, and graham flour. Add the yeast mixture. Beat until smooth, about 3 minutes. Add the remaining unbleached flour ½ cup at a time until a soft dough is formed that clears the sides of the bowl, switching to a wooden spoon when necessary.

3. Turn out the dough onto a lightly floured work surface and knead to form a soft, springy dough that is resilient to the touch, adding 1 tablespoon of flour at a time as necessary to prevent sticking. The dough should retain a slightly tacky, soft quality, yet hold its own shape. Place in a greased deep container, turning once to coat the top, and cover with plastic wrap. Let rise at room temperature until doubled, about 1½ hours. Meanwhile, preheat the oven to 350°. Spread the pine nuts in a jelly roll pan and bake until lightly toasted, 8 to 10 minutes. Let cool.

4. Turn the dough out onto the work surface. Without punching it down, pat it into a large oval and sprinkle evenly with half the figs and toasted pine nuts. Roll up the dough. Pat it into an oval once again and sprinkle evenly with the remaining figs and nuts. Roll it up again. Shape into a round loaf or loaves, gently pulling the surface taut from the bottom. Place on a greased or parchment-lined baking sheet or a baker's paddle sprinkled with cornmeal. Cover loosely with plastic wrap and let rise until doubled, about 1 hour. Twenty minutes before baking, preheat the oven to 425°, with a baking stone if desired.

5. Slash the loaf or loaves quickly with a serrated knife no deeper than ¼ inch. Slide the loaf or loaves onto the baking stone, or place the baking sheet directly on the stone or oven rack for 15 minutes. Lower the heat to 375° and bake 35 minutes more. The bread will be brown, crusty, and sound hollow when tapped on the bottom. Let cool completely on a rack.

Potato and Rye Vienna Twist

This is a humble name for a spectacular and delicious bread from Austria, where it is known as *Verheiratesbrot*. Two distinctly different doughs, one a creamy potato with anise seed and the other a beer rye uniquely flavored with ground coriander, are twisted together to form a two-toned earth-colored bread. It is adapted from a recipe developed by master baker Diane Dexter of the East Bay's Metropolis Bakery.

Yield: 2 long twists

Rye Dough
2 teaspoons active dry yeast
½ cup warm water (105° to 115°)
1 cup flat beer, heated slightly to burn off some of the alcohol
1 tablespoon barley malt syrup
1 egg
1½ teaspoons salt
1 tablespoon ground coriander
1 cup medium rye flour
3 cups unbleached all-purpose or bread flour

Potato Dough
One unpeeled 6-ounce russet potato, cut into large chunks
1½ teaspoons active dry yeast
¼ cup warm potato water (105° to 115°)
⅞ cup warm milk (105° to 115°)
4 tablespoons unsalted butter at room temperature
1 tablespoon sugar
1 egg
1½ teaspoons whole aniseed
1½ teaspoons salt
3½ to 3¾ cups unbleached all-purpose or bread flour

1. To make the rye dough: In a large bowl, sprinkle the yeast over the warm water and stir until smooth. Add the warm beer, malt, egg, salt, spice, and rye flour. Beat with a whisk until smooth, about 1 minute. Add all the unbleached flour at once and beat with a wooden spoon to make a smooth dough that clears the sides of the bowl, about 3 minutes. Turn the dough out onto a lightly floured surface and knead until smooth and springy, about 10 kneads. Add no more flour; this dough is soft.

   Place the rye dough in a greased deep container and turn once to coat the top. Cover with plastic wrap and let rise at room temperature until doubled in bulk, about 1½ hours.

2. To make the potato dough: In a medium saucepan, cover the potato chunks with water. Bring to a boil, reduce heat to low, and cook until tender, about 20 minutes. Drain, reserving ¼ cup of the potato water. Let the water cool to warm, 105° to 115°. Meanwhile, peel the potato and puree with a food mill or electric mixer to make ⅔ cup of puree.

3. In a large bowl, sprinkle the yeast over the warm potato water and stir until smooth. Add the potato puree, milk, butter, sugar, egg, aniseed, salt, and 1 cup of the flour. Beat with a whisk until smooth, about 1 minute. Add 2½ cups more unbleached flour and beat with a wooden spoon to make a smooth dough that clears the sides of the bowl, about 3 minutes. Turn the dough out onto a lightly floured surface and knead until smooth and springy, about 10 kneads, adding flour 1 tablespoon at a time as necessary to prevent sticking.

   Place the potato dough in a greased deep container and turn once to coat the top. Cover with plastic wrap and let rise at room temperature until doubled in bulk, about 1 hour.

4. Turn the doughs out onto a lightly floured work surface. Divide each dough into 2 equal portions. Roll each piece into a log about 14 inches long. Lay 1 log each of rye and potato dough side by side and pinch the ends together. Twist each log and wrap around each other with 4 or 5 turns. Pinch the ends and tuck them under. Place the loaf on a greased or parchment-lined baking sheet, arranging the loaf so that it is neat and even. Repeat to form a second twist. Cover loosely with plastic wrap and let rise until almost doubled, about 40 minutes. Twenty minutes before baking, preheat the oven to 450° if using a baking stone, or 400° without a stone.

5. Mist the loaves with water and sieve them all over with 1 to 2 tablespoons of unbleached flour. Reduce the oven temperature to 400° if using a baking stone, and bake in the preheated oven for 35 to 40 minutes, or until golden brown and crusty. Cool on racks before slicing.

Yam Country Bread with Sesame

The yam is more than a candied accompaniment at turkey time; it is a versatile, delicious vegetable on its own. True yams are of the genus *Dioscorea* and not usually available in this country. What we call yams are a member of the sweet potato genus, *Ipomoea,* the same as the morning glory. American yams are distinguished from sweet potatoes by their darker flesh. For this recipe, look for the ruby yam. Yams combine well with different flours, especially rye and cornmeal, adding texture, flavor, and moistness. Sesame is one of the oldest cultivated plants and the seeds are a favorite seasoning for bread. This is an exquisite country bread to serve during the winter months and a nice accompaniment to hearty soups and meat stews. The recipe also makes very nice individual rolls to be served with tangy, soft cheeses such as chèvre, or used to sandwich smoked poultry.

Yield: 1 large or 2 medium round loaves

One 8-ounce ruby yam
2 tablespoons (2 packages) active dry yeast
Pinch brown sugar
1½ cups warm water (105° to 115°)
2 tablespoons cold-pressed sesame oil or melted unsalted butter
1 tablespoon salt
½ teaspoon ground white pepper
¼ cup rye flour
½ cup yellow cornmeal
4 to 4½ cups unbleached all-purpose or bread flour
Cornmeal for sprinkling

Egg Glaze, page 155
Sesame seeds

1. Preheat the oven to 350° and bake the yam for 50 minutes, or until tender (test by inserting a paring knife into the center). Let cool. Scoop out the flesh and puree in a blender or food processor, or force through a sieve. You should have 1 cup of puree; set aside.

2. In a small bowl, sprinkle the yeast and sugar over ½ cup of the warm water. Stir until dissolved and let stand until foamy, about 10 minutes.

3. In a large bowl, whisk together the remaining 1 cup water, yam puree, oil or butter, salt, white pepper, rye, and cornmeal. Add the yeast mixture. Beat until smooth, about 2 minutes. Add the unbleached flour ½ cup at a time to form a soft dough that just clears the side of the bowl, switching to a wooden spoon when necessary. This bread may also be made in a heavy-duty electric mixer.

4. Turn the dough out onto a lightly floured work surface and knead to form a soft, gently tacky dough that holds its own shape, about 3 minutes, adding 1 tablespoon of flour at a time as necessary to prevent sticking. Place in a greased deep container, turning once to coat the top, and cover with plastic wrap. Let rise at room temperature until doubled, about 1½ to 2 hours.

5. Sprinkle the work surface with cornmeal. Turn the dough out onto the work surface and form into a round loaf or loaves. Cover loosely with plastic wrap and let rise until doubled, about 40 minutes. Twenty minutes before baking, preheat the oven to 450° with a baking stone or 400° without a stone.

6. Slash the top of the loaf or loaves gently with a serrated knife. Brush the entire surface with the egg glaze and sprinkle

with as many sesame seeds as will adhere. If using a baking stone, place the baking sheet directly on the hot stone, and reduce heat to 400°. Bake for about 45 to 50 minutes, or until brown, crusty, and hollow sounding when tapped. Let cool on a rack.

Cornmeal Brioche

Slices of brioche make the ultimate sandwich, especially when the bread is made with crunchy, flavorful cornmeal. Using a heavy-duty electric mixer in place of long, arduous hand mixing and kneading, this loaf is one of the easiest yeast breads to make, baking into an unbelievably soft, rich, and uniformly textured bread (see page 29 for instructions on making brioche by hand if you do not have a mixer).

Cornmeal Brioche makes impeccable BLTs, is good spread with Vegetable Cream Cheese (page 161) topped with fresh arugula for canapés, or served toasted alongside pan-fried fresh trout for breakfast. Fluffy brioche sandwich buns are very special with the addition of capers or bits of sun-dried tomato.

Yield: Two 8-by-4-inch loaves or a dozen sandwich buns

3½ cups unbleached all-purpose flour
1 cup yellow cornmeal
1 tablespoon (1 package) active dry yeast
2 tablespoons sugar
2 teaspoons salt
½ cup hot water (120°)
5 eggs at room temperature
1 cup (2 sticks) unsalted butter at room temperature, cut into small chunks

1. In the bowl of a heavy-duty electric mixer fitted with the paddle attachment, combine ½ cup of the flour, and the cornmeal, yeast, sugar, and salt. Add the hot water and beat at medium speed for 2 minutes, or until smooth.
2. Add the eggs one at a time, beating well after each addition. Gradually add 1½ cups more of the flour.
3. When well blended, add the butter a few pieces at a time. Beat until just incorporated. Gradually add the remaining 1½ cups flour at low speed. Beat until throughly blended and creamy, about 1 minute. The dough will have a soft, batter-like consistency.
4. With a spatula, scrape the dough into a greased deep container. Cover lightly with plastic wrap and let rise at a cool room temperature until doubled, about 3 hours.
5. Gently deflate the dough with a spatula, cover tightly, and refrigerate for 12 hours or overnight to chill the dough for easier handling.
6. Turn the chilled dough out onto a very lightly floured work surface. Divide into 2 equal portions and form into standard loaves. Place in 2 greased loaf pans, filling no more than half full. (To make buns, divide into 12 equal portions and form into rounds. Place on greased or parchment-lined baking sheets at least 2 inches apart. Press with your palm to flatten.) Let rise at a cool room temperature until doubled in bulk, about 1½ hours, or until the dough is level with the tops of the pans. *Note:* The butter will separate from the dough if it is risen in the traditional "warm place" called for in most bread recipes. Twenty minutes before baking, preheat the oven to 375°.
7. Bake on the center rack of the preheated oven for 35 to 40 minutes, or until golden brown and a cake tester comes out clean when inserted into the center. Remove immediately from the pan to cool completely on racks before eating. Reheat to serve.

Cornmeal Brioche with Sun-dried Tomatoes
Add ½ cup oil-packed sun-dried tomatoes, drained and coarsely chopped, to the dough after incorporating the eggs in Step 2.

Cornmeal Brioche with Capers
Add ¼ cup small (nonpariel) capers (or chopped large capers), rinsed and drained, to the dough after incorporating the eggs in Step 2.

French Bread
(Pain Ordinaire)

Pain ordinaire is really a bread of multiethnic origins, as it is the basis for all simple yeast breads made with wheat flour. Its depth of character is based exclusively on the purity of its ingredients and the long rising time to develop the dough's flavor. *Pain ordinaire* can be either a homemade bread or a commercial bread with equal success. Originally published in my first book, *Bread*, this is an important recipe to master, as it lends itself to a great variety of beautiful shapes, and can be the basis for both hard rolls and many savory picnic breads with fillings. The addition of whole-wheat and quinoa flour or Hopi blue cornmeal are untraditional variations but make delicious breads with a surprisingly soft, tender crumb.

Yield: 3 long baguettes or round *boules*

1½ tablespoons (1½ packages) active
    dry yeast
1 tablespoon sugar
2 cups warm water (105° to 115°)
3 cups unbleached bread flour
1 tablespoon salt
About 3 cups unbleached all-purpose flour
Cornmeal for sprinkling

Egg Glaze, page 155

1. In a large bowl, sprinkle the yeast and sugar over the water. Stir until combined. Let stand until dissolved and foamy, about 10 minutes.
2. Add 2 cups of the bread flour and salt. Beat hard with a whisk for 3 minutes, or until smooth. Add the remaining 1 cup bread flour and most of the all-purpose flour ½ cup at a time with a wooden spoon. The dough will form a shaggy mass and clear the sides of the bowl. This dough may also be made in a heavy-duty electric mixer.
3. Turn the dough out onto a lightly floured work surface and knead until the dough becomes soft, silky, and resilient, about 5 minutes, adding flour 1 tablespoon at a time as necessary to prevent sticking. The dough should not be sticky.
4. Place the dough in a greased deep bowl and turn once to coat the top. Cover with plastic wrap and let rise in a cool area until tripled in bulk, 1½ to 2 hours. If you have time, punch the dough down and allow it to rise again for about 1 hour. The dough may also rise in the refrigerator overnight.
5. Turn the dough out onto the work surface and divide it into 3 equal portions.

Knead in more flour now if the dough seems sticky. Form into tight round balls for *boules*. To make baguettes, flatten each portion into a rectangle and roll it up tightly with your thumbs to form a long sausage shape; roll back and forth with your palms to adjust the length. Place the loaves 4 inches apart on a greased or parchment-lined baking sheet sprinkled with cornmeal.

6. **Quick Method:** Directly after forming the loaves, slash the tops diagonally with a serrated knife no deeper than ¼ inch and brush the entire surface with the egg glaze. Place in a cold oven on the middle or lower rack. Turn the oven temperature to 400° and bake for 35 to 40 minutes, or until crusty.
7. **Standard Method:** Loosely cover the loaves with plastic wrap and let rise until puffy and doubled, about 30 to 40 minutes. Preheat a baking stone at 450° for at least 20 minutes, if desired; otherwise, preheat the oven to 400°. Slash the tops of the loaves diagonally no deeper than ¼ inch and brush the entire surface with the egg glaze. Spray a mist of water into the oven, or throw a few ice cubes onto a gas oven floor to crisp the crust, if desired. Turn the oven temperature to 400° and bake for 35 to 40 minutes, or until crusty and hollow sounding when tapped. Eat immediately or cool on a rack.

Whole-Wheat and Quinoa French Bread

In Step 2, replace 2 cups of the all-purpose flour with 1 cup whole-wheat flour and 1 cup raw quinoa ground to flour in a blender or food processor; add 1 tablespoon sesame or olive oil. Continue to mix, knead, let rise, form, and bake as directed for French Bread.

Hopi Blue Corn French Bread

Substitute 1¼ cups fine- to medium-ground Hopi blue cornmeal or flour for an equal amount of all-purpose flour, and add 2 tablespoons corn oil in Step 2. Sprinkle the baking sheets with blue cornmeal to keep the loaves from sticking. Continue to mix, knead, let rise, form, and bake as directed for French Bread.

Grilled Flatbread with Herbs

Prepare French Bread through Step 4. Turn the dough out onto a lightly floured work surface and divide it into 8 equal portions. Roll the dough out to 8-inch free-form rounds with a rolling pin. Sprinkle with a few tablespoons chopped fresh basil, marjoram, thyme, parsley, olive pieces, or strips of sun-dried tomatoes, as desired. Use a rolling pin to press the herbs into the dough surface. Drizzle with 1 tablespoon olive oil and flip over onto a sheet of aluminum foil or parchment paper. Sprinkle again with herbs and oil. Repeat with the remaining rounds, stacking the flatbreads to store. Wrap in plastic and refrigerate for up to 2 hours if not grilling immediately.

Prepare an outdoor charcoal or wood fire. When the coals are covered with gray ash, throw a few branches of rosemary, thyme, or lavender on top of the coals for extra aromatics while grilling. Place a clean grill 4 inches above the fire and flip the flatbread onto the grill. Remove the foil or parchment immediately. Grill as many breads as will fit on your grill at once. Cook 5 minutes, then turn once to grill the other side, for a total of about 10 minutes. Sprinkle with Parmesan cheese, if desired. Remove with a large spatula or insulated mitts. Serve warm in a basket with extra olive oil, or cold with a garbanzo or cannellini bean puree for dipping. Serves 8 to 10.

To Dry Fresh Herbs

Gently wash the herbs with cool to tepid water, as hot water can dissolve precious aromatic oils. Strip the leaves from the stems, unless the herbs will be hung to dry or used as a *bouquet garni*. Spread the leaves on a double layer of paper towels placed on a plate or flat basket. Let air-dry at room temperature 3 days or up to 1 week, away from direct sunlight. Store in airtight containers no longer than 1 year. Home-dried herbs are coarser in texture than commercial dried herbs. This method is especially good for tarragon, thyme, rosemary, bay, oregano, and savory.

To Freeze Fresh Herbs

For a close-to-fresh flavor, freezing is a good way to preserve delicate herbs. Wash the herbs and strip the leaves from the stems as for drying. Chop the leaves or leave them whole, as desired. Place in small plastic freezer bags and label. Break off frozen portions when needed. Frozen herbs can be used frozen or defrosted, but should not be kept for more than 3 months. Do not refreeze herbs. This method is especially good for chives, chervil, parsley, and basil.

Brioche

The round loaves of various sizes with topknots found in bakery cases can only be *la brioche*. Originally a homemade egg- and butter-rich loaf designed to bake free-form in the descending heat of wood-fired ovens, over the centuries it has evolved to the rich bread we now know. Its texture is a cross between pastry and bread, with an even crumb and a dairy-sweet flavor. The best loaves are baked in tin or metal molds, rather than earthenware or tempered glass, to create the desired hairline-thin crust.

Traditionally made by hand with the arduous incorporation of the ingredients (see Techniques, page 27), brioche is easily made by even beginning bakers in a heavy-duty electric mixer. The dough must stay cold at all stages of mixing, rising, and forming in order to keep the high percentage of butter from melting. The rises are slow, but the loaf will rise dramatically in the oven due to the eggs. Another basic recipe from *Bread*, this brioche is used as a case for delicately flavored sweet and savory fillings in a wide variety of shapes. The full-sized braid, *nanterre*, and *parisienne* loaves are beautifully patterned breads to pull apart at the table.

Add 1 tablespoon coarsely ground fresh black pepper to the dough during mixing to create a savory Black Pepper Brioche that is good served with meats and cheeses for entertaining. Brioche keeps up to 4 days at room temperature and freezes perfectly.

Yield: 16 *petites brioches à tête* (individual size)

4½ cups unbleached all-purpose flour
1 package (1 tablespoon) active dry yeast
¼ cup sugar
2 teaspoons salt
½ cup hot water (120°)
6 eggs at room temperature
1 cup (2 sticks) unsalted butter at room temperature, cut into small pieces and softened

Rich Egg Glaze, page 155

1. In the bowl of a heavy-duty mixer fitted with a paddle attachment, combine 1 cup of the flour, yeast, sugar, and salt. Add the hot water and beat at medium speed for 2 minutes, or until smooth.
2. Add the eggs one at a time, beating well after each addition. Gradually add 2 more cups of the flour.
3. When well blended, add the butter a few pieces at a time. Beat just until completely incorporated. Gradually add the remaining 1½ cups flour at low speed. Beat until thoroughly blended and creamy in consistency. The dough will be very soft and have a batter-like consistency.
4. With a spatula, scrape the dough into a greased bowl. Cover tightly with plastic wrap and let rise at a cool room temperature until doubled in bulk, about 3 hours.
5. Gently deflate the dough with a spatula, cover tightly, and refrigerate for 12 hours or overnight. (The dough may be frozen at this point for up to 2 weeks. When ready to use, place in the refrigerator to thaw for 1 day.)
6. Turn the chilled dough out onto a lightly floured work surface and divide it into fourths. Roll each portion into a rope about 12 inches long and 1 inch in diameter. Divide each into four 2-inch pieces and four 1-inch pieces. Round the pieces with your fingers to make 16 larger balls and 16 small ones. Do not worry if the rolls vary slightly in size.

  Place the larger balls in well-buttered 3½-inch fluted molds or standard muffin cups and snip an X on top of each with scissors. Push your finger through the middle of the dough to the bottom. Place a small ball in each center. It is convenient to place the individual molds

on a baking sheet for easier handling. Let rise at a *cool* room temperature until doubled, about 45 minutes. *Note:* The butter will separate from the dough if it is risen in the traditional "warm place" called for in most bread recipes. Twenty minutes before baking, preheat the oven to 400°.

7. Brush each brioche gently with the egg glaze. Bake in the preheated oven for 10 to 15 minutes, or until golden brown. Remove from the molds to cool completely on a rack before eating. Brioche is best when reheated.

Large Brioche à Tête

Yield: Two 8-inch *grosses brioches*

Divide the preceding brioche dough into halves. Divide each piece in 2 unequal pieces as for the *petites,* shape into rounds, and follow directions for forming the *petites.* Place in 2 greased 8-inch fluted tin molds, charlotte pans, or round baking dishes. Let rise until doubled, about 1½ hours. Brush gently with the egg glaze. Bake in a preheated 375° oven for 35 to 40 minutes, or until golden brown and a cake tester inserted into the center of the brioche comes out clean. Remove from the pans and cool completely on racks. Slice in wedges to serve with fine fruit preserves or pâté. *Note:* If using the brioche for a croustade to be filled or for bread pudding, bake the day before needed. For bread crumbs, toast day-old brioche slices on a baking sheet at 250° until lightly golden brown around the edges and evenly crisp, about 45 minutes. Cool. Whirl in a food processor until fine crumbs are formed. Store in an airtight container in the refrigerator.

Pain Brioche

Yield: One large braided loaf, or two 9-by-5-inch standard or pull-apart *(nanterre* or *parisienne)* loaves.

To form a large braided loaf, divide the preceding brioche dough into 3 equal portions. Roll each section into a 14-inch rope, tapering towards the ends. Lay the ropes side by side on a greased or parchment-lined baking sheet. Working from the center, weave into a thick 3-strand braid. Pinch the ends and tuck them under.

To form a traditional loaf good for sandwiches, divide the preceding brioche dough into halves. Pat each section of dough into a flat rectangle and roll up tightly to form a fat log the length of the loaf pan. Pinch the seams to seal and place each in a lightly greased loaf pan, seam down. Flatten to fill the pans.

To form *nanterre* loaves, divide each half of the dough into 6 or 8 equal pieces. Shape each piece into a smooth ball 2 to 3 inches in diameter, pulling the surface taut to the underside. Pinch the bottoms. Place 6 balls, seam-side down, in each lightly greased loaf pan to form two even rows of 3 to 4 balls or place in a zigzag pattern to fill the pan. Flatten to fill the pans.

To form *parisienne* loaves, divide each half of the dough into 5 equal pieces. Flatten each into a small rectangle and roll up from the short edge to form fat cylinders of dough about 5 inches in length to fit the width of the pans. Lay cylinders tightly side by side in a parallel pattern to fill the pans.

Let the loaves rise until doubled, covered lightly with buttered plastic wrap, about 1½ to 2 hours. Twenty minutes before baking, preheat the oven to 375°. Just before baking, glaze the surface of the loaves gently. Bake in the center of the preheated oven for 35 to 40 minutes, or until golden brown and a cake tester inserted into the center of a loaf comes out clean. Remove from pans and cool completely on a rack.

Brie in Brioche

Brie cheese baked in brioche is an elegant presentation on a buffet or hors d'oeuvre table. Besides plain Brie, consider herbed, pepper, or mushroom Brie for variety. This bread can be baked several hours before serving and stored at room temperature. An 8-inch wheel will serve about 30 people with a selection of other hors d'oeuvres. Brie in Brioche can be assembled and refrigerated overnight before baking. Or wrap it in aluminium foil and freeze, then let stand at room temperature for 3 hours before baking. For smaller parties, use a 4-inch wheel of Brie. (This size serves 4 to 6.) The one-half recipe of brioche dough used here will be enough to wrap 3 small 4-inch Bries. Serve with thin-sliced French bread or crackers and fresh fruit such as apples, pears, figs, grapes, or berries.

Yield: 1 round loaf

½ recipe Brioche dough
One 8-inch wheel 60 percent fat Brie cheese (about 2.8 pounds), rind on
1 egg beaten with a pinch of salt

1. Prepare the Brioche dough and refrigerate overnight. Divide the chilled dough into 2 equal portions, reserving one portion for another use. On a lightly floured work surface, roll out the dough to 16 inches in diameter and no less than ¼ inch thick. Place the wheel of Brie in

the exact center and fold the edges of dough up around the cheese. Enclose the Brie by trimming away the excess dough (save the scraps for decorations) and press the edges together to seal.

2. Turn the cheese over and place on a large greased or parchment-lined baking sheet. Brush with the beaten egg. Cut a small hole in the top of the dough to allow steam to escape. Brush the top and sides with the egg. Decorate the top with dough forms, if desired, fastening them with the beaten egg. A grape and tendril pattern works well. Preheat the oven to 375°.

3. Let the Brie stand at room temperature for 15 minutes. Bake in the center of the preheated oven for about 40 minutes, or until golden brown and puffy. Cool on a rack. Serve warm or at room temperature.

Pizza Dough

Pizza evolved from northern Etruscan flatbreads that were baked beneath hot hearth stones as ashcakes. This bread is now known as *focaccia*. When the Greeks, known as the greatest bakers of ancient times, colonized Southern Italy, they baked toppings on the flatbread and created a food very similar to the pizza we eat today. Italians also bake *calzone* (turnovers) and *mezzalune* (half moons), which are made of pizza dough that is folded and stuffed. Sicilians roll their pizzas, which are called *bonate* and *stromboli*. Stuffed pizzas are known as *pizza rustica* and *torta rustica* (see Picnic Breads). In the South of France, the French make *pissaladière* and *pizza provençale* with their own special flair for local ingredients.

Making pizza dough utilizes the same techniques as regular bread dough; the difference comes in the forming and baking. Although it is hard to reproduce a pizzeria-style pizza without an extremely hot brick oven, a homemade pizza is still very good, as well as lots of fun to make. The crusts are flavorful, chewy, and crisp, the toppings savory and delectable with quality ingredients. For best results, use tin-lined heavy-gauge aluminum pans with Swiss cheese–sized holes, metal screens, or black-finished metal pizza pans, all known in professional circles as "power pans."

Pizza may also be made with excellent results on top of the stove in any size of cast-iron skillet with a cover, which is convenient for camping aficionados. Roll out the risen pizza dough with a rolling pin, or an empty bottle, if necessary, to fit the bottom of the pan. Preheat the pan over medium-high heat. Remove the pan from the heat and sprinkle the pan bottom with cornmeal to prevent sticking. Immediately lay the round of dough in a flat layer about ¼ to ½ inch thick in the bottom of the pan and place over medium-high heat. Cook the dough until it is crusty and black spots appear on the underside, about 3 minutes. Check the dough at this point: if the heat is too high, the dough will blacken too quickly and the center will still be doughy. Flip over gently with a spatula. Top as for oven pizzas, leaving a small border around the edge, and cover. Cook until the crust is crusty and the toppings are hot and melted, about 3 to 5 minutes. Slide out of the pan onto a cutting board and cut into wedges immediately.

There are lots of recipes these days for toppings; in fact you'll find entire books and magazine articles dedicated just to pizza, but my all-time favorite is still

Tomato-Basil Sauce, page 165, with a layer of fresh whole-milk mozzarella and lots of chopped fresh basil and garlic.

Yield: One 16- to 18-inch crust, two 10- to 12-inch crusts, three 8-inch crusts, or ten 4-inch appetizer *pizzette*

2 teaspoons active dry yeast
Pinch sugar, honey, or barley malt
2½ to 3 cups unbleached all-purpose flour
1 cup warm water (105° to 115°)
2 tablespoons good olive oil
½ teaspoon salt

1. In a small bowl, sprinkle the yeast, sweetening, and 1 tablespoon of the flour into the warm water. Stir until dissolved and let stand until foamy, about 15 minutes.

2. **By Hand:** In a large bowl, place the oil, salt, 1 cup flour, and the yeast mixture. Whisk hard until smooth, about 3 minutes. Add the remaining flour ½ cup at a time with a wooden spoon until a soft, sticky dough is formed that just clears the sides of the bowl. Remove the dough from the bowl.

   By Electric Mixer: In the workbowl of a heavy-duty electric mixer fitted with the paddle attachment, combine the salt and 1 cup flour. Pour in the yeast mixture, and stir on low to combine. Add the olive oil. Beat for 2 minutes, adding the remaining flour ½ cup at a time, until the dough just clears the sides of the bowl. Remove from the bowl.

   By Food Processor: Place 2½ cups of the flour and salt in the workbowl of a food processor fitted with a metal blade. Add the oil to the yeast mixture and, with the machine running, pour this mixture through the feed tube. Process

bination of dried or fresh herbs marinated in good olive oil. Variations on this flatbread are known by many names: in Tuscany it is called *schiacciata*, in Emilio-Romagna *piadina*, in France *fouace* or *fougasse*. It makes a simple, yet satisfying appetizer or sandwich bread, or it can be cut into chunks to be served alongside roast meats and salads. Serve focaccia the same day it is baked.

Yield: Eight 6-inch rounds, or one 11-by-17-inch rectangle

2 recipes Pizza Dough, page 54

Cornmeal for sprinkling
⅓ cup olive oil
1 tablespoon crumbled dried whole rosemary or sage, or 2 tablespoons finely chopped fresh, or to taste
1 tablespoon crumbled dried oregano or basil, or 2 tablespoons finely chopped fresh, or to taste

1. Prepare the pizza dough and let rise.
2. Place the dough ball on a lightly floured work surface. Use the heel of your hand to press and flatten the dough. Lift and gently pull the dough, stretching it to fit a greased and cornmeal-sprinkled 11-by-17-inch baking sheet or eight 6-inch round cake pans at least 1 inch deep. Cover gently with plastic wrap and let rise at room temperature until doubled in bulk, 30 minutes to 1 hour.
3. Meanwhile, combine the oil and herbs in a small bowl. Let sit 30 minutes at room temperature. Place a baking stone on the lowest rack of a cold oven and preheat it to 450° for 20 minutes; otherwise preheat the oven to 400°.
4. Using your fingertips or knuckles, gently poke some indentations all over the dough surface about ¼-inch deep. Drizzle the herbed oil over the dough, letting it pool in the indentations. Reduce the oven heat to 400° if using a stone. Bake the pan directly on the hot stone or an oven rack for 20 to 25 minutes for small rounds and 35 to 40 minutes for the large rectangle, or until nicely browned. Let cool in the pan. Serve warm from the oven plain or sprinkled with coarse salt.

AMERICAN COUNTRY BREADS

Home-style White Bread with Poppy Seeds

This is a quintessential American country bread made with all unbleached flour. Wheat produces bread with a light, even texture and delicate flavor. There is no comparison between store-bought and homemade white bread. If you can obtain fresh stone-ground unbleached white flour from a small mill, you're in for a unique taste treat. This bread is also exceptional made in pullman pans for a rectangular shape good for croûtons and sandwiches such as Croque Monsieur. Pullman pans have lids that slide over the top, sealing the pan and keeping the bread in a perfectly rectangular shape. Serve spread with fruit preserves, or layered with slices of prosciutto, fresh California mozzarella, and a dab of olive paste.

The Stuffed Bread with Italian Cheeses variation (following) is a substantial turnover loaf similar to a *calzone, mezzaluna,* or French *chausson,* and is excellent for lunch or entertaining.

1 tablespoon (1 package) active dry yeast
Pinch sugar
¾ cup warm water (105° to 115°)
1½ cups warm milk (105° to 115°)
½ cup (1 stick) unsalted butter at room
    temperature, cut into pieces
2½ teaspoons salt
5 to 5½ cups unbleached all-purpose or
    bread flour

Rich Egg Glaze, page 155
2 tablespoons poppy seeds

1. In a small bowl, sprinkle the yeast and sugar over the warm water. Stir to dissolve and let stand until foamy, about 10 minutes.
2. In a large bowl, combine the milk, butter, salt, 2 cups of the flour, and yeast mixture. Whisk hard to combine. Add the remaining flour ½ cup at a time, beating with a wooden spoon after each addition, until a shaggy dough is formed that clears the sides of the bowl.
3. Turn the dough out onto a lightly floured surface and knead for 3 to 5 minutes, or until the dough is smooth and satiny, adding flour 1 tablespoon at a time as necessary to prevent sticking. Place in a greased deep container, turn once to coat the top, and cover with plastic wrap. Let rise in a warm place until doubled in bulk, about 1 to 1¼ hours.
4. Gently deflate the dough, turn it out onto the work surface, and divide it into 2 equal portions. Form into round or standard loaves. Place in 2 greased 9-by-5-inch clay or metal loaf pans or on a greased or parchment-lined baking sheet. Cover lightly with plastic wrap and let rise in a warm place until fully doubled in bulk, 30 to 45 minutes. Twenty minutes before baking, preheat the oven to 375°.
5. In a small bowl, beat the egg and milk with a small whisk or fork. Brush the glaze gently over the top of the loaves. Immediately sprinkle each loaf evenly with 1 tablespoon of the poppy seeds. Bake on the center rack of the preheated oven for about 40 to 45 minutes, or until the loaves are browned and pull away from the pans. Remove from the pans to cool on racks before slicing.

Stuffed Bread with Italian Cheeses

Dissolve the yeast in ¼ cup of the warm water. Substitute 2 eggs for ½ cup of the water during mixing in Step 2. Continue to mix and let rise as for the above recipe.

Combine 1 pound diced whole-milk mozzarella, 1 pound diced Italian Fontina, and 4 ounces of crumbed fresh goat cheese, such as Montrachet, in a medium bowl.

In Step 4, roll out each portion of the dough into a 12-by-15-inch oval. Sprinkle the cheese on the long half of each oval, leaving a 1-inch rim, mounding the cheese in the center of the lower half. Brush the edge with egg glaze and fold over to form a half-moon shape. Pinch the edges to seal and, starting with the top edge, roll in sections to form a rope-like edge.

Place the loaves on a greased or parchment-lined baking sheet, prick the top for steam vents, and brush with egg glaze. Sprinkle each with 1 teaspoon sesame seeds or grated Parmesan cheese, if desired. Let the loaves rest for 15 minutes while preheating the oven to 400°. Bake in the preheated oven for about 25 to 30 minutes, or until browned. Remove from the pans to cool on racks. Serve warm.

Old-Fashioned 100 Percent Whole-Wheat Bread

The flavor of this all-whole-wheat loaf is sweet, wholesome, and nutty. The secret to a moist, fine-textured loaf is a technique known as the sponge method and wholewheat flour that has been finely ground. The sponge method evenly moistens and slightly ferments whole-grain batter before it is mixed and kneaded. A coarse grind of flour has lots of big bran flecks, which makes for a more crumbly loaf. It is important to retain the moisture in the dough by using plastic wrap during all risings; this prevents the formation of a crust, which would dry out the top of the loaf and prevent it from attaining a full, rounded dome during baking. Mastering this loaf is satisfying indeed. Serve slices topped with a layer of cottage cheese and Spiced Honey, page 165, for breakfast.

Yield: 3 medium round loaves

Sponge
3 cups warm water (105° to 115°)
1 cup dried buttermilk
2 tablespoons (2 packages) active dry yeast
¾ cup mild honey
3 cups whole-wheat flour

Dough
½ cup vegetable oil (not olive or peanut)
1¼ tablespoons salt
5 to 5½ cups whole-wheat flour
Sponge, above

Rolled oats for sprinkling

1. To prepare the sponge: In a large bowl, whisk together the water, dried buttermilk, yeast, honey, and the 3 cups whole-wheat flour until smooth. Scrape down the sides with a spatula and cover with plastic wrap. Set in a warm place for about 1 hour. The sponge will double in bulk and be bubbly. Gently stir it down with a wooden spoon.
2. Sprinkle the oil, salt, and 2 cups of the flour over the sponge and beat hard with a whisk for 1 minute, or until smooth. Add the remaining flour ½ cup at a time with a wooden spoon until a soft dough is formed that just clears the sides of the bowl. This bread may also be made in the workbowl of a heavy-duty electric mixer fitted with the paddle attachment, if you prefer.
3. Turn the dough out onto a lightly floured work surface and knead until smooth and springy, yet slightly sticky, about 3 minutes, adding flour 1 tablespoon at a time as necessary to keep the dough from sticking to the work surface. Do not add too much flour, as the dough must retain a definite sticky quality, which will smooth out during the rising process. The dough will also have a slightly abrasive quality due to the whole grains. Place in a greased deep container, turn once to coat the top, and cover with plastic wrap. Let rise in a warm place until doubled in bulk, about 1½ to 2 hours.
4. Turn the dough onto the work surface and divide it into 3 equal portions. Shape into 3 round balls and place at least 4 inches apart on a greased or parchment-lined baking sheet that has been sprinkled with rolled oats. Cover loosely with plastic wrap and let rise until not quite doubled in bulk, about 45 minutes. Twenty minutes before baking, preheat the oven to 375°.
5. Bake in the center of the preheated oven for about 40 to 45 minutes, or until the loaves are deep brown and hollow sounding when tapped. Place a piece of aluminum foil over the tops to control browning, if necessary. Cool on racks completely before slicing.

Whole-Wheat Bread with Apricots and Seeds
In Step 2, replace ½ cup of whole-wheat flour in the recipe with ¼ cup each of whole raw millet and oat bran, 3 tablespoons each wheat germ and raw sesame seeds, ½ cup raw sunflower seeds, and 1 cup finely chopped dried apricots. Proceed to mix, let rise, shape, and bake as for Old-Fashioned 100 Percent Whole-Wheat Bread.

Pumpkin Seed Wheat Bread
Add 1¾ cups toasted pumpkin seeds during the mixing in Step 2. Proceed to mix, let rise, shape, and bake as for Old-Fashioned 100 Percent Whole-Wheat Bread.

To Toast Pumpkin Seeds
On an ungreased baking sheet lined with parchment or aluminum foil, toss 1¾ cups unsalted raw pumpkin seeds with 3 tablespoons vegetable oil to evenly coat. Bake in the center of a preheated 300° oven until crisp and golden, about 20 to 30 minutes, stirring occasionally. Let cool before using in bread recipes.

Farmhouse White Bread with Cardamom

Known for years around the house as Judy Larsen's Mother's White Bread from Sweden, this was the first bread I mastered over twenty years ago. This country white bread from the heartland is perfect for beginning bakers, and it makes 4 big loaves: one to eat immediately, one for the next day's sandwiches and toast, one to give away, and one for the freezer. It may also be made into 2 or 3 large braids drizzled with Powdered Sugar Glaze, page 155, and decorated for the holidays.

Yield: Four 9-by-5-inch loaves

4 cups boiling water
1⅔ cups instant nonfat dried milk
4 tablespoons unsalted butter
1 tablespoon salt
1 cup sugar
2 tablespoons (2 packages) active dry yeast
Pinch sugar
½ cup warm water (105° to 115°)
10 dried cardamom pods
About 12 cups unbleached all-purpose or
 bread flour

Rich Egg Glaze, page 155

1. In a very large bowl, combine the boiling water, dried milk, butter, salt, and sugar with a whisk. Stir until the butter melts and let stand at room temperature until lukewarm, about 20 minutes.
2. In a small bowl, sprinkle the yeast and pinch of sugar over the warm water. Stir to dissolve and let stand until foamy, about 10 minutes. Remove the seeds from the cardamom pods and crush with a rolling pin on a piece of waxed paper. Set aside.
3. Add 4 cups of the flour, cardamom seeds, and yeast mixture to the milk and butter mixture. Beat hard with a whisk for 2 minutes, or until smooth and creamy. Switch to a wooden spoon and add the remaining flour ½ cup at a time to form a soft, shaggy dough that clears the sides of the bowl.
4. Turn out onto a lightly floured work surface and knead until the dough is smooth and resilient to the touch but

not dry, 5 to 8 minutes, adding the flour 1 tablespoon at a time as necessary to prevent sticking. Place the dough in a greased deep container, turn once to coat the top, and cover with plastic wrap. Let rise at room temperature until doubled in bulk, about 1½ hours.
5. Turn the dough out onto the work surface and divide into 4 equal portions. Shape into rectangular loaves and place in four greased 9-by-5-inch loaf pans. Cover loosely with plastic wrap and let rise again at room temperature until 1 inch above the rim of the pans, about 40 minutes. Twenty minutes before baking, preheat the oven to 350°.
6. With a serrated knife, score the tops decoratively not more than ¼ inch deep and brush with egg glaze. Bake in the center of the preheated oven until browned and hollow sounding when tapped, about 40 to 45 minutes. Remove from the pans immediately to cool on racks.

California Walnut Bread

Walnut breads have their roots in the baking traditions of France, where they are immensely popular. Walnut oils come in the cold-pressed variety, which is clear and light-flavored, or the imported variety made from toasted nuts, which is a striking dark amber in color and assertively flavored. Choose as your palate dictates to control the character of this bread. The common English walnut, *Juglans regia*, or "Jupiter's acorn," was known to the Romans. Native American species include the thick-shelled *nigra*, or black walnut, and the *cinerea*, or

butternut. Each has its own particular flavor, but they may be used interchangeably in recipes. This recipe will also yield about 20 delicious dinner rolls, which are perfect for entertaining or picnics. Serve warm with fresh pears and Brie and Walnut Spread, page 161.

Yield: Two 8-by-4-inch loaves, or 3 round loaves

Sponge
2 tablespoons (2 packages) active dry yeast
¼ cup warm water (105° to 115°)
2 cups unbleached all-purpose or bread flour
3 tablespoons honey or sugar
2 cups milk at room temperature

Dough
1½ cups walnuts
½ cup walnut oil
1 tablespoon salt
About 3 cups unbleached all-purpose or
 bread flour
Sponge, above

1. To prepare the sponge: In a large bowl, whisk together the yeast, water, 2 cups of the flour, honey or sugar, and milk. Beat hard until smooth and creamy. Cover loosely with plastic wrap and let rest at room temperature for about 1 hour, or until bubbly.
2. Meanwhile, preheat the oven to 350°. Chop the walnuts and spread them evenly on a baking sheet. Bake until lightly toasted, about 8 minutes. Remove from the oven and let cool.
3. Add the oil, salt, and 1 cup of the flour to the sponge and stir with a wooden spoon to combine. Add the walnuts and the remaining flour ½ cup flour at a time until a soft, shaggy dough is formed that

clears the sides of the bowl. This dough may also be made in a heavy-duty electric mixer, if you prefer.

4. Turn the dough out onto a lightly floured work surface and gently knead until smooth and springy, about 3 minutes, adding 1 tablespoon of flour at a time as necessary to prevent sticking. Push any walnuts that fall out back into the dough. This dough should be moist and soft, yet hold its own shape. Take care not to add too much flour, or the loaf will be dry. Place in a greased deep container and turn once to coat the top. Cover with plastic wrap and let rise at room temperature until doubled in bulk, about 1½ to 2 hours.

5. Gently turn the dough out onto the work surface and divide into 2 or 3 equal portions. Shape into round or standard loaves. Place on a greased or parchment-lined baking sheet or in greased loaf pans. Cover loosely with plastic wrap and let stand at room temperature to rise until double, about 45 minutes. Twenty minutes before baking, preheat the oven to 375°.

6. Bake on the center rack of the preheated oven for about 35 to 40 minutes, or until brown and hollow sounding when tapped. Cool completely on a rack before slicing.

Walnut Rolls

In Step 4, divide the dough into 4 equal portions. Cut each portion into 5 portions and roll each into a ball. Place the balls 1 inch apart on a greased or parchment-lined baking sheet. Press each with your palm to flatten. With clean kitchen scissors dipped in flour, make 4 evenly spaced cuts around the edge of each roll almost to the center. The rolls should stay connected in the cen-

ter and be shaped like a Maltese cross. Cover loosely with plastic wrap and let rise at room temperature until almost doubled, about 30 minutes. With the scissors, snip the center of each cross with an X to allow room for expansion. Bake as directed, for about 15 to 18 minutes. Serve warm.

Olive Bread

Olive trees abound throughout the Mediterranean, where the fruit is a dietary staple. This hearty, colorful country loaf is studded with sharp-flavored green and mellow ripe black olives. Choose your favorite varieties: wizened, salt-cured Greek; tiny, pungent niçoise; minute chunks of picoline; purple-black Calamata; California olives flavored with garlic or chilies. Although traditional European loaves are often baked with the whole olive, I prefer to remove the pits. Serve with egg dishes or as a base for hors d'oeuvre toppings. Serve plain or toasted with unsalted butter, or with Goat Cheese Spread, page 162, drizzled with a bit of extra-virgin olive oil.

Yield: Two round or 9-by-5-inch loaves

1 tablespoon (1 package) active dry yeast
Pinch sugar
¾ cup warm water (105° to 115°)
1½ cups warm milk (105° to 115°)
⅓ cup good olive oil
1½ teaspoons salt
5 to 5½ cups unbleached all-purpose or bread flour
1 cup Spanish-style pimiento-stuffed green olives, drained, patted dry, and halved
2 cups pitted black olives, drained, patted dry, and halved

1. In a small bowl, sprinkle the yeast and sugar over the warm water. Stir to dissolve and let stand until foamy, about 10 minutes.

2. In a large bowl, using a whisk, or in the workbowl of a heavy-duty electric mixer fitted with the paddle attachment, combine the milk, olive oil, yeast mixture, salt, and 2 cups of the flour. Beat hard for 1 minute, or until creamy and smooth. Add the remaining flour ½ cup at a time to form a soft, shaggy dough that clears the sides of the bowl, switching to a wooden spoon when necessary if mixing by hand.

3. Turn the dough out onto a lightly floured work surface and knead for 2 to 3 minutes, adding flour 1 tablespoon at a time as necessary to prevent sticking. The dough should be smooth and springy, but not dry. Place in a greased deep container and turn once to coat the top. Cover with plastic wrap and let rise at room temperature until doubled in bulk, about 1½ hours.

4. Gently deflate the dough by turning it out onto the work surface. Divide into 2 equal portions and pat into flat ovals. Scatter a mixture of both kinds of olives evenly over the dough and press them in lightly. Roll the dough to encase the olives. Form into tight rounds or standard rectangular loaves. Place on a greased or parchment-lined baking sheet or in 2 greased loaf pans (clay pans are nice). Cover lightly with plastic wrap and let rise at room temperature until doubled in bulk, about 45 minutes. Twenty minutes before baking, preheat the oven to 375°.

5. Bake on the center rack of the preheated oven for 40 to 45 minutes, until the bread is browned and pulls away from

the sides of the pan. Remove from pans and cool completely on a rack before slicing.

Olive Toasts for Hors d'Oeuvres

Cut day-old or frozen loaves into thin slices or fat fingers. Place on an ungreased baking sheet. Bake on the center rack of a preheated 325° oven for about 25 minutes, or until just crisp and golden around the edges. Serve warm, or make a day ahead and store in an airtight container at room temperature. Good with wine before dinner.

Lemon Whole-Wheat Egg Bread with Nasturtium Butter

Originally from India, the colorful, familiar lemon adds a refreshing, zesty counterpoint to sweet whole grains and honey in baking when added in small amounts. Both the yellow zest and the juice are used for flavoring. Nasturtiums are a common summer flower originally from the jungles of Mexico and Peru. Their aromatic, spicy watercress-like flavor turns plain unsalted butter into a seasonal specialty. Be certain to use only unsprayed blossoms, wash them thoroughly, and let dry on paper towels before preparing tangy Nasturtium Butter.

Yield: Two 9-by-5-inch loaves

Nasturtium Butter, page 157

Sponge
1 tablespoon (1 package) active dry yeast
2 cups warm water (105° to 115°)
¾ cup instant nonfat dried milk
½ cup honey
3 cups whole-wheat flour, finely ground if possible

Dough
1 large lemon
About 3 cups whole-wheat pastry flour
6 tablespoons unsalted butter, melted and cooled
1 tablespoon salt
Sponge, above
4 eggs
¼ cup rolled oats for sprinkling

1. Prepare the Nasturtium Butter and chill.
2. To prepare the sponge: In a large bowl or plastic container, whisk together the yeast, water, dried milk, honey, and whole-wheat flour. Beat hard until smooth and creamy. Scrape down the sides with a spatula and cover with plastic wrap. Let sit at room temperature for about 2 hours, or until bubbly. Gently stir down.
3. Remove the yellow zest of the lemon with a sharp knife, a fine grater, or a zester, taking care to avoid the white part, which is bitter. Place in a food processor or blender with ½ cup of the whole-wheat pastry flour and process until the zest is incorporated into the flour.
4. Sprinkle the lemon flour, butter, and salt over the sponge and beat hard with a wooden spoon to combine. Add the eggs one at a time then ½ cup of the pastry flour. Beat hard again to make a smooth batter. Continue to add the remaining flour ½ cup at a time to form a shaggy dough that clears the sides of the bowl. The dough also may be mixed in a heavy-duty electric mixer, if desired.
5. Turn the dough out onto a lightly floured work surface and knead until a soft, slightly sticky yet springy dough is formed, about 3 minutes, adding pastry flour 1 tablespoon at a time as necessary to prevent sticking. This dough will also have a mildly abrasive quality due to the whole grains. The dough must remain soft, or the baked loaf will be dry. The dough should just be able to hold its own shape. Place in a greased deep container, turn once to coat the top, and cover with plastic wrap. Let rise at room temperature until doubled in bulk, about 1½ to 2 hours.
6. Sprinkle the bottom and sides of each of 2 greased loaf pans (clay is nice for these) with half of the rolled oats. Turn the dough out onto the work surface and divide into 4 equal portions. With the palms of your hands, roll into 4 fat oblongs, about 10 inches long. Place 2 oblongs side by side. Starting in the center, wrap each around the other to create a fat twist effect. Place in one of the greased loaf pans and repeat to make the second loaf. Let rise at room temperature, uncovered, for about 30 minutes, or until level with the sides of the pans. The loaves should not completely double. Meanwhile, preheat the oven to 375°.
7. Place on the center rack of the preheated oven and bake for about 35 to 40 minutes, or until deep brown and hollow sounding when tapped. Place a piece of aluminum foil over the tops if the loaves seem to be browning too fast. Remove immediately from the pans to cool completely on racks before slicing.

Yogurt Pumpernickel

This is a rye bread with no seeds and a naturally sour tang due to the addition of yogurt. Bake one large country-style loaf, or use an 11-by-5-inch pullman pan or two smaller 9-by-5-inch pullman pans to create a rectangular loaf with a smooth, dense crumb suitable for slicing. Serve cut thin with Date Cream Cheese (page 162) for a delightful taste combination.

Yield: One large round loaf, or one large or two small pullman loaves

1½ tablespoons (1½ packages) active
    dry yeast
1 teaspoon molasses or brown sugar
1 cup warm water (105° to 115°)
1 tablespoon unsweetened cocoa powder
1 tablespoon salt
½ cup miller's bran
1 cup whole-wheat flour
1½ cups pumpernickel or coarse rye flour
2 cups plain yogurt at room temperature
4 tablespoons unsalted butter, melted
3½ to 4 cups unbleached all-purpose or
    bread flour
2 tablespoons miller's bran for sprinkling

1. In a small bowl, combine the yeast, molasses or brown sugar, and warm water. Stir to dissolve and let stand until foamy, about 10 minutes.
2. In a large bowl, using a whisk, or in the workbowl of a heavy-duty electric mixer fitted with the paddle attachment, combine the cocoa, salt, bran, whole-wheat flour, and pumpernickel or rye flour. Add the yogurt, butter, and yeast mixture. Beat hard for 1 minute. Add the unbleached flour ½ cup at a time to form a soft dough that just clears the sides of the bowl, switching to a wooden spoon when necessary if mixing by hand.
3. Turn the dough out onto a lightly floured work surface and knead until smooth and springy, about 3 minutes. The dough will have a slight tacky, moist quality. At this stage, add flour only 1 tablespoon at a time as necessary to prevent sticking. Take care not to add too much flour, or the bread will be too dry. Place in a greased deep container, turn once to coat the top, and cover with plastic wrap. Let rise in a warm place until doubled in bulk, about 1½ hours.
4. Turn the dough onto the work surface and form it into a tight round, or form a 10-by-5-inch rectangle of dough and roll up to form a long loaf. Place in a greased pullman pan (the pan should be only two-thirds full), or on a greased or parchment-lined baking sheet sprinkled with bran. The dough may also be divided into 2 equal portions, patted into 8-by-5-inch rectangles, and rolled up to fit 2 greased pullman pans. Cover loosely with plastic wrap and let rise in a warm place again until doubled, about 30 to 40 minutes. If baking in pullman pans, when the loaves are level with the top of the pans, cover them with their well-greased lids. Meanwhile, preheat the oven to 375°.
5. Bake in the preheated oven until brown and crusty, about 45 to 50 minutes. For pullman loaves, remove the lids after baking for 25 minutes and continue baking until brown and solid to the touch when tapped. Remove from the pan or pans and cool completely on a rack.

Squaw Bread

Rye will grow in places most other grains won't. It thrives in almost every type of soil and needs less water than wheat. A favorite grain for home gardeners, it is sown from August to September and harvested in June or July of the next year. Cultivated from a wild grain by the Romans, rye became the predominant bread-making grain, combined with barley, throughout Europe, Scandinavia, and Russia. Being naturally low in gluten, rye is usually combined with wheat for a light yeasted loaf. Squaw Bread's unique flavor comes from the addition of "raisin water," which adds a very special sweetening to the grains. Serve spread with Honeyed Ricotta, page 162.

Yield Four medium round or oval loaves

2 cups warm water (105° to 115°)
⅓ cup oil
¼ cup honey
¼ cup brown sugar
¼ cup dark raisins
1½ tablespoons (1½ packages) active
    dry yeast
Pinch brown sugar
¼ cup warm water (105° to 115°)
3 to 3¼ cups unbleached all-purpose or
    bread flour
1½ cups whole-wheat flour
1½ cups medium rye flour
½ cup instant nonfat dried milk
2½ teaspoons salt
Cornmeal for sprinkling
2 tablespoons unsalted butter, melted for
    brushing

1. In a blender or food processor, combine ½ cup of the water, the oil, honey, brown sugar, and raisins. Let stand for 5 minutes to soften the raisins, then puree. Add the rest of the water and process to just combine. Set the raisin water aside.
2. In a small bowl, sprinkle the yeast and pinch of sugar over the warm water. Stir to dissolve and let stand until foamy, about 10 minutes.
3. In a large bowl, using a whisk, or in the workbowl of a heavy-duty electric mixer fitted with the paddle attachment, combine 1 cup of the unbleached flour, all the whole-wheat and rye flours, dried milk, and salt. Add the raisin water and yeast mixture. Beat hard for 1 minute. Gradually add the remaining unbleached flour ½ cup at a time to form a soft dough that just clears the sides of the bowl, switching to a wooden spoon when necessary if mixing by hand.
4. Turn the dough out onto a lightly floured work surface and knead until springy and smooth, about 3 minutes, adding flour 1 tablespoon at a time as necessary to prevent sticking. The dough will have a tacky quality. Place in a greased deep container, turn once to coat the top, and cover with plastic wrap. Let rise at room temperature until doubled in bulk, about 1½ hours.
5. Turn the dough out onto the work surface and divide into 4 equal portions. Form into tight round loaves and place seam-sides down on two greased or parchment-lined baking sheets sprinkled with coarse cornmeal. Cover loosely and let rise again at room temperature until doubled, about 45 minutes. Twenty minutes before baking, preheat the oven to 425° with a baking stone, or to 375° without a stone.

6. With a serrated knife, slash the tops with an X about ¼ inch deep. Brush the tops with melted butter. Reduce the oven heat to 375° if using a baking stone. Bake in the preheated oven for 35–40 minutes or until crusty, browned, and hollow sounding when tapped. Remove from the pans to cool on racks before serving.

Poppy Seed and Prune Braids

This barely sweet bread has the surprise flavor of chopped prunes and the crunch of poppy seeds. Plums were introduced to the Santa Clara Valley of California before the Gold Rush by a Frenchman, and in their dried form as prunes (the word *prune* is French for "plum") they are as popular as raisins for eating and baking. This bread makes excellent toast and is good with mild jack or goat cheeses. This recipe will also make 10 to 12 miniature 2-by-4-inch individual loaves, if desired.

Yield: Two 9-by-5-inch braids

1½ tablespoons (1½ packages) active dry yeast
3 tablespoons brown sugar
1 cup warm water (105° to 115°)
1 cup warm milk (105° to 115°)
4 tablespoons unsalted butter, melted
2½ teaspoons salt
2 eggs
5½ to 6 cups unbleached all-purpose or bread flour
⅓ cup poppy seeds
1½ cups pitted moist prunes, snipped into pieces
Grated zest of 1 large lemon

1. In a small bowl, sprinkle the yeast and a pinch of sugar over the warm water. Stir to dissolve and let stand until foamy, about 10 minutes.
2. In a large bowl, using a whisk, or in the workbowl of a heavy-duty electric mixer fitted with a paddle attachment, combine the milk, butter, salt, eggs, and 1 cup of the unbleached flour. Beat hard until creamy, about 1 minute. Stir in the yeast mixture, poppy seeds, prunes, and lemon zest. Add the remaining flour ½ cup at a time until a soft dough is formed that just clears the sides of the bowl, switching to a wooden spoon when necessary if mixing by hand.
3. Turn the dough out onto a lightly floured work surface and knead until soft and springy, about 3 minutes, adding flour 1 tablespoon at a time as necessary to prevent sticking. Place in a greased deep container, turn once to coat the top, and cover with plastic wrap. Let rise in a warm area until doubled in bulk, about 1½ hours.
4. Turn the dough out onto the work surface. Divide into 4 equal portions. Roll 2 portions into fat ropes about 12 inches long. Wrap the ropes around each other to form a twist. Place in a greased clay or other standard loaf pan, tucking the ends under to form a neat loaf. Repeat with the remaining dough. Cover loosely with plastic wrap and let rise in a warm place until almost doubled (the dough should be 1 inch over the rim of the pan), about 40 minutes. Twenty minutes before baking, preheat the oven to 375°.
5. Bake in the preheated oven until the bread is golden brown and a cake tester inserted into the center comes out clean, about 35 to 40 minutes. Remove immediately from the pans to cool on racks.

Pecan Wheat-Berry Bread

According to Middle Eastern folk tales, the forbidden fruit of the Garden of Eden was not an apple, but a stalk of wheat with gigantic kernels. Whole-wheat berries are the very hard whole grains of wheat. They will keep stored indefinitely in a cool, dry place. This hearty bread is chewy with the combination of whole grains and sweet pecans. Wheat berries are available in natural foods stores or the bulk section of some supermarkets.

Yield: Two 8-by-4-inch loaves

¼ cup wheat berries
2 cups water
1 tablespoon (1 package) active dry yeast
Pinch brown sugar
1½ cups warm water (105° to 115°)
3 tablespoons honey
2 tablespoons oil or unsalted butter, melted
2 teaspoons salt
¾ cup pecans, chopped
¾ cup whole-wheat flour
3 to 3½ cups unbleached all-purpose or
    bread flour

1. In a medium saucepan, combine the wheat berries and 2 cups water. Bring to a boil. Remove from heat and let the berries soak for 1 hour. Return to a boil, immediately reduce heat, cover, and simmer until tender, about 30 minutes. Add more water if necessary to cover the berries. Drain and set aside to cool. You should have about ¾ cup.
2. In a large bowl or the workbowl of a heavy-duty electric mixer fitted with the paddle attachment, sprinkle the yeast and pinch brown sugar over the warm water. Stir to dissolve and let stand until foamy, about 10 minutes.
3. Stir in the wheat berries, honey, oil or butter, salt, pecans, and whole-wheat flour. Beat hard with a whisk or the mixer until smooth, about 1 minute. Stir in the unbleached flour ½ cup at a time until a soft dough is formed that just clears the sides of the bowl, switching to a wooden spoon when necessary if mixing by hand.
4. Turn the dough out onto a lightly floured work surface and knead until smooth and springy, about 3 minutes, adding flour only 1 tablespoon at a time as necessary to prevent sticking. The dough will have a nubby, tacky quality due to the whole grains. Place in a greased deep container, turn once to coat the top, and cover with plastic wrap. Let rise at room temperature until doubled in bulk , about 1½ hours.
5. Turn the dough out onto the work surface and divide into 2 equal portions. Form into rectangular loaves and place in greased 8-by-4-inch loaf pans. Cover loosely with plastic wrap and let rise at room temperature until the dough is about 1 inch above the rim of the pan, about 40 minutes. Twenty minutes before baking, preheat the oven to 375°.
6. With a serrated knife, slash the tops no more than ¼ inch deep. Bake in the preheated oven until brown and hollow sounding when tapped, about 35 to 40 minutes. Remove from the pans immediately and cool on a rack.

Seven-Grain Honey Bread

The commercial seven-grain cereal blend of cracked wheat, rye, oats, barley, millet, flax, and corn makes a delicious bread. Our word *honey* is from the Germanic word *hunaga*, which means "golden." Until modern times, it was the only source of sweetening available. Use a local honey: apple blossom or blueberry in New England, sage in the Southwest, orange blossom in Florida, eucalyptus in California, spearmint or clover in the Midwest. This much-requested recipe bakes into a light, even-textured bread that is excellent for sandwich making. It is a good recipe for novice bakers.

Yield: Three medium round, or two 9-by-5-inch loaves

1½ cups boiling water
1 cup seven-grain cereal
1½ tablespoons (1½ packages) active
    dry yeast
Pinch sugar
¼ cup warm water (105° to 115°)
¼ cup warm buttermilk (105° to 115°)
⅓ cup local honey
3 tablespoons corn or other vegetable oil
2 tablespoons unsalted butter, melted
3 eggs
1 tablespoon salt
4½ to 5 cups unbleached all-purpose or
    bread flour

1. In a small bowl, pour boiling water over the seven-grain cereal. Let stand for 1 hour to soften and come to room temperature.

2. In a small bowl, sprinkle the yeast and pinch of sugar over the warm water. Stir to dissolve and let stand until foamy, about 10 minutes.

3. In a large bowl, using a whisk, combine the buttermilk, honey, oil, butter, eggs, salt, and 1 cup of the flour. Beat hard until smooth, about 1 minute. Add the cereal and yeast mixture. Add the remaining unbleached flour ½ cup at a time until a soft, sticky dough is formed that just clears the sides of the bowl, switching to a wooden spoon when necessary. This dough may also be mixed in a heavy-duty electric mixer, if desired.

4. Turn the dough out onto a lightly floured work surface and knead until a soft and springy dough is formed, about 3 minutes, adding 1 tablespoon of flour at a time as necessary to prevent sticking. The dough will have a nubby and slightly tacky feel. Place in a greased deep container, turn once to coat the top, and cover with plastic wrap. Let rise at room temperature until doubled in bulk, about 1 to 1¼ hours.

5. Turn the dough out onto the work surface. Divide into 3 equal portions and form into round loaves, or divide into 2 equal portions and form into 9-by-5-inch loaves. Place the round loaves on a greased or parchment-lined baking sheet and the standard loaves in greased clay or metal loaf pans. Cover loosely with plastic wrap and let rise at room temperature until doubled in bulk, about 30 to 40 minutes. Twenty minutes before baking, preheat the oven to 375°.

6. Bake in the center of the preheated oven until golden brown and hollow sounding when tapped, about 35 to 40 minutes. Remove from the pans to cool on racks before slicing.

Polenta-Millet Sunflower Bread

Sunflower seeds, along with pumpkins and corn, are pure Americana, originally native to the American Southwest and Mexico. Each tall, delightfully top-heavy golden sunflower blossom bears a surprising number of seeds which may be eaten whole or crushed for a flavorful cooking oil. In France the sunflower is known as *tournesol*, and in Italy as *girasol;* both translate as "turning toward the sun." The combination of sunflower seeds and grains in this bread is sweet, crunchy, and addicting. Serve toasted or use for sandwiches.

Yield: Two 9-by-5-inch loaves

2 tablespoons (2 packages) active dry yeast
Pinch sugar or drop honey
2¼ cups warm water (105° to 115°)
½ cup honey
¼ cup corn or sunflower seed oil
1 egg
1 tablespoon salt
⅓ cup raw millet
½ cup polenta (coarse cornmeal)
½ cup raw sunflower seeds
2 cups whole-wheat flour
3½ to 4 cups unbleached all-purpose or bread flour

Egg Glaze, page 155
½ cup raw sunflower seeds for sprinkling

1. In a small bowl, sprinkle the yeast and sugar or honey over ½ cup of the water. Stir to dissolve and let stand until foamy, about 10 minutes.

2. In a large bowl, using a whisk, or the workbowl of a heavy-duty electric mixer fitted with the paddle attachment, combine the remaining 1¾ cups water, honey, oil, egg, salt, millet, polenta, sunflower seeds, and whole-wheat flour. Add the yeast mixture and beat for 1 minute. Add unbleached flour ½ cup at a time until a soft dough is formed that just clears the sides of the bowl, switching to a wooden spoon when necessary if mixing by hand.

3. Turn the dough out onto a lightly floured work surface and knead until smooth and elastic, about 3 minutes, adding flour 1 tablespoon at a time as necessary to prevent sticking. The dough will retain a nubby, tacky quality. Place in a greased deep container, turn once to coat the top, and cover with plastic wrap. Let rise at room temperature until doubled in bulk, about 1½ hours.

4. Turn the dough out onto the work surface and divide into 2 equal portions. Form into rectangular loaves and place in 2 greased 9-by-5-inch loaf pans. Cover loosely with plastic wrap and let rise at room temperature until level with the tops of the pans, about 45 minutes. Twenty minutes before baking, preheat the oven to 375°.

5. Brush the tops gently with egg glaze and sprinkle with sunflower seeds. Bake in the preheated oven until crusty and golden, 35 to 40 minutes. Turn out of the pans to cool on racks completely before slicing.

Dakota Bread with Ancient Grains

Similar in texture to couscous and millet, quinoa is technically an herb. Used extensively by the Incan civilization, the seeds are usually a variegated beige in color, but there is also a black variety that looks nice in this bread. Amaranth is the minute grain of the Aztecs. Together these native plants are known as the "super-grains," as they are so high in protein. Sesame seeds graced the banquets of the pharaohs, and poppy seeds come from one of the most ancient medicinal plants. The combination of ancient and modern grains in this recipe creates a noble loaf with unique taste, crunchy character, and chewy texture. It is not only beautiful, but nourishing. Serve toasted, with red currant or blackberry jelly.

Yield: Two 9-by-5-inch loaves

1 large russet potato (about ¾ pound)
2 cups water
¼ cup yellow cornmeal
2 tablespoons unsalted butter
1½ tablespoons (1½ packages) active
*   dry yeast*
1 cup warm milk (105° to 115°)
2 tablespoons sugar
1 tablespoon salt
1 tablespoon poppy seeds
2 tablespoons sesame seeds, stirred in a dry
*   skillet over medium heat until lightly*
*   toasted*
¼ cup rolled oats
¼ cup popped amaranth (following)
½ cup quinoa nuggets (following)
1 cup whole-wheat flour
5 to 5½ cups unbleached all-purpose or
*   bread flour*
¼ cup rolled oats for sprinkling

1. Peel the potato and cut it into large pieces. Place in a medium saucepan, cover with the water, bring to a boil, and cook over low heat until tender, about 20 minutes. Drain and reserve the liquid. In a small bowl, combine ½ cup of the hot potato water and the cornmeal. Set aside. Puree the potato until smooth with the butter. Set aside.

2. Cool the remaining potato water to 105° to 115° and add warm water as needed to make 1 cup total. Sprinkle with the yeast, stir to dissolve, and let stand until foamy, about 10 minutes.

3. In a large bowl, using a whisk, or the workbowl of a heavy-duty electric mixer fitted with the paddle attachment, combine the potato, cornmeal, yeast mixture, milk, sugar, salt, seeds, oats, amaranth, quinoa, whole-wheat flour, and 1 cup of the unbleached flour. Beat until smooth, about 1 minute. Add the remaining unbleached flour ½ cup at a time to form a soft dough that just clears the sides of the bowl, switching to a wooden spoon when necessary if mixing by hand.

4. Turn the dough out onto a floured work surface and knead until springy and smooth yet with a tacky, nubby quality, about 3 minutes, adding flour 1 tablespoon at a time as necessary to prevent sticking. Do not let the dough get too dry. Place in a greased deep container, turn once to coat the top, and cover with plastic wrap. Let rise at room temperature until doubled in bulk, about 1½ to 2 hours.

5. Turn the dough out onto the work surface and divide into 2 equal portions. Sprinkle the bottom and sides of 2 greased 9-by-5-inch loaf pans with the rolled oats. Form the dough into loaves and place in the prepared pans. Cover loosely with plastic wrap and let rise at room temperature until 1 inch above the rim of the pans, about 40 minutes. (The dough may also be made into 1 free-form round and baked on a preheated baking stone for a hearth loaf.) Twenty minutes before baking, preheat the oven to 400°.

6. Bake the loaves in the preheated oven for 10 minutes, reduce heat to 350°, and bake another 30 to 35 minutes, or until deep brown, crusty, and hollow sounding when tapped. Remove immediately from the pans to cool on a rack.

Popped Amaranth

When heated, amaranth seeds pop like tiny kernels of popcorn. They can be added to bread and cereals whole or ground.

Yield: ¼ cup grain equals 1 cup popped

Heat a deep cast-iron pot or other heavy saucepan over medium heat. Add 1 tablespoon amaranth to the dry, hot pan. Immediately begin stirring constantly with a natural-bristle pastry brush. When the popping stops, empty the pan and continue to make more if needed. Store at room temperature in an airtight container. Use whole or ground to a meal in a blender or food processor.

Quinoa Nuggets

Yield: ½ cup

Place ⅓ cup quinoa in a large bowl and fill with cold water. Rinse and drain about five times to dissolve the bitter saponin coating. In a small saucepan, bring ¼ cup of water to a boil and add the quinoa. Cover with plastic wrap and set aside for 10 to 15 minutes before adding to dough.

Pumpkin–Blue Corn Rye Bread

This is an adaptation of an early Colonial multi-grain loaf known as "rye n' injun bread," with pureed fresh pumpkin for added color, moisture, and flavor. Use canned pumpkin, or puree the cooked flesh of an orange, white, aqua, or even blue pumpkin. Use parched Hopi Blue kernels, home ground if possible, for a particularly nutty flavor reminiscent of corn parched over smoky open fires or in outdoor ovens. I also like the coarse-ground blue cornmeal from Los Chileros (see Source Directory), as it has almost luminescent flecks of different-colored corn in the meal. Serve this hearty, satisfying, daily bread with Whipped Honey Butter, page 157, made with a raspberry or blueberry honey.

Yield: Two 9-by-5-inch standard or round loaves

½ cup coarse-ground blue cornmeal
1 cup water
⅓ cup molasses or sage blossom honey
5 tablespoons unsalted butter
½ cup fresh or canned pumpkin puree
    (following)
2½ teaspoons salt
1½ tablespoons (1½ packages) active
    dry yeast
Drop molasses or honey
1 cup warm water (105° to 115°)
¾ cup medium rye flour
¾ cup whole-wheat flour
4 to 4½ cups unbleached all-purpose or
    bread flour
¼ cup coarse-ground blue cornmeal for
    dusting pans

1. In a medium saucepan, combine the cornmeal and water. Cook over medium heat until bubbly and thickened, stirring constantly with a whisk. Stir in the molasses or honey, butter, pumpkin, and salt. Stir until the butter is melted. Remove from heat and let cool to lukewarm.
2. In a large bowl or the workbowl of a heavy-duty electric mixer fitted with the paddle attachment, sprinkle the yeast and molasses over the warm water. Stir to dissolve and let stand until foamy, about 10 minutes.
3. With a whisk or the mixer, add the cornmeal-pumpkin mixture, rye flour, whole-wheat, and 1 cup of unbleached flour. Beat hard 1 minute until creamy. Continue to add unbleached flour ½ cup at a time until a soft dough is formed that just clears the sides of the bowl, switching to a wooden spoon when necessary if mixing by hand.
4. Turn the dough out onto a lightly floured work surface and knead until a soft, springy dough is formed, about 3 minutes, adding flour 1 tablespoon at a time as necessary to prevent sticking. The dough will retain a coarse, somewhat tacky texture due to the whole grains. Do not add too much flour; the dough should remain soft. Place in a greased deep container, turn once to coat the top, and cover with plastic wrap. Let stand at room temperature until doubled in bulk, about 1½ to 2 hours.
5. Turn the dough out onto the work surface and divide into 2 equal portions. Form into rectangular loaves and place in 2 greased and cornmeal-dusted 9-by-5-inch loaf pans, or form into round loaves and place on a greased or parchment-lined baking sheet. Cover loosely with plastic wrap and let rise at room temperature until doubled in bulk, about 40 minutes. Twenty minutes before baking, preheat the oven to 350°.
6. With a serrated knife, slash the loaves decoratively not more than ¼ inch deep. Bake in the preheated oven for 40 to 45 minutes, or until browned and hollow sounding when tapped. Remove from the pans immediately to cool on racks.

Fresh Pumpkin Puree

Yield: About ½ pound of raw pumpkin will yield about ½ cup puree

Wash a medium-sized sugar or other cooking pumpkin and cut off the top. Cut in half and then into large cubes, leaving the skin intact. Scoop out the seeds and fibers. Place flesh down in a baking dish with about 1 inch of water. Cover and bake at 350° for 1 to 1½ hours, or until tender. Let cool. Peel off and discard the skin. Puree the pulp until smooth in a blender, food mill, or food processor. Cool, cover, then refrigerate or freeze.

To Parch and Grind Dried Corn

Buy dried whole blue or yellow corn kernels at a local natural foods store or through mail order (see Source Directory), or obtain homegrown. Place in a cast-iron skillet over low heat and stir constantly with a wooden spoon until the kernels are a golden brown. Cool and grind in the grinding attachment of a heavy-duty electric mixer, or in an electric or hand grinder, to the desired texture. Parching makes the high-starch kernels easier to digest and gives them a delightful toasted flavor.

Miller's Hearth Bread

Whole brown rice and barley ground with oats and whole-wheat flour in a food processor or home grinder creates a nutty whole-grain flour with lots of fiber and hearty flavor. Barley can be grown at the highest elevation of any grain and is commonly seen in cold to temperate areas from Norway down to the Equator. Serve this bread for brunch with fresh-squeezed orange juice, and a wedge of honeydew melon.

Yield: Two round or 9-by-5-inch loaves

¼ cup raw pearl barley
½ cup raw brown rice
½ cup rolled oats
½ cup whole-wheat flour
1½ tablespoons (1½ packages) active
*   dry yeast*
¼ cup brown sugar
2¼ cups warm water (105° to 115°)
4 tablespoons unsalted butter, melted
1 tablespoon salt
3½ to 4 cups unbleached all-purpose or
*   bread flour*
¼ cup yellow cornmeal for sprinkling

1. In a food processor or an electric or hand grinder, combine the barley, rice, oats, and whole-wheat flour and grind until a medium to fine flour is formed.
2. In a small bowl, sprinkle the yeast and a pinch of brown sugar over ½ cup of the warm water. Stir to dissolve and let stand until foamy, about 10 minutes.
3. In a large bowl, using a whisk, or in the workbowl of a heavy-duty electric mixer fitted with the paddle attachment, combine remaining 1¾ cups water, brown sugar, butter, salt, and whole-grain flour mixture. Beat until creamy, about 1 minute. Add the yeast mixture and 1 cup unbleached flour. Beat again for 1 minute. Add the remaining flour ½ cup at a time to form a soft dough that just clears the sides of the bowl, switching to a wooden spoon when necessary if mixing by hand.
4. Turn the dough out onto a lightly floured work surface and knead until a soft, springy dough is formed, about 3 minutes, adding 1 tablespoon flour at a time as necessary to prevent sticking. It is important not to add too much flour or the bread will be dry. Place in a greased deep container, turn once to grease the top, and cover with plastic wrap. Let rise at room temperature until doubled in bulk, about 1½ to 2 hours.
5. Turn the dough out onto the work surface and divide into 2 equal portions. Form into round loaves and place on a greased or parchment-lined baking sheet sprinkled with cornmeal. Or form into rectangular loaves and place in 2 greased 9-by-5-inch loaf pans. Cover loosely with plastic wrap and let rise again at room temperature until doubled in bulk, about 45 minutes. Twenty minutes before baking, preheat the oven to 400°, with a baking stone if you desire.
6. With a serrated knife, slash the tops decoratively not more than ¼ inch deep. Place the baking sheet or pans directly on the baking stone, if using, and bake in the preheated oven until the bread is deep brown and hollow sounding when tapped, 35 to 40 minutes. Remove from the pans to cool on racks.

Mixed Rice Bread

This bread, inspired by master chef Narsai David, uses the Lundberg Farms mixture of wehani, brown, black, and wild rices grown in California's Central Valley. You can customize the recipe by using any combination of rices you fancy. Originally descended from the wild newaree plant, rice has been cultivated in Southeast Asia since five thousand years before Christ. Along with millet, barley, wheat, and soybeans, it was considered one of the five sacred crops of China. Now that rice is part of gastronomic chic, different varieties are available in most supermarkets. Here, each rice contributes its own unique flavor, accentuating the moist texture and earthy color of this special loaf.

Yield: Two 8-by-4-inch loaves

2 cups water
1 cup mixed raw rices (see above)
¾ cup whole-wheat flour
1 tablespoon (1 package) active dry yeast
1 tablespoon fennel seed
1 tablespoon cumin seed
1 tablespoon salt
4 to 4½ cups unbleached all-purpose or
*   bread flour*
3 tablespoons barley malt or molasses
3 tablespoons vegetable oil

1. In a medium saucepan, bring the water to a boil and add the rice. Lower the heat, cover, and simmer for 40 minutes. Pour into a 1-quart measure and add water to make a total of 3 cups of liquid and rice. Let cool to 120°.
2. In a large bowl, using a whisk, or in the workbowl of a heavy-duty electric mixer

fitted with the paddle attachment, combine the whole-wheat flour, yeast, seeds, salt, and 1 cup unbleached flour. Add the rice mixture, malt or molasses, and oil. Beat 1 minute, or until creamy. Continue to add the remaining unbleached flour ½ cup at a time to form a soft dough that just clears the sides of the bowl, switching to a wooden spoon when necessary if mixing by hand.

3. Turn the dough out onto a lightly floured work surface and knead until a smooth, springy dough is formed, about 3 minutes, adding 1 tablespoon flour at a time as necessary to prevent sticking. The dough will have a distinctly nubby texture due to the rice. Place the dough in a greased deep container, turn once to coat the top, and cover with plastic wrap. Let rise at room temperature until doubled in bulk, 1 to 1½ hours.

4. Turn the dough out onto the work surface and divide into 2 equal portions. Form into loaves and place in 2 greased 8-by-4-inch loaf pans. Cover loosely with plastic wrap and let rise at room temperature until doubled in bulk or 1 inch above the rims of the pans, about 40 minutes. Twenty minutes before baking, preheat the oven to 375°, with a baking stone, if you desire.

5. With a serrated knife, slash the tops of the loaves decoratively no more than ¼ inch deep. Place in the preheated oven (directly on the baking stone, if used) and bake until crusty and hollow sounding when tapped, about 40 to 45 minutes. Remove immediately from the pans and cool on a rack.

Maple, Oatmeal, and Oat Bran Bread

Oatmeal breads are everyday loaves, hearty with lots of whole grain, not too sweet, yet light enough in texture for toast or sandwiches. Originally found growing wild in fields of barley throughout the northern hemisphere, oats were carried to all parts of the Roman Empire, including the chilly, wet hinterlands of the British Isles, where they proliferated. The classic oat bread recipes we enjoy today are related to the breads of that region.

Yield: Two round or 8-by-4-inch loaves

2 tablespoons (2 packages) active dry yeast
½ cup pure maple syrup
1½ cups warm water (105° to 115°)
1 cup warm milk (105° to 115°)
¼ cup vegetable oil
2½ teaspoons salt
⅓ cup wheat bran
½ cup oat bran
½ cup whole-wheat flour
1½ cups rolled oats
4½ to 5 cups unbleached all-purpose or bread flour

1. In a small bowl, sprinkle the yeast and 1 teaspoon of the maple syrup over ½ cup of the warm water. Stir to dissolve and let stand until foamy, about 10 minutes.

2. In a large bowl, using a whisk, or in the workbowl of a heavy-duty electric mixer fitted with the paddle attachment, combine the remaining 1 cup of water, milk, oil, salt, brans, whole-wheat flour, oats, and 1 cup of unbleached flour. Add the yeast mixture. Beat for 1 minute, or until creamy. Continue to add the remaining unbleached flour ½ cup at a time until a soft dough is formed that just clears the sides of the bowl, switching to a wooden spoon when necessary if mixing by hand.

3. Turn the dough out onto a lightly floured work surface and knead until a soft, springy dough is formed, about 3 minutes, adding flour 1 tablespoon at a time as necessary to prevent sticking. Do not let the dough get too dry, as the brans will absorb moisture during the rising process. Place the dough in a greased deep container, turn once to coat the top, and cover with plastic wrap. Let rise at room temperature until doubled in bulk, about 1½ to 2 hours.

4. Turn the dough out onto the work surface and divide into 2 equal portions. Form into round or standard loaves. Place in 2 greased loaf pans or on a greased or parchment-lined baking sheet. Cover loosely with plastic wrap and let rise at room temperature until doubled in bulk, about 45 minutes. Twenty minutes before baking, preheat the oven to 375°.

5. With a serrated knife, slash the tops of the loaves decoratively no more than ¼ inch deep. Bake in the center of the preheated oven until deep brown and hollow sounding when tapped, 35 to 40 minutes. Remove from the pans immediately to cool on racks.

Anadama Bread with Tillamook Cheddar Cheese

Cornmeal may be bought either stone-ground from whole dried corn, or degerminated by a process that removes part of the bran and germ to allow for longer storage. Seek out the best stone-ground cornmeal you can find for this traditional Early American bread. Cornmeal mush is combined with robust, nut-like cheddar cheese and thick honey and made into a super-delicious bread with a hairline-thin swirl of sweet paprika. Serve with roast meats or soups for a winter holiday dinner.

Yield: Two 9-by-5-inch loaves

½ cup yellow cornmeal, stone-ground if
    possible
1⅓ cups water
2 cups (8 ounces) shredded Tillamook cheddar
    cheese
½ cup mild local honey
4 tablespoons unsalted butter at room
    temperature
1 tablespoon (1 package) active dry yeast
⅔ cup warm water (105° to 115°)
6 to 6½ cups unbleached all-purpose or
    bread flour
2 teaspoons salt
2 teaspoons ground paprika
Melted unsalted butter for brushing
Cornmeal for dusting

1. In a medium saucepan, combine the cornmeal and water. Cook over medium heat, stirring constantly with a whisk, until bubbly and thickened. Remove from heat. Stir in the cheese, honey, and 2 tablespoons of the butter. Stir until the butter is melted. Set aside and let cool to warm.

2. In a large bowl or the workbowl of a heavy-duty electric mixer fitted with the paddle attachment, sprinkle the yeast over the warm water and stir to dissolve. Let stand until foamy, about 10 minutes. Using a whisk or the mixer, slowly mix in the cornmeal-cheese mixture, 2 cups of the flour, and salt. Beat for 2 minutes. Add the remaining flour ½ cup at a time until a soft dough is formed that just clears the sides of the bowl, switching to a wooden spoon when necessary if mixing by hand.

3. Turn the dough out onto a lightly floured work surface and knead until a soft, smooth dough with a grainy texture is formed, about 3 minutes, adding flour 1 tablespoon at a time as necessary to prevent sticking. Place in a greased deep container, turn once to coat the top, and cover with plastic wrap. Let rise at room temperature until doubled in bulk, about 1½ hours.

4. Turn the dough out onto the work surface and divide in half. Working with one half at a time, pat or roll the dough out to a 9-by-5-inch-thick rectangle. Spread evenly with 1 tablespoon of the remaining soft butter and sprinkle lightly with 1 teaspoon ground paprika. Roll up jelly-roll fashion, starting with the short side. Pinch the seams to seal. Place seam-side down in a greased and cornmeal-sprinkled 9-by-5-inch loaf pan. Repeat to make the second loaf. Brush each loaf with the melted butter and sprinkle lightly with cornmeal. Cover loosely with plastic wrap and let rise at room temperature until doubled in bulk or 1 inch above the rims of the pans, about 45 minutes. Twenty minutes before baking, preheat the oven to 350°.

5. Bake in the preheated oven until browned and hollow sounding when tapped, 45 to 50 minutes. Remove from the pans immediately to cool on a rack before slicing.

Fresh Corn and Cornmeal Egg Bread

If an East Coast Native American made this loaf in the traditional manner, it most certainly would contain only maple syrup, ground corn, and water. There would be no wheat, leavening, or dairy products, which are European additions. It would be baked on a hot stone, wrapped around a green twig and cooked over an open fire, or boiled in a corn husk. Our familiar American corn had its beginnings in what is now Central America about eighty thousand years ago, although no wild form of corn has ever been discovered. *Maize* made up 85 percent of the native diet, as well as providing fuel, jewelry, religious symbolism, and medicine.

Indian corn is known as *grano turco*, or "Turkish corn," in Italy. Fresh Corn and Cornmeal Egg Bread is an exceptional late-summer bread inspired by a bread eaten in the Swiss-Italian Alps. With the substitution of frozen baby corn for fresh, it can grace the autumn table as well.

Yield: 2 large braided loaves

1½ tablespoons (1½ packages) active
　dry yeast
Pinch sugar
2 cups warm water (105° to 115°)
⅓ cup pure maple syrup
6 tablespoons corn oil or unsalted butter,
　melted
3 eggs
1 tablespoon salt
1¼ cups yellow cornmeal
4½ to 5 cups unbleached all-purpose or
　bread flour
1½ cups fresh raw white or yellow corn
　kernels

Rich Egg Glaze, page 155

1. In a small bowl, sprinkle the yeast and
　sugar over the warm water. Stir to dis-
　solve and let stand until foamy, about 10
　minutes.
2. In a large bowl, using a whisk, or in the
　workbowl of a heavy-duty electric mixer
　fitted with the whisk attachment, com-
　bine the maple syrup, oil, and eggs. Add
　the salt, cornmeal, yeast mixture, and 1
　cup of the flour. Beat hard for 1 minute,
　or until creamy. Switch to a wooden
　spoon or paddle attachment for the
　mixer and add the corn kernels, then the
　remaining flour ½ cup at a time until a
　soft dough is formed that just clears the
　sides of the bowl.
3. Turn the dough out onto a lightly
　floured work surface and knead until
　smooth and springy, adding flour 1
　tablespoon at a time as necessary to pre-
　vent sticking. The dough will be grainy
　and nubby in texture, retaining a slightly
　sticky quality. Place in a greased deep
　container, turn once to coat the top, and

cover with plastic wrap. Let rise at room
temperature until doubled in bulk,
about 1 to 1½ hours.
4. Turn the dough out onto the work sur-
　face and divide into 6 equal portions.
　Roll each section into a strip with your
　palms and lay 3 strips side by side. Braid
　from the middle to taper the ends. Pinch
　the ends together and tuck them under.
　Place on a greased or parchment-lined
　baking sheet. Repeat to braid the second
　loaf. Cover loosely with plastic wrap and
　let rise at room temperature until *almost*
　doubled in bulk, about 40 minutes.
　Because of the eggs, this loaf should not
　completely double during rising, as it
　will rise a lot in the oven during baking.
　Twenty minutes before baking, preheat
　the oven to 350°.
5. Brush with the egg glaze for a shiny
　brown crust. Bake in the center of the
　preheated oven until deep golden brown
　and hollow sounding when tapped, 40
　to 45 minutes. Carefully lift the braids
　off the baking sheet with a large spatula
　to cool completely on a wire rack.

Oatmeal–Bulgur Wheat Bread

Bulgur, also known as "bulgur cracked
wheat," consists of steamed, then dried and
coarsely crushed wheat berries, which were
known to the Romans as cerealis. It was a
staple food in the ancient world, especially
for the wandering tribes and armies of the
Mediterranean, Middle East, and North
Africa. Please note that bulgur, which has
been partially precooked to cook quickly
with a minimum of fuel, is entirely different

from plain cracked wheat, which has not
been precooked and has its bran and germ
intact. The crunchy quality bulgur gives to
bread is most satisfying when combined
with sweet, mild oats to make a great-
tasting old-fashioned homemade bread.

Yield: 3 round or 8-by-4-inch loaves

Sponge
1 tablespoon (1 package) active dry yeast
2 tablespoons brown sugar
⅔ cup bulgur wheat, fine or medium grind
2¼ cups warm water (105° to 115°)
2 cups unbleached all-purpose or bread flour

Dough
Sponge, above
1¼ cups regular rolled oats
¼ cup wheat bran
¼ cup brown sugar
3 tablespoons vegetable oil
1 tablespoon salt
3 to 3½ cups unbleached all-purpose or
　bread flour

1. To prepare the sponge: In a large bowl
　or the workbowl of a heavy-duty electric
　mixer fitted with the paddle attachment,
　sprinkle the yeast, 2 tablespoons of the
　brown sugar, and bulgur wheat over the
　warm water and let stand for 5 minutes.
　Add 2 cups of the flour and beat hard
　with a whisk or the mixer until well
　moistened and creamy. Cover with plas-
　tic wrap and let stand at room tempera-
　ture until bubbly, about 1 hour.
2. To make the dough: To the sponge, add
　the rolled oats, bran, brown sugar, oil,
　and salt. Beat hard for about 1 minute.
　Add more flour ½ cup at a time and beat
　for another 1 minute, or until stretchy
　and well-moistened. Add more flour ½

cup at a time until the dough pulls away from the sides of the bowl, switching to a wooden spoon when necessary if mixing by hand.

3. Scrape the dough out onto a lightly floured work surface and knead until the dough is smooth and elastic, about 3 minutes, adding flour 1 tablespoon at a time as necessary to prevent sticking. Place the dough in a greased deep container, turn once to coat the top, and cover with plastic wrap. Let dough rise at room temperature until doubled in bulk, about 1½ to 2 hours.

4. Turn the dough out onto the work surface and divide into 3 equal portions. Shape each into a round or rectangular loaf and place on a greased or parchment-lined baking sheet, or in 3 well-greased 8-by-4-inch loaf pans. Cover loosely with plastic wrap and let rise in a warm place until doubled, about 45 minutes. Twenty minutes before baking, preheat the oven to 375°.

5. With a serrated knife, slash the tops of the loaves decoratively no more than ¼ inch deep. Bake in the preheated oven until the loaves are browned and hollow sounding when tapped, 35 to 40 minutes. Let cool in the pans for 5 minutes, then turn out onto racks to cool completely.

Wild Rice and Oatmeal Bread

A field of cultivated oats grows luxuriously to be about as tall as a man. Although originally grown for animal feed, this satisfying source of essential carbohydrates became popular as food for humans because of its good sweet flavor. Oats are low in gluten, so they need to be combined with wheat flour for a high-risen yeast bread, but as they contain a large percentage of fat, a loaf made with oats will have good keeping qualities. This special daily bread is made with rolled oats, earthy wild rice, and a bit of cornmeal for texture, and is sweetened with pure maple syrup.

Yield: 3 round loaves

2 tablespoons (2 packages) active dry yeast
Pinch sugar
½ cup warm water (105° to 115°)
2 cups warm milk (105° to 115°)
½ cup pure maple syrup
4 tablespoons unsalted butter, melted
5 to 5½ cups unbleached all-purpose or bread flour
1 tablespoon salt
1 cup cooked wild rice (see page 77)
½ cup cornmeal
1½ cups rolled oats
2 tablespoons each oatmeal and cornmeal, and 1 tablespoon of flour for sprinkling

1. In a small bowl, sprinkle the yeast and sugar over warm water. Stir to dissolve and let stand until foamy, about 10 minutes.

2. In a large bowl, using a whisk, or in the workbowl of a heavy-duty electric mixer fitted with the paddle attachment, combine the milk, maple syrup, and butter. Add 1 cup of the flour, salt, wild rice, cornmeal, and oats. Beat until smooth, about 1 minute. Add the yeast mixture and ½ cup more flour. Beat for 2 minutes. Continue to add the remaining flour, ½ cup at a time, until a soft dough is formed that just clears the sides of the bowl, switching to a wooden spoon when necessary if mixing by hand.

3. Turn the dough out onto a lightly work floured surface and knead until smooth and springy, about 3 minutes, adding 1 tablespoon of flour at a time as necessary to prevent sticking. The dough will have a delicate tacky, yet nubby quality. Place in a greased deep container, turn once to coat the top, and cover with plastic wrap. Let rise at room temperature until doubled in bulk, about 1½ hours.

4. Turn the dough out onto the work surface and divide into 3 portions. Form into tight rounds and place on a greased or parchment-lined baking sheet sprinkled with the mixture of oats, cornmeal, and flour. Roll the loaves to coat them about 1 inch up the sides with the grains. Cover loosely with plastic wrap and let rise at room temperature until doubled in bulk, about 45 minutes. Twenty minutes before baking, preheat the oven to 375°.

5. With a serrated knife, slash a cross on the top of each loaf no deeper than ¼ inch. Bake in the preheated oven until brown and hollow sounding when tapped, 35 to 40 minutes. Remove from the pan to cool on a rack before slicing.

Wild Rice–Molasses Bread

This whole-grain loaf is rich-flavored and light-textured, yet chewy and as soul-satisfying as good bread gets. It never fails to get lots of kudos in baking classes. Add flour judiciously to keep the dough very soft. For best results, use an unsulphured Barbados molasses, which is light and sweet, rather than the strong blackstrap variety. Enjoy with dinner, for sandwiches the next day, or toasted with soft cheeses.

Yield: 2 round loaves

2 tablespoons (2 packages) active dry yeast
Pinch brown sugar
1¼ cups warm water (105° to 115°)
1 cup warm milk (105° to 115°)
½ cup walnut oil or melted butter
½ cup molasses
1½ cups cooked wild rice (following)
2½ teaspoons salt
2½ cups whole-wheat flour
About 4½ cups unbleached all-purpose or
  bread flour

1. In a small bowl, sprinkle the yeast and sugar over the warm water. Stir to dissolve and let stand until foamy, about 10 minutes.
2. In a large bowl, using a whisk, or in the workbowl of a heavy-duty electric mixer fitted with the paddle attachment, combine the milk, oil or butter, molasses, wild rice, salt, and whole-wheat flour. Add the yeast mixture. Beat hard 3 minutes. Add the unbleached flour ½ cup at a time until a soft dough is formed that just clears the sides of the bowl, switching to a wooden spoon when necessary if mixing by hand.
3. Turn the dough out onto a well-floured work surface and knead until firm, yet quite soft and still springy, about 3 minutes, adding 1 tablespoon of flour at a time as necessary to prevent sticking. Because of the whole-grain flour, the dough will retain a tacky quality. Do not add too much flour, or the dough will be hard and the bread will be dry. Place in a greased deep container, turn once to coat the top, and cover with plastic wrap. Let rise in a warm place until doubled in bulk, about 1½ to 2 hours. Do not worry if rising takes a bit longer.
4. Turn the dough out onto a lightly floured work surface and divide into 2 equal portions. Form into round loaves and place on a greased or parchment-lined baking sheet. Cover loosely with plastic wrap. Let rise in a warm place until doubled in bulk, about 40 to 50 minutes. Twenty minutes before baking, preheat the oven to 375°.
5. With a serrated knife, slash 3 parallel gashes on the tops of each loaf no more than ¼ inch deep. Bake in the preheated oven until brown and hollow sounding when tapped, 40 to 45 minutes. Remove from the pans to cool on a rack.

To Cook Wild Rice

Yield: About 1½ to 2 cups cooked rice

In a medium saucepan, bring 1½ cups water to a rolling boil over high heat. Add ¾ cup wild rice. Bring back to a rolling boil. Cover tightly and reduce heat to the lowest setting. Cook 55 minutes for paddy-cultivated rice, 30 minutes for hand-harvested rice, or until the rice is tender and all liquid has been absorbed. Set aside to cool or refrigerate up to 3 days.

PICNIC BREADS

An old-fashioned picnic creates a world of its own, and people who love picknicking are dedicated to its simple, spontaneous pleasures. The French call this meal a *picque-nicque* or *dejeuner sur l'herbe*. I call it a celebration of the earth. Whether miles from home in the wine country, viewing the sunset from a neighboring mountain, under a park's big shade oak, or at a table spread in your own backyard, a picnic is a shared adventure, a free-spirited style of eating.

Picnic fare demands abundance, contrasting textures, and strong flavors to satisfy robust appetites. The natural beauty of the food itself sets the table. Bread is an essential part of any picnic; the Latin phrase *cum panum,* "with bread," is the root of the word "companion," meaning to break bread together. Think beyond the traditional sandwich to make-ahead main-dish breads that are easy to pack, beautiful to look at, and delicious to eat. Meat or fish, cheese, and vegetables are baked into these breads, incorporating all elements into one dish. The emphasis is on substantial and nourishing seasonally fresh ingredients.

Picnic food is a specialized art. You can spend as much time planning a picnic as an elegant dinner party, but keep it simple by packing foods that are easy to carry and can be eaten at room temperature, preferably with the fingers. The vital little things such as salt, wine openers, and serving spoons are easily forgotten, so keep a backup supply along with your favorite disposable plates, cups, flatware, and napkins for impromptu portable meals. Have a sturdy hamper or insulated chest for easy transporting.

Menu Suggestions

Pancetta-Onion Gruyère Ring
Steamed artichokes and sliced tomatoes
White bean salad with olives and basil
Figs and melon wedges
Coconut-date bars
Sparkling water/Fumé Blanc

Shallot and Poppy Seed Braid
Beet, apple, and endive salad
Cold roast Cornish hens stuffed with grapes and garlic
Pecan tartlets
Chilled sparkling wine

Eggplant, Pepper, and Artichoke Torta
Hard-cooked chicken or quail eggs
Green beans vinaigrette
Sliced fresh tomatoes with olive oil and basil
Asiago cheese, fresh grapes, cherries, strawberries, and watermelon
Zinfandel

Ham in Rye Buns
Dill pickles or cornichons/champagne dill mustard
Beefsteak tomatoes stuffed with cold basil rice
Crudités (cold carrots, celery hearts, mushrooms, rings of red and yellow peppers)
Peach cobbler
Cold ale and soft drinks

Coulibiac in Buckwheat Brioche with Watercress Dill Sauce
Marinated sun-dried tomatoes and cracked olives
Five lettuces with virgin olive oil and lemon
Cold lemon soufflé with fresh raspberries
Chilled Sauvignon Blanc

Shallot and Poppy Seed Braid

The common shallot is a pear-shaped bulb about the size of a large nut. Its flavor is more delicate than that of the onion and less pungent than garlic. Shallots are easy to digest and claim no tears when being chopped. The Latin name *Allium*, or "large pearl," is a derivative of the Celtic word *all*, which translates to "burning hot." The shallot is unsurpassed as an ingredient in this very popular savory stuffed bread.

Yield: 1 large or 2 small braids

Dough
1 tablespoon (1 package) active dry yeast
3 tablespoons sugar
2 teaspoons salt
4 to 4½ cups unbleached all-purpose or bread flour
1 cup hot milk (120°)
½ cup hot water (120°)
1 egg
½ cup (1 stick) unsalted butter at room temperature, cut into small pieces

Shallot–Poppy Seed Filling
4 tablespoons unsalted butter
2 tablespoons olive oil
⅔ cup (about 6 medium to large) chopped shallots
⅔ cup (4 small) chopped white onions
3 tablespoons grated Parmesan cheese
5 tablespoons poppy seeds

Egg Glaze, page 155
1 tablespoon poppy seeds for sprinkling

1. To prepare the dough: In a large bowl, using a whisk, or in the workbowl of a heavy-duty electric mixer fitted with the paddle attachment, combine the yeast, sugar, salt, and 1½ cups of the flour. Add the milk and water and beat for 1 minute, or until creamy. Add the egg and butter pieces with ½ cup more flour. Beat until the butter is incorporated. Add the remaining flour ½ cup at a time to form soft dough that just clears the sides of the bowl, switching to a wooden spoon when necessary if mixing by hand.

2. Turn the dough out onto a lightly floured work surface and knead gently to form a soft, yet springy dough, adding flour 1 tablespoon at a time as necessary to prevent sticking. Place in a greased deep container, turn once to coat the top, and cover with plastic wrap. Let rise in a warm place until doubled in bulk, about 1½ hours.

3. Meanwhile, prepare the filling: In a medium skillet or sauté pan, melt the butter and oil. Add the shallots and white onions. Sauté until just limp and translucent but not browned, or the filling will be bitter. Remove from heat and stir in the cheese and poppy seeds. Set aside to let cool to room temperature.

4. Turn the dough out onto the work surface. Roll the dough out with a rolling pin to a 12-by-18-inch rectangle, moving the dough frequently to prevent sticking. Cut lengthwise into three 4-inch-wide strips. Carefully spread the filling over the center of each strip, leaving a 1-inch margin of dough all the way around. Fold over the edges and pinch them together, encasing the filling.

5. Lift the ropes gently onto a greased or parchment-lined baking sheet, placing them 1 inch apart. Beginning in the middle, braid each rope loosely to each end. Pinch the ends and tuck them under securely. Cover loosely with plastic wrap and let rise in a warm place until doubled in bulk, about 30 minutes. Meanwhile, preheat the oven to 350°.

6. Gently brush the dough with egg glaze and sprinkle lightly with poppy seeds. Bake in the center of the preheated oven until golden brown and a cake tester inserted in the center of a loaf comes out clean, about 35 to 40 minutes. Remove from the baking sheet to cool completely on a rack before serving.

Eggplant, Pepper, and Artichoke Torta

A *torta rustica* is an Italian-style savory pie. This one, adapted from a recipe by Bay Area food writer Cynthia Scheer, is one of the most delicious and attractive stuffed breads I have ever eaten. Don't let the long list of ingredients put you off. The torta is quickly assembled, making it easy for beginning bakers. This deep-dish mixed vegetable pie with a tender whole-wheat crust is suitable for both winter and summer entertaining. Serve hot or at room temperature.

Yield: One 8-inch torta serving about 6

Light Wheat Torta Dough
2 teaspoons active dry yeast
Pinch sugar
⅓ cup warm water (105° to 115°)
⅓ cup whole-wheat flour
½ teaspoon salt
2 eggs
1⅔ cups unbleached all-purpose flour
½ cup (1 stick) unsalted butter at room temperature, cut into small pieces

Vegetable Filling

1/4 cup olive oil
1 medium yellow or white onion, chopped
1 red bell pepper, cored, seeded, and cut into thin strips
4 unpeeled Japanese or baby eggplants, cut into cubes
2 garlic cloves, peeled and chopped
2 teaspoons dried mixed Italian herbs
1/2 teaspoon each salt and freshly ground black pepper
Two 9-ounce packages frozen artichokes, defrosted
One 14 1/2-ounce can Italian-style plum tomatoes, drained (liquid reserved) and chopped
3 eggs
1 1/2 cups (6 ounces) shredded Swiss or Gruyère cheese
1/2 cup grated Parmesan cheese, plus 1 tablespoon for sprinkling

1. To prepare the torta dough: In a medium bowl or the workbowl of a heavy-duty electric mixer fitted with the paddle attachment, sprinkle the yeast and sugar over the warm water. Stir to dissolve and let stand until bubbly, about 10 minutes. Add the whole-wheat flour and salt. Beat with a whisk or the mixer for 30 seconds, or until creamy.

2. Beat in the eggs one at a time until incorporated. Add the unbleached flour 1/2 cup at a time to make a soft dough that just clears the sides of the bowl, switching to a wooden spoon when necessary if mixing by hand. Beat in the butter 1 tablespoon at a time, beating well after each addition. The dough will be soft and sticky. Remove from the bowl, place on a lightly floured surface, and knead about six times to form a smooth ball. Use only a few teaspoons more flour if the dough is very sticky; it is important that the dough be moist and resilient. Place in a greased deep container and cover with plastic wrap. Let rise at room temperature until doubled, about 1 hour.

3. To prepare the filling: In a large skillet or sauté pan, heat the oil over medium heat. Add the onion, red pepper, and eggplants, stirring until soft and beginning to brown. Add the garlic, herbs, salt, pepper, and artichoke hearts. Stir and add the tomatoes and their liquid. Bring to a boil, reduce heat to medium, and cook until the vegetables are tender and the liquid is evaporated, about 10 minutes. Remove from heat and set aside to cool to room temperature. Preheat the oven to 375°.

4. In a large mixing bowl, beat the eggs. Add the cooled vegetables and cheeses. Stir to blend evenly. Turn the dough out onto a lightly floured work surface. Divide into 1 large and 1 small portion, about two thirds and one third of the dough respectively. Roll out the larger portion to a 12-inch round and place in a greased 8-inch springform pan. Press the dough up and over the sides of the pan and let the excess hang over the edge. Add the vegetable mixture and fold in the overhanging dough. Turn the dough under and gently crimp. Roll out the remaining portion of dough to an 8-inch square and cut it into 1-inch-wide strips. Space half the strips evenly over the top of the torta and the other half over the top in the opposite direction to form a lattice weave. Tuck the dough edges under and recrimp. Sprinkle the top with 1 tablespoon of the Parmesan cheese.

5. Place immediately in the preheated oven on the center rack and bake until browned and set, 50 minutes to 1 hour. Cool in the pan on a rack for 10 minutes before removing the sides of the pan. Let stand for 1 hour before cutting into wedges. Serve warm or at room temperature. Store in the refrigerator.

Individual Fresh-Tomato Tarts

These French-style tarts are based on a delicate yeasted pastry formed into 6- or 7-inch rounds and baked on cookie sheets. They may also be fitted into the requisite fluted tin molds to form individual quiches. The pastry may be mixed and formed, covered tightly with plastic wrap, and refrigerated the day before topping and baking, which is helpful for entertaining.

Yield: 5 entrée tarts

Yeasted Herb Pastry
2 teaspoons active dry yeast
1 teaspoon sugar
1/2 cup warm milk (105° to 115°)
2 tablespoons fine-ground yellow cornmeal
2 to 2 1/4 cups unbleached all-purpose flour
1 tablespoon minced fresh chives or thyme
1/2 teaspoon salt
1 large egg
1/2 cup (1 stick) unsalted butter at room temperature, cut into tablespoonfuls

Topping
4 large ripe fresh tomatoes, cut into thick slices
2 tablespoons chopped fresh herbs of choice
1/4 cup good olive oil

1. To prepare the pastry: In a medium bowl, sprinkle the yeast and sugar over the warm milk. Stir to dissolve and let stand until bubbly, about 10 minutes. Add the cornmeal, ½ cup of the flour, chives or thyme, salt, and egg. Beat with a whisk until smooth. Add 1½ cups more of the flour a little at a time until a soft dough is formed, switching to a wooden spoon when necessary. Add the butter 1 tablespoon at a time and beat until incorporated. The dough should be moist, yet hold together when patted into a round. Chill in plastic wrap for at least 1 hour or up to 1 day. Reserve any extra flour.

2. Divide the pastry into 5 equal portions. On a lightly floured work surface, roll out each piece to a 6- or 7-inch round. Place the pastry round on a greased or parchment-lined 10-by-15-inch baking sheet. Fold about ½ inch of the edge onto the pastry and crimp to seal the edges, forming a shallow rim. Repeat to shape the remaining rounds, using a second baking sheet. Let stand uncovered for 15 minutes at room temperature, or until the rims are puffy. Meanwhile, preheat the oven to 425°.

3. To make the topping: Fan the tomato slices on top of each round, sprinkle with herbs, and drizzle with olive oil. Bake one sheet on the lowest rack and the other on the upper rack in the preheated oven, switching them halfway through baking. Bake a total of 6 to 10 minutes, or until the bottoms are browned. Let stand for 5 minutes before removing with a spatula to serve warm.

Individual Mushroom and Cheese Tarts
In a large skillet or sauté pan, sauté 1 pound fresh mushrooms and ¼ cup chopped shallots in 4 tablespoons unsalted butter over medium-high heat until the mushrooms are lightly browned and the liquid is evaporated. Set aside while forming the tarts as above. Using 2½ cups (10 ounces) shredded Swiss cheese, sprinkle each pastry with an equal portion. Top each with one fifth of the sautéed mushrooms and some chopped fresh flat-leaf parsley. Continue to bake as above.

Torta d'Erbe

(Italian Green Tart)

Torta d'erbe is a rustic savory yeasted pie filled with cheeses, eggs, fresh herbs, chard, parsley, and summer squash. Based on a medieval tart, it is related to the French quiche. Borage, sorrel, spinach, or beet greens may be substituted for any of the vegetables. This makes a wonderful picnic dish or a light supper, served with sliced fresh tomatoes and olives, with oranges and biscotti for dessert.

Yield: One 10-inch tart; 4 to 6 servings

Yeasted Olive Oil Pastry
1 teaspoon active dry yeast
Pinch sugar
⅓ cup warm water (105° to 115°)
3 tablespoons olive oil
1 egg
¼ teaspoon salt
1½ to 1⅔ cups unbleached all-purpose flour

Savory Green Filling
3 tablespoons olive oil
2 small shallots, minced
½ cup diced zucchini or yellow summer squash
2 bunches spinach or Swiss chard, washed, stemmed, and coarsely chopped
Dash fresh black pepper and fresh-grated nutmeg
¼ cup chopped fresh basil leaves
¼ cup chopped fresh parsley
8 ounces (1 cup) whole-milk ricotta
½ cup coarsely shredded whole-milk mozzarella
3 eggs
½ cup heavy (whipping) cream
¼ cup grated Parmesan or Asiago cheese

1. To prepare the pastry: In a large bowl, with whisk, or the workbowl of a heavy-duty electric mixer fitted with the paddle attachment, sprinkle the yeast and sugar over the warm water. Stir to dissolve and let stand until foamy, about 10 minutes. Add the olive oil, egg, and salt.

2. Gradually beat in 1½ cups of the unbleached flour to make a soft dough, about 1 minute, switching to a wooden spoon when necessary if mixing by hand. Turn the dough out onto a lightly floured work surface and knead no more than ten times to make a soft, springy ball, adding no more than 2 tablespoons or so of flour to keep the dough from sticking. Place in a greased container and cover with plastic wrap. Let rise in a warm area until puffy, about 1 hour.

3. While the dough is rising, make the filling: Heat the oil in a medium skillet or sauté pan and sauté the shallots and zucchini or squash until soft. Add the spinach or chard and stir until just wilted. Drain off any accumulated liquid. Stir in the pepper, nutmeg, basil, and parsley. Set aside and let cool to room temperature. Preheat the oven to 375°. In a separate bowl, combine the ricotta, mozzarella, eggs, cream, and cheese.

Add the cooled vegetable mixture and stir until blended.

4. Roll the dough out on a lightly floured work surface to a 10-inch round. Line a greased and cornmeal-dusted 10-inch tart pan with dough, pressing the dough up the sides. Let rest 10 minutes. Gently scrape the filling into the prepared tart shell. Bake immediately on the center rack of the preheated oven for 35 to 40 minutes, or until the filling is set and the crust is golden. Let cool for 15 minutes before cutting into wedges to serve.

Pancetta-Onion Gruyère Ring

The ivory-colored Gruyère is a prince among cheeses, as tasty for eating in thin wedges cut from the sienna-coated wheel as for melting in its signature dish, fondue. Gruyère is still made in the Jura Mountains bordering France and Switzerland, where it originated hundreds of years ago. Here it's paired with smoky pancetta and onion bulbs to make a very special ring-shaped bread that is the essence of a perfect picnic loaf.

Yield: One 10-inch tube pan, serving 8

Dough
1½ tablespoons (1½ packages) active dry yeast
1 tablespoon sugar
¼ cup bran
4 to 4½ cups unbleached all-purpose or bread flour
2 teaspoons salt
½ cup hot water (120°)
1 cup hot milk (120°)
2 eggs
2 tablespoons Dijon mustard
½ cup (1 stick) unsalted butter at room temperature, cut into pieces

Filling
10 slices, ¼-inch thick, pancetta (round Italian bacon)
1 medium yellow onion, chopped
8 ounces cream cheese
2 eggs
½ pound (2 cups) shredded Gruyère cheese

Reserved egg white
1 tablespoon water
¼ cup sesame seeds

1. In a large bowl, using a whisk, or in the workbowl of a heavy-duty mixer fitted with paddle attachment, combine the yeast, sugar, bran, 1 cup of the flour, and salt. Add the water, milk, eggs, and mustard. Beat until evenly moistened, about 1 minute. Add 1 cup more of the flour and the butter in pieces, beating to incorporate it into the dough. Beat in the remaining flour ½ cup at a time until a soft dough just clears the sides of the bowl, switching to a wooden spoon when necessary if mixing by hand.

2. Turn the dough out onto a lightly floured work surface and knead until a smooth, soft dough is formed, about 2 minutes, adding 1 tablespoon of flour at a time as necessary to prevent sticking. Place in a greased deep container, turn once to coat the top, and cover with plastic wrap. Let rise at room temperature until doubled in bulk, about 1 hour.

3. Meanwhile, make the filling: In a large skillet or sauté pan, cook the pancetta and onion over medium heat until well browned. Drain on a paper towel. Let cool.

4. Separate the yolk and white of 1 of the eggs (reserve the white for glazing). In a medium bowl, beat the cream cheese with 1 egg and 1 egg yolk until smooth. Fold in the bacon-onion mixture and the shredded cheese.

5. Turn the dough out onto a lightly floured work surface and roll out into an 8-by-18-inch rectangle. Mound the cheese mixture down the center of the rectangle. Fold each short side over the filling, overlapping the dough 2 inches. With the palms of your hands, form the dough into a long cylinder and spiral it, seam side down, into a greased tube or fluted kugelhopf mold, forming 2 layers. The dough should fill the mold about two-thirds full. Cover with plastic wrap and let rest at room temperature for about 30 minutes, or until puffy. Meanwhile, preheat the oven to 375°.

6. Beat the egg white with the water until foamy. Brush the top of the dough with egg glaze and sprinkle with sesame seeds. Bake in the center of the preheated oven until golden brown and hollow sounding when tapped, about 50 minutes to 1 hour. Remove immediately from the pan onto a rack to cool, right side up. Let cool for at least 30 minutes before serving.

Roasted Chili, Black Olive, and Jack Cheese Bread

I've always referred to this loaf as "California bread," as it combines mild fresh green chilies, good black table olives, cocoa-dusted dry jack, and Monterey jack, a whole-milk cheese first made by Spanish missionaries in the 1800s. Encased in a simple French bread dough, it is easy to assemble. Prepare at the last minute for an afternoon repast with a California zinfandel and cool tossed greens with lots of crunchy endive and spicy arugula.

Yield: 1 large rectangular loaf; serves about 6

*1 recipe French Bread dough (page 49), with
¼ cup fruity California olive oil added to
the dough during mixing*

Chili and Olive Filling
2 tablespoons olive oil
2 shallots, minced
*½ cup California black olives, pitted and
chopped*
*1 red bell pepper, roasted, peeled, and chopped
(see page 154)*
*One 4-ounce can roasted green chilies, diced,
or ¾ cup roasted, peeled, and seeded
poblano or Anaheim chilies*
½ teaspoon dried oregano
1 garlic clove, minced
*8 ounces (2 cups) shredded Monterey jack
cheese*
½ cup grated dry jack cheese
Cornmeal for grinding
Olive oil for brushing (optional)

1. Prepare the French Bread dough and let rise until doubled in bulk, about 1 to 1½ hours at room temperature. While the dough is rising, prepare the filling: In a small skillet or sauté pan, heat the oil and sauté the shallots until soft. In a medium bowl, combine the sautéed shallots and the oil, olives, roasted red pepper, diced green chilies, oregano, and garlic. Set aside at room temperature. Preheat the oven to 400°, with a baking stone if you like.

2. Gently deflate the dough, turn it out onto a lightly floured surface, and pat into a 14-by-10-inch rectangle. Spread the chili mixture evenly over the center third of the dough. Sprinkle with the cheeses. Fold into a rectangle by bringing the two long ends together and pinching them closed. Fold each short end over about 1 inch and pinch tightly to close. Lay seam-side down on a greased or parchment-lined baking sheet sprinkled with cornmeal. With a serrated knife, slash or snip the dough, 1 inch deep and at an angle, in 3 places along the top. Brush with extra olive oil if a soft crust is desired.

3. Let the dough rest for 10 minutes, then bake immediately in the preheated oven until brown, 40 to 45 minutes. Cool completely on a rack before slicing.

Vegetable and Mozzarella Torta Rustica

Layers of *pane di mais*, cured meat, cheeses, eggs, and vegetables form a mosaic of flavor and color in this Italian-style deep-dish pie. Cut into thick wedges and serve at room temperature as a one-dish meal with fruit and wine.

Yield: One 8-inch torta; serves 10 to 12

*One recipe Cornmeal Brioche (plain or with
sun-dried tomatoes or olives added to the
dough), page 49*

Filling
4 tablespoons unsalted butter
1 shallot, minced
*2 bunches spinach, washed, stemmed, and
chopped*
Salt, pepper, and grated nutmeg to taste
4 large eggs
1 cup (8 ounces) whole-milk ricotta cheese
10 thin slices prosciutto
*One 7½-ounce jar roasted red peppers,
drained*
*1½ pounds whole-milk mozzarella cheese, cut
into thin slices*

Egg Glaze, page 155
*Homemade Lemon-Mustard Mayonnaise,
page 164*

1. Prepare the Cornmeal Brioche the day before and let it rise in the refrigerator overnight. Preheat the oven to 375°, with a baking stone if you like.

2. To make the filling: In a large skillet or sauté pan, heat 2 tablespoons of the butter. Add the shallot and spinach. Cook

until the spinach is wilted and the liquid is evaporated. Season with salt, pepper, and nutmeg. Set aside to cool.

3. Meanwhile, beat 2 of the eggs. Melt 1 tablespooon of the butter in an 8-inch skillet and cook the beaten eggs as an omelet. Set the omelet aside to cool, and repeat to make a second omelet with the remaining 2 eggs and 1 tablespoon butter; let cool.

4. Turn the dough out on a lightly floured surface and divide it into 2 portions, one about two thirds of the whole, and the other about one third. Roll out the large section to a 14-inch round about 1 inch thick. Line a greased 8-inch springform pan, letting the extra dough fall over the sides of the pan.

5. Place one omelet into the bottom of the dough-lined pan. Cover with one half of the spinach in an even layer. Continue to layer with one half each of the ricotta, prosciutto, and red peppers. Cover with one half of the mozzarella. Cover with the remaining ricotta. Repeat with the remaining prosciutto and red peppers. Top with the second omelet and the remaining spinach. Top all with a thick layer of the remaining mozzarella. The contents should fill the pan to the rim and be heaped in the center.

6. Roll out the remaining third of the dough into a 9-inch round. Place on top of the torta. Pinch the edges to make a fluted edge that seals the torta. Cut 3 small slashes on top for steam to escape. Brush with egg glaze.

7. Place immediately in the preheated oven and bake until golden brown, 40 to 45 minutes. Let cool completely in the pan. Wrap the pan in aluminum foil and let sit at toom temperature until ready to serve the same day. To serve, unwrap,

then release the pan sides, leaving the torta on the base. Serve with Lemon-Mustard Mayonnaise. This is best eaten the same day it is made. Refrigerate any leftovers.

Coulibiac in Buckwheat Brioche with Watercress-Dill Sauce

Coulibiac is an extravagant stuffed bread from Eastern Europe. In this version, the combination of buckwheat and wild rice gives the dough an earthy flavor that goes well with the salmon and mushrooms. The preparation may be done over a period of 2 days. The most crucial step for a perfect coulibiac is to have all the components cold before assembling them on the chilled dough. Warm ingredients will melt the butter in the delicate brioche dough, significantly altering its special texture. This outstanding savory creation is perfect for the Easter season. The recipe may also be used to make individual stuffed breads.

Yield: Serves 6

1 recipe Brioche dough (page 51) substituting ⅔ cup buckwheat flour for an equal amount all-purpose flour

Court Bouillon
1 cup chopped yellow onion
2 tablespoons unsalted butter
2 cups chicken broth
2 cups dry white wine

2 pounds skinless, boneless fresh salmon fillet, cut crosswise into 2-inch-thick strips

¼ cup fresh lemon juice
¼ cup olive oil
½ cup wild rice, rinsed and drained
¾ cup converted long-grain white rice

Duxelles
6 tablespoons butter
1¼ pounds cultivated mushrooms, sliced
1 teaspoon crumbled dried thyme
3 shallots, minced

12 quail eggs or 3 chicken eggs
1½ cups cooked fresh peas or thawed frozen petit peas
½ cup chopped fresh flat-leaf parsley leaves
Salt and pepper to taste
¼ cup fine dry bread crumbs

Rich Egg Glaze, page 155
Dill, flat-leaf parsley, and watercress sprigs for garnish
Watercress-Dill Sauce, page 164
Lemon wedges

1. The day before serving, prepare the brioche dough. Refrigerate overnight.

2. Early on the serving day or 1 day in advance, prepare the court bouillon: In a saucepan large enough to hold the salmon in one layer, cook the onion in the butter over moderately low heat, stirring occasionally until it is softened. Add the broth and wine, bringing the liquid to a boil. Add the salmon and lay a buttered round of waxed or parchment paper on top. Cover and poach the salmon at a bare simmer for 5 to 6 minutes, or until it barely flakes. Remove the salmon with a slotted spatula to a deep plate. Strain and reserve the court bouillon. Sprinkle the salmon with the lemon juice, oil, and salt and pepper to taste.

Turn the salmon to coat it with the lemon marinade, and cover the bowl with plastic wrap. Covered and chill until needed.

3. While the salmon is marinating, in a medium saucepan bring 2 to 2 ½ cups of the court bouillon to a boil. Add the wild rice, cover, and simmer for 30 minutes. Add the white rice, cover, and simmer for 20 minutes more, stirring occasionally. The rice should be just tender and all the liquid should be absorbed. Set aside to cool to room temperature.

4. While the rice is cooking, make the duxelles: In a large skillet or sauté pan, heat the butter over moderate heat and sauté the mushrooms, thyme, and shallots until all the mushroom liquid is evaporated. Combine the duxelles with the rice mixture. Refrigerate. The mushroom-rice mixture may also be made 1 day in advance and kept covered and chilled.

5. Place the quail eggs in a pot and cover with 1 inch of cold water. Bring to a boil. The eggs will be done when the water begins to boil. The yolks will be soft, but not runny. (Place the chicken eggs in a pot and cover with 1 inch of cold water. Bring to a boil and reduce to a simmer for 12 to 15 minutes.) Remove 1 egg and cut it open to test. Immediately drain and cool the remaining eggs under cold running water. Peel and wrap in a clean tea towel. Refrigerate.

6. In a bowl, combine the mushroom-rice mixture, peas, parsley, salt and pepper.

7. About 2 hours before serving time, assemble the coulibiac. Preheat the oven to 375°. Remove the brioche dough from the refrigerator. Reserve one fourth of the dough for decoration, wrap it in plastic wrap, and refrigerate. Halve the remaining dough on a lightly floured work surface and roll out each half into an approximately 16-by-10-inch-long oval, ⅓ inch thick. Transfer one of the rectangles to a greased or parchment-lined baking sheet. Sprinkle the dough with the bread crumbs, leaving a 2- to 3-inch border along the edges. Spread half of the mushroom-rice mixture over the crumbs. Arrange the salmon in 1 layer on the mushroom-rice mixture and spread the remaining rice mixture over the salmon, patting it firmly in place. Place a line of eggs lengthwise down the center and press them into the dough.

8. Brush the 1-inch band of the dough around the edges of the filling with some of the egg wash. Lay the second layer of brioche dough over the filling, fitting it gently, and press the 2 pieces of dough together at the base of the filling. Cut away the excess dough, reserving it for decorating. Cut a 1-inch hole in the top of the coulibiac. Roll out the reserved one fourth of brioche dough ¼ inch thick on a lightly floured surface and cut out leaf shapes for decorating the top, and long strips for forming braids along the bottom border. Brush the entire surface of the dough with some of the remaining egg wash. Apply the decorations, pressing firmly, and brush them with the remaining egg wash. Chill the coulibiac for 30 minutes.

9. Bake the coulibiac in the center of the preheated oven until a rich, golden brown, about 50 minutes. Cover loosely with aluminum foil if the crust begins to brown too fast. Remove from the oven and let sit on the baking sheet for 15 minutes before transferring the coulibiac to a serving platter. Garnish with dill, Italian parsley, and watercress sprigs. Serve with the Watercress-Dill Sauce and lemon wedges.

Ham in Rye Buns

A ready-made sandwich of savory ground ham, wrapped in a slightly sour, light-textured rye bun. Served with Champagne Herb Mustard, page 165, this is an exotic picnic entree. The fiery mustard complements the sweetness of the well-seasoned ham mix.

Yield: 12 buns

1 tablespoon (1 package) active dry yeast
Pinch brown sugar
1 cup warm water (110° to 115°)
2 tablespoons brown sugar
4 tablespoons unsalted butter at room temperature
1 teaspoon salt
1 egg
¾ cup medium rye flour
2½ to 3 cups unbleached all-purpose or bread flour

Ham and Sour Cream Filling
2 shallots, finely chopped
2 tablespoons unsalted butter
1 garlic clove, minced or pressed
1 pound smoked, Black Forest, or honey-baked ham, ground in a food processor (3 cups ground)
½ cup sour cream
2 tablespoons cognac or brandy
1 teaspoon white Worcestershire sauce
2 tablespoons capers, drained, or chopped pecans

1. In a large bowl or the workbowl of a heavy-duty electric mixer fitted with the paddle attachment, sprinkle the yeast and pinch of sugar over the warm water. Let stand for 10 minutes, or until bubbly.

2. Add the sugar, butter, salt, egg, and rye flour. Mix with a whisk or the mixer to blend. Add 1 cup of the unbleached flour. Beat hard until smooth, about 1 minute. Add the remaining unbleached flour ½ cup at a time until soft dough is formed and just clears the sides of bowl, switching to a wooden spoon when necessary if mixing by hand.

3. Turn the dough out onto a lightly floured work surface and knead until just smooth, about 1 to 2 minutes, adding 1 tablespoon of flour at a time as necessary to prevent sticking. The dough should be soft. Place the dough in a greased deep container, turn once to coat the top, and cover with plastic wrap. Let rise in a warm area until doubled in bulk, about 1 hour.

4. Prepare the Ham and Sour Cream Filling: In a medium saucepan, sauté the shallots in butter until soft but not brown. Add the garlic and cook only about 1 minute more. Stir in the ground ham, sour cream, Cognac or brandy, Worcestershire sauce, and capers or pecans. Refrigerate until needed.

5. Turn the dough out onto a lightly floured work surface and roll into a 12-by-16-inch rectangle. With a sharp knife, divide the dough into twelve 4-inch squares. Place about ¼ cup ham filling in the center of each square. Bring the opposite corners together and pinch to seal.

6. Grease 12 standard-size muffin cups. Place a square of filled dough in each muffin cup, seam side down. Cover loosely with plastic wrap and let rise in a warm place until the buns are puffy and doubled, about 30 to 40 minutes. Twenty minutes before baking, preheat the oven to 400°.

7. Bake in the preheated oven until well browned and springy to the touch, about 20 to 25 minutes. Let stand in the cups for 5 minutes, then remove to racks to cool. To bake the rolls a day or more ahead, refrigerate or freeze them, then reheat at 325° on a baking sheet loosely covered with aluminum foil. Wrap warm buns in foil to transport. Or the rolls may be shaped and filled the night before, covered loosely with plastic wrap, and refrigerated overnight. Let stand at room temperature while preheating the oven for 20 minutes in the morning. Bake as directed.

Pumpernickel Rolls with a Tillamook Cheddar Heart

A recipe I have made for many years, these little breads are adapted from a bread created by baking maven Bernard Clayton. This pumpernickel combines the sweet and savory tastes of balsamic vinegar, unsweetened cocoa, thick molasses, spicy caraway, and aromatic espresso coffee powder. Tillamook is a superior medium-sharp raw-milk cheddar from Oregon, but in a pinch a Wisconsin longhorn, Vermont Colby, or New York sharp can be substituted. These rolls freeze well, enabling the baker to prepare them a week in advance for a tailgate party or country jaunt.

Yield: 1 dozen rolls

1½ tablespoons (1½ packages) active dry yeast
Pinch sugar
2 cups warm water (105° to 115°)
4 tablespoons unsalted butter, melted
3 tablespoons molasses
2 tablespoons balsamic vinegar
1 tablespoon instant espresso coffee powder
2 teaspoons salt
2 teaspoons caraway seed
⅓ cup yellow cornmeal
¼ cup unsweetened cocoa
½ cup pumpernickel or coarse rye flour
3 to 3½ cups unbleached all-purpose or bread flour
One 12-ounce block medium or sharp Tillamook cheddar cheese

1. In a small bowl, sprinkle the yeast and sugar over ¼ cup of the warm water. Stir to dissolve. Let stand until foamy, about 10 minutes.

2. In a large bowl, place all the remaining ingredients except the unbleached flour and cheese. Whisk until smooth and add the yeast mixture. Beat hard for 2 minutes, or until creamy. Add the unbleached flour ½ cup at a time and continue beating until the dough just clears the sides of the bowl, switching to a wooden spoon when necessary.

3. Turn the dough out onto a lightly floured work surface and knead until smooth, springy, and no longer sticky, about 3 minutes, adding flour 1 tablespoon at a time as necessary to prevent sticking. Place in a greased deep container, turning once to coat the top.

Cover with plastic wrap and let rise in a warm place until doubled in bulk, about 1 to 1½ hours.

4. Turn the dough out onto a lightly floured work surface and divide into 12 equal portions. Cut the cheese into 12 equal chunks, each about 1 to 1½ inches square. Form each portion of the dough into a ball, then flatten to about a 4-inch round with your palm. Place a chunk of cheese in the center and bring the edges up around the cheese. Pinch to close the seams and place, seam-side down, about 2 to 3 inches apart on a greased parchment-lined baking sheet. Cover loosely with plastic wrap and let rise in a warm place until doubled in bulk, 30 to 40 minutes. Twenty minutes before baking, preheat the oven to 375°.

5. Bake on the middle rack of the preheated oven until slightly browned and firm to the touch, 30 to 35 minutes. Place on a rack to cool before serving.

Sesame Burger Buns

Although any good yeast bread recipe may be divided into small portions and formed into a sandwiching roll, this is the quintessential burger bun. It is fine-textured, moist, and not too chewy, so that the filling can be showcased. Bake a double batch and keep plenty in the freezer for your barbecue picnics.

Yield: 12 rolls

1 tablespoon (1 package) active dry yeast
½ teaspoon sugar
1¾ cups warm water (105° to 115°)
⅓ cup instant nonfat dried milk

2 tablespoons sugar
2½ teaspoons salt
3 tablespoons unsalted butter, melted
4½ to 5 cups unbleached all-purpose or bread flour

Egg Glaze, page 155
¼ cup sesame seeds

1. In a small bowl, sprinkle the yeast and sugar over ½ cup of the warm water. Stir to dissolve and let stand until foamy, about 10 minutes.

2. In a large bowl, whisk together the remaining 1¼ cups water, dried milk, sugar, salt, and butter. Add 2 cups of the flour. Beat hard until creamy, about 1 minute. Add the remaining flour, ½ cup at a time, until a soft, shaggy dough is formed that just clears the sides of the bowl, switching to a wooden spoon when necessary.

3. Turn the dough out onto a lightly floured work surface. Knead for about 3 minutes, adding flour 1 tablespoon at a time as necessary to make a smooth, soft dough. Place in a greased deep container, turn once to coat the top, and cover with plastic wrap. Let rise at room temperature until doubled in bulk, 1 to 1¼ hours.

4. Turn the dough out onto the work surface and divide it into 12 equal pieces. Form each into a tight round ball and place seam-side down and at least 2 inches apart on a greased or parchment-lined baking sheet. Flatten each ball with your palm. Use a second baking sheet rather than crowd the rolls. Cover loosely with plastic wrap and let rise in a warm place until puffy, about 20 minutes.

5. Brush each roll with egg glaze and sprinkle the surface with sesame seeds. Bake in the center of the preheated oven until slightly brown and firm to the touch, about 20 to 25 minutes. Place on a rack to cool before splitting.

DINNER ROLLS

Classic dinner rolls are fine-textured, soft and chewy, golden and fragrant, and individually shaped. Whether a few bites or a miniature pull-apart loaf, they are meant to accent a meal with a buttery, mellow wheat flavor, rather than be eaten alone. Fresh from the oven, savory dinner rolls slathered with butter are a traditional accompaniment to the American meal. Because they are best eaten very fresh and hot, the convenience of refrigerating or freezing the shaped dough makes homemade rolls adaptable to the busiest schedule. Making doughs ahead allows home baking to be relaxing and gratifying.

Essentially the same in composition as their big brother the yeasted loaf, dinner rolls can be soft and almost crustless, or dense, hard rolls good for mopping up a delicate sauce. The art of forming rolls is fascinating, even to the experienced baker, as it is the perfect arena for exhibiting personal style. The pieces of dough may seem very small and slightly awkward to shape at first, but the rising and baking cycles will correct many irregularities. Shaping techniques for a wide range of twists, fans, crescents, pinwheels, and knobby clusters are easy for even the most timid baker.

A batch of yeast dough made with about 3 cups of flour will produce 12 to 16 small dinner rolls of about 2 ounces each, or 6 sandwich-size buns. Expect hand-formed rolls to vary slightly in size and shape. For easiest handling, the dough should be left a bit softer than for regular loaves, but it must be able to hold its own shape. If the dough becomes overly springy or resists being shaped while working, cover it with a clean cloth and let it rest on the work surface for about 10 minutes. The dough may rise a bit, but it will relax enough for you to continue shaping. When forming these little breads, tuck any stray ends under, and always place the rolls seam-side down on a greased or parchment-lined baking sheet with a bit of room between them for expansion during the final rising and baking. Be certain to allow for the full rising time required in each recipe, as this helps to create a light texture.

Any yeast dough may take advantage of a slow rise in the refrigerator. The low temperature, from about 40° to 45°, of home refrigerators is perfect for retarding the action of yeast. During this cold period, doughs will continue to rise, although over a longer period of time than if at room temperature; this is known as the "cool-rise" method (see page 32). Always place the dough in a container that has plenty of room for it to double or triple in bulk. Grease the top surface of the dough thoroughly, and tightly cover it with plastic wrap to keep it from drying out. The chilled dough will be ready at any time, up to 4 days, to be formed, risen, and baked as directed by the recipe. While the dough is returning to room temperature, the yeast will resume activity and the dough will continue to rise.

Store leftover room-temperature baked dinner rolls by wrapping them tightly in plastic so that no air remains. To freeze, wrap them again in an outer layer of aluminum foil. Do not wrap breads directly in foil for the freezer, or they will be subject to freezer burn. Use frozen baked rolls within 3 months for best flavor and texture. To reheat, defrost the fully wrapped rolls at room temperature for about 2 to 3 hours. Remove the plastic wrap, rewrap the rolls in aluminum foil to preserve moisture, and reheat them in a preheated 300° oven for about 20 minutes. Rolls heated in a microwave must be served and eaten quickly, as they tend to harden when cool.

To freeze raw doughs, place a single layer of formed rolls in a freezer-proof or disposable aluminium pan, cover with plastic wrap, and place in the freezer immediately after shaping. After the rolls are frozen, cover the pan with a layer of foil, or remove the frozen rolls to a plastic freezer bag for longer storage. To make your own doughs ahead, follow the recipes, adapting them according to the directions for Refrigerator Rolls and Freezer Rolls.

REFRIGERATOR ROLLS:
Method One: After kneading the dough, place it in a greased deep container, bowl, or gallon-size plastic food storage bag. Brush the surface of the dough with melted butter or oil. Cover tightly with plastic wrap or seal the bag, leaving room for the dough to expand. Refrigerate up to 4 days, deflating the dough as necessary.

To form rolls, remove the amount of dough desired about 3 hours before serving. Shape as desired. Place on greased or parchment-lined baking sheets or pans, cover loosely with plastic wrap, and let rise at room temperature until almost doubled, about 1½ to 2 hours. Bake as directed in the recipe.

Method Two: After the dough has risen as directed in the recipe, gently deflate it and shape the rolls. Place on prepared pans and brush the tops with melted butter. Cover loosely with oiled waxed paper or parchment, then with plastic wrap, taking care to cover all edges tightly. Immediately refrigerate for 2 to 24 hours.

When ready to bake, remove the pans from the refrigerator, uncover, and let stand at room temperature for 20 to 30 minutes while preheating the oven. Bake as directed in the recipe.

FREEZER ROLLS

Mix, rise, and shape the rolls as directed in the recipe. Place on a nonstick, disposable, or parchment-lined baking sheet that will fit into your freezer. Cover tightly with plastic wrap. Freeze until firm, about 2 to 3 hours. Remove the rolls from the baking sheet, if desired, and transfer to a plastic freezer bag. Freeze the rolls for up to 2 weeks and no longer, as the leavening power of the yeast will begin to decrease at that time.

To serve: Unwrap the frozen rolls and place in a greased or parchment-lined baking pan. Cover loosely with plastic wrap and let stand at warm room temperature to rise until doubled in bulk, about 4 to 6 hours. The dough may also be thawed out overnight in the refrigerator. Bake as directed.

BROWN-AND-SERVE ROLLS

Mix, rise, and shape the rolls as directed in the recipe. Disposable aluminum baking pans are perfect to use. Let rise until doubled in bulk. Bake on the center rack of a preheated 300° oven until the rolls are fully baked, but not browned, about 15 to 20 minutes. Remove from the pan and cool the rolls on a wire rack. Place the rolls in a heavy-duty plastic bag and refrigerate for up to 3 days, or freeze for up to 3 weeks.

To serve: Let the frozen rolls thaw at room temperature in the bag. Place in a single layer on an ungreased or parchment-lined baking sheet. Bake in a preheated 375° oven until golden brown, 10 to 15 minutes.

DINNER ROLL SHAPES

Crescent Rolls: Cut the dough in half. On a lightly floured work surface, roll each half into an 8-inch circle. Brush with corn oil. With a knife or pastry wheel, cut each circle into 6 equal wedges. Beginning at the wide end, firmly roll each wedge up towards the point. Place point-side down on the prepared baking sheet and curve the ends inward.

Cloverleaf Rolls: Pinch off pieces of the dough and shape each into a 1-inch ball. Place 3 smooth balls in each of 12 greased standard muffin cups.

Double Crescents: Cut the dough in half. Roll each piece into a 10-by-6-inch rectangle about ¼ to ½ inch thick. Cut each into 3 long strips. Roll each strip into a 10-inch rope. Divide each rope into 3 equal pieces. Roll each piece and taper the ends. Shape into a half circle. Lay 2 crescents back to back on the prepared baking sheet. The crescents should just be touching. Lay a small strip of dough over the center and tuck it underneath on each side.

Rosettes: To make a bow knot: Cut the dough in half and divide each portion into 6 equal portions. Roll each piece into an 8-inch rope ½ inch in diameter. Tie loosely in a knot, leaving 2 long ends. Tuck one end over and under the roll; bring the bottom end up and over to tuck into the roll center. Place the rolls about 2 inches apart on the prepared baking sheet.

Snails: Cut the dough in half. and divide it into 6 equal portions. Roll each portion into a 8-inch-long rope ½ inch in diameter. Starting at one end, wind the strip of dough around itself to form a spiral. Tuck the edge firmly under.

Cottage: Divide each piece of dough into 2 uneven pieces approximately three fourths and one fourth of the dough. Shape each piece into a tight ball. Place the larger round on the prepared baking sheet and top with the smaller round. With the floured handle of a wooden spoon, poke a hole directly through the center of both rounds down to the baking sheet.

Ovals: Divide the dough into 12 to 16 equal portions. Shape each piece of dough into a small oval. With a serrated knife, gently cut 2 or 3 diagonal slashes no more than ¼ inch deep on the top of each.

Braids: Divide the dough into 3 equal portions. Roll each portion into a long rope about 24 inches in length. Place the ropes side by side and braid them loosely. Cut the braids into 12 equal portions and pinch the ends to taper them.

Mango Butterhorns

Mangos are known for their apricot-colored fibrous flesh and fragrant perfume. The oval fruit, related to the cashew, hails from Southeast Asia and is a staple in tropical countries. Mango puree is a silky smooth, lusciously sweet, and unusual ingredient in these tender dinner rolls, losing none of its uniqueness in the cooking process. Select a mango by smelling the stem end; it should be sweet and perfumey. Mango puree freezes perfectly for 6 months.

Yield: 40 dinner rolls

1 tablespoon (1 package) active dry yeast
1 cup warm milk (105° to 115°)
2 medium mangos (about 1¾ pounds total)
1 egg
1 tablespoon salt
6 to 6¼ cups unbleached all-purpose or
*   bread flour*
½ cup (1 stick) unsalted butter at room
*   temperature, cut into small pieces*

1. In a small bowl, sprinkle the yeast over the warm milk and stir to dissolve. Let stand until bubbly, about 10 minutes.
2. Peel and cube the mangos. Puree in a blender or food processor and strain through a sieve into a bowl to make 1 cup puree.
3. In a large bowl with a whisk or the workbowl of a heavy-duty electric mixer fitted with the paddle attachment, combine the mango puree, egg, salt, and 1 cup of the flour. Beat hard with a whisk or the mixer to combine. Add the yeast mixture and 2 more cups of the flour. Beat hard for 1 minute. Add the butter a few pieces at a time, beating until incorporated.

Add flour ½ cup at a time to make a soft dough that just clears the sides of the bowl, switching to a wooden spoon when necessary if mixing by hand.

4. Turn the dough out on a lightly floured work surface and knead to make a smooth dough, about 2 to 3 minutes, adding flour 1 tablespoon at a time as necessary to prevent sticking. Place in a greased deep container, turn once to coat the top, and cover with plastic wrap. Let rise in a warm place until doubled, about 1½ to 2 hours.
5. Gently deflate the dough, turn it out onto the work surface, and divide into 5 equal portions. Roll each portion into a circle about ¼ inch thick. Cut each into 8 pie-shaped sections, each measuring about 2½ to 3 inches across the wide end. Roll the wedges into a crescent shape from long side to point. Place, with the tip of crescent down, 1 inch apart on 3 greased or parchment-lined baking sheets. Cover loosely with plastic wrap and let rise in a warm place until just doubled, about 30 minutes. Meanwhile, preheat the oven to 375°.
6. Brush the rolls with melted butter, if desired, and bake in the preheated oven for 15 to 18 minutes, or until golden. Cool on racks.

Wild Rice Bread Sticks

The harvesting of wild rice takes place in Minnesota in late August and early September. Local Chippewa tribes process the rice using traditional techniques, such as hand-parching in galvanized tubs over open fires. This brown-green rice has very large, uneven kernels with a mild, rich, sweet flavor and soft texture. Hand-harvested wild rice is never black; this distinguishes it from cultivated paddy rice, which is left out in the weather to cure. During the fall harvest months, after you have received your winter stash of wild rice, make and serve these crunchy bread sticks with dinner, for snacking or for antipasti (spread with Pesto Butter, page 159). The sticks may be plainly shaped or snipped to form "stalks," which look very special on a buffet table.

Yield: 2 dozen bread sticks

1 tablespoon (1 package) active dry yeast
Pinch brown sugar
1½ cups warm water (105° to 115°)
¼ cup olive oil
2 teaspoons salt
1 cup cooked wild rice (see page 14)
½ cup whole-wheat flour
3½ to 4 cups unbleached all-purpose or
*   bread flour*

Egg Glaze, page 155
Coarse salt
Olive oil for brushing

1. In a large bowl or the workbowl of a heavy-duty electric mixer fitted with the paddle attachment, sprinkle the yeast and brown sugar over the warm water.

Stir to dissolve and let stand until bubbly, about 10 minutes.

2. Stir in the oil, salt, wild rice, and whole-wheat flour and beat with a whisk or the mixer until smooth, about 1 minute. Add the unbleached flour ½ cup at a time to form a soft dough that just clears the sides of the bowl, switching to a wooden spoon when necessary if mixing by hand.

3. Turn the dough out onto a lightly floured work surface and knead until smooth, about 2 minutes, adding flour 1 tablespoon at a time as necessary to prevent sticking. The dough will be nubby from the rice and not stiff. Place in a greased deep container, turn once to coat the top, and cover with plastic wrap. Let rise at room temperature until doubled, about 1 hour.

4. Turn the dough out onto the work surface and divide into 4 equal portions. Cut each portion into 6 equal pieces. With your palms, roll each piece into a long rope, preferably the size of your baking sheet. Place the sticks parallel and no less than 1 inch apart on a greased or parchment-lined baking sheet. Brush the surfaces with olive oil. Let stand at room temperature for about 20 minutes, or until puffy. Meanwhile, preheat the oven to 375°.

5. Gently brush the glaze on the surface of the sticks. Sprinkle with coarse salt, if desired. Bake in the preheated oven until crisp and golden brown, about 20 to 25 minutes. These sticks will not be soft like a roll, but a bit dry. Remove from the baking sheet to cool on a rack. Cover air-tight and store at room temperature.

Fresh Corn and Cornmeal Yeast Muffins in Corn Husks

Fresh corn kernels and stone-ground corn-meal are a dynamite flavor combination in these yeasted muffins. Mixed as for a batter bread and baked in muffin tins, they are easy to serve to a large crowd of summer-time bread lovers. They are also good during the winter made with defrosted frozen baby white corn kernels. Dried corn husks are available in the Mexican food section of many supermarkets. Bake these early in the day and reheat to serve warm with sweet butter or a tangy, fresh goat cheese.

Yield: 36 muffins

2 cups milk
1½ cups yellow or blue cornmeal
½ cup (1 stick) unsalted butter
½ cup sugar
2 teaspoon salt
16 dried or fresh corn husks
1 tablespoon (1 package) active dry yeast
Pinch sugar
⅓ cup warm water (105° to 115°)
2 eggs
Exactly 4¾ cups unbleached all-purpose flour
2 cups fresh yellow, white, or mixed corn
*   kernels (about 4 ears), parcooked 1 minute*

1. In a medium saucepan, scald the milk. Stir in the cornmeal, butter, sugar, and salt. Stir with a whisk and let cool to warm (105° to 115°), about 20 minutes. Soak the dried corn husks in boiling water until pliable, about 10 minutes. Drain on paper towels until needed.

2. In a small bowl, sprinkle the yeast and sugar over the warm water. Stir to dissolve and let stand until bubbly, about 10 minutes.

3. Add the yeast mixture to the cornmeal and place in a large bowl or the work-bowl of a heavy-duty electric mixer fitted with the paddle attachment. Add the eggs and 2 cups of the flour. Beat with a whisk or the mixer on low speed for 1 minute. Add the remaining flour ½ cup at a time to form a soft batter, switching to a wooden spoon when necessary if mixing by hand. Add the corn and stir until evenly incorporated. Cover with plastic wrap and let sit at room temperature until doubled in bulk, about 45 minutes to 1 hour.

4. Stir the batter down. Grease 36 standard muffin cups with butter. Drain the husks, pat them dry, and cut into 1½-inch-thick strips. Lay 2 strips in each cup to form a cross that comes up above the rim of each muffin cup. Spoon the batter evenly into the prepared cups, filling each one half full. Let rise, uncovered, until doubled, about 45 minutes longer. Twenty minutes before baking, preheat the oven to 375°.

5. Bake in the preheated oven for 25 to 30 minutes, or until a cake tester inserted in the center comes out clean and the tops are springy to the touch. Let stand for 5 minutes before turning out onto a rack to cool. Serve warm.

California Olive Rolls

Olives grow on the gnarled branches of *Olea europaea,* a tree with willow-like leaves. It thrives in mild regions with compact, clay-like soil. The precious fruit does not begin to appear until the tree is about 10 years old, but the tree will produce for generations. The firm black olive is exclusively for the table, being sun dried and cured in olive oil and salt or in brine, while many of the smaller green species are crushed or pressed for oil. Use a flavorful California olive, such as Santa Barbara Olive Company's Italian or country-style, or Fusano's Sicilian-style, paired with a fruity oil for this crusty, yet elegant dinner roll. These are also good served with slivers of a young Asiago cheese and a glass of wine.

Yield: 12 rolls

1 tablespoon (1 package) active dry yeast
Pinch sugar
½ cup rye flour
3 to 3¼ cups unbleached all-purpose or
  bread flour
1¼ cups warm water (105° to 115°)
⅓ cup fruity domestic olive oil
1 tablespoon unsalted butter at room
  temperature
1 teaspoon salt
¾ to 1 cup domestic black olives, pitted and
  coarsely chopped

1. To prepare the sponge: In a large bowl or the workbowl of a heavy-duty electric mixer fitted with the paddle attachment, sprinkle the yeast, sugar, rye and ½ cup of the unbleached flour over the warm water and beat well with a whisk or the mixer until smooth and creamy. Cover loosely with plastic wrap and let rise at room temperature for 30 minutes to 1 hour, or until bubbly.
2. Add ½ cup more of the flour, oil, butter, salt, and olives, and beat until smooth, about 1 minute. Add the remaining flour ½ cup at a time until a soft dough is formed that just clears the side of the bowl, switching to a wooden spoon when necessary if mixing by hand.
3. Turn the dough out onto a lightly floured work surface and knead until smooth and springy, about 2 minutes, adding flour 1 tablespoon at a time as necessary to prevent sticking. Place in a greased deep container, turn once to coat the top, and cover with plastic wrap. Let rise for 1 hour, or until puffy.
4. Turn the dough out onto the work surface and divide into 12 equal portions. Form each into an oval and place at least 2 inches apart on a greased or parchment-lined baking sheet. Cover loosely with plastic wrap and let rise at room temperature for 20 minutes. Meanwhile, preheat the oven to 450° with a baking stone or to 425° without a stone.
5. With kitchen shears, snip the top of each roll 3 times at a 45-degree angle down the center. Reduce the oven temperature to 425° if using a baking stone and bake the rolls for 25 to 30 minutes, or until crusty and brown. Serve immediately, or cool on racks to reheat later.

Rustic Cornmeal-Graham Dinner Rolls

One bite of these wholesome, yet delicate, grain-sweet dinner rolls will persuade you to make them many times. Graham flour is a different grind of whole-wheat flour that is particularly nutty in flavor, so it is worth seeking out. Cornmeal by itself has no gluten, so to produce a light-textured roll, it must be combined with wheat flour. Use a fresh stone-ground yellow cornmeal (also known as johnnycake meal) from a small gristmill such as Gray's or Kenyon Mill (see Source Directory) for an extra flavor treat.

Yield: 12 rolls

1 package (1 tablespoon) active dry yeast
Pinch sugar
½ cup warm water (105° to 115°)
3 tablespoons instant nonfat dried milk
1 teaspoon salt
¾ cup graham or whole-wheat flour
⅓ cup yellow cornmeal
¼ cup corn oil
½ cup plain yogurt
2 tablespoons molasses
1 egg
About 2 cups unbleached all-purpose or
  bread flour

Egg Glaze, page 155 (optional)

1. In a small bowl, sprinkle the yeast and sugar over the warm water and stir until dissolved. Let stand until foamy, about 10 minutes.
2. In a large bowl, using a whisk, or in the workbowl of a heavy-duty electric mixer fitted with the paddle attachment, combine the dried milk, salt, graham or

whole-wheat flour, and cornmeal. Add the corn oil, yogurt, molasses, egg, and yeast mixture and beat hard until creamy, about 3 minutes. Add the unbleached flour ½ cup at a time to form a soft dough, switching to a wooden spoon when necessary if mixing by hand. The dough should just clear the sides of the bowl.

3. Turn the dough out onto a lightly floured work surface and knead for about 2 to 3 minutes, or until a soft, springy dough is formed that is slightly sticky to the touch; add flour 1 table-spoon at a time as necessary to prevent sticking. The dough should have a rough, tacky quality. Place in an greased deep container, turn once to coat the top, and cover with plastic wrap. Let rise in a warm place until doubled in bulk, 45 minutes to 1 hour.

4. Turn the dough out onto the work surface, divide into 12 equal portions, and form into balls for round rolls, or into other shapes as desired (see page 92). Place 1 inch apart on a greased or parchment-lined baking sheet. Brush the tops with extra corn oil and cover loosely with 2 layers of plastic wrap, taking care to secure the edges. Immediately refrigerate for 2 to 24 hours.

5. When ready to bake, let stand at room temperature no longer than 20 minutes; meanwhile, preheat the oven to 375°. Brush with Egg Glaze, if desired, for a shiny crust. Bake in the preheated oven for 20 to 25 minutes, or until browned. Serve immediately, or cool on a rack to reheat later.

Squash Cloverleaf Rolls

During the fall I enjoy cooking with a wide assortment of winter squash. This group of vegetables takes its name from the Narraganset Indian word *askutasquash*. You can make these delicious and subtly orange-tinged dinner rolls from mashed cooked globular green acorn, tapered tan butternut, ribbed Gold Nugget sugar pumpkin, smooth calabazas, striped turban, or the dense oval Blue Hubbard with equal success. Serve Squash Cloverleaf Rolls with vegetable or bean soups, roast onions, meat stews, and roast turkey.

Yield: About 20 cloverleaf rolls

1 tablespoon (1 package) active dry yeast
Pinch brown sugar
¼ cup warm water (105° to 115°)
¾ cup warm milk (105° to 115°)
¼ cup orange liqueur, such as Grand Marnier
1 cup pureed cooked winter squash (following), or one defrosted 12-ounce package frozen cooked winter squash
3 tablespoons brown sugar
Grated zest of 1 orange
2 teaspoons salt
6 tablespoons unsalted butter, melted
4 to 4½ cups unbleached all-purpose or bread flour
Melted butter for brushing (optional)

1. In a small bowl, sprinkle the yeast and sugar over the warm water. Stir to dissolve and let stand until foamy, about 10 minutes.
2. In a large bowl, using a whisk, or in the workbowl of a heavy-duty electric mixer fitted with the paddle attachment, combine the milk, liqueur, squash, brown sugar, orange zest, salt, and butter. Add the yeast mixture and 2 cups of the flour. Beat for 2 minutes, or until smooth and creamy. Gradually add the remaining flour ½ cup at a time until a soft dough is formed that just clears the sides of the bowl, switching to a wooden spoon when necessary if mixing by hand.

3. Turn the dough out onto a lightly floured work surface and knead until satiny and elastic, about 2 minutes, adding flour 1 tablespoon at a time as necessary to prevent sticking. This should be a very smooth dough. Place in a greased deep container, turn once to coat the top, and cover with plastic wrap. Let rise at room temperature until doubled in bulk, about 1 hour.

4. Turn the dough out onto the work surface and divide into 4 equal portions. Divide each portion into 5 equal portions. Divide each of these portions into 3 portions, and form these into small balls about the size of a walnut (about 1 inch in diameter). Arrange 3 balls of dough in each of 20 lightly greased miniature (1⅝-inch diameter) muffin cups. Cover loosely with plastic wrap and let rise until doubled, about 20 minutes. Meanwhile, preheat the oven to 400°.

5. Bake in the preheated oven for 12 to 15 minutes, or until golden brown. Remove from the muffin cups immediately to cool on racks or serve warm.

6. **Refrigerator Method:** Brush the tops with melted butter and cover loosely with 2 layers of plastic wrap with some room for expansion, taking care to tightly wrap all the edges. Immediately refrigerate for 2 to 24 hours. When

ready to bake, uncover and let stand at room temperature no more than 20 minutes. Meanwhile, preheat the oven to 400°. Bake as directed above.

Winter Squash Puree

Yield: 1 pound of raw winter squash yields 1 cup puree

Wash a whole winter squash and cut off the top. Take care when cutting, as some varieties are very hard. Some small varieties, such as Gold Nugget, may be cooked whole. Cut in half and scrape out seeds and spongy fibers. Cut into large cubes, leaving the skin intact. Place in a baking dish, flesh down, with a little water. Cover and bake at 350° for 1 to 1½ hours, or until the flesh is tender when pierced with a knife. Drain, cool, then peel off and discard the skin. Puree the pulp until smooth in a blender, food mill, or food processor. Cool, cover, then refrigerate or freeze.

Olive Oil–Potato Rolls

Solanum tuberosum, better known as the humble potato, is one of the great food plants of the world. The best varieties to use for bread are those high in starch, such as the russet, developed by Luther Burbank. For unsurpassed flavor, order some organic heirloom potatoes, such as Buttes, Yukon Gold, Yellow Finns, or Bintje, from the Wood Prairie Farm in Maine (see Source Directory) during the fall harvest, or grow your own.

Yield: 20 dinner rolls

1 large russet potato (½ to ¾ pound), peeled and cut into chunks
½ cup milk
1 tablespoon (1 package) active dry yeast
2 tablespoons sugar
1 tablespoon salt
2 eggs
⅓ cup olive oil
¾ cup rolled oats
4½ to 5 cups unbleached all-purpose or bread flour
Olive oil for brushing
Flour for dusting

1. In a medium saucepan, cover the potatoes with water. Cover, bring to a boil, reduce heat to low, and cook until tender, about 20 minutes. Drain, reserving ½ cup of the potato water. Let the water cool to warm, 105° to 115°. Meanwhile, with an electric mixer, beat the potatoes with the milk until smooth. Make certain there are no lumps. Let cool to warm, 105° to 115°.
2. In a small bowl, sprinkle the yeast over the warm potato water. Stir to dissolve and let stand until foamy, about 10 minutes.
3. In a large bowl, using a whisk, or in the workbowl of a heavy-duty electric mixer fitted with the paddle attachment, combine the potatoes, sugar, salt, eggs, olive oil, oats, and 2 cups of the unbleached flour. Beat until smooth and add the yeast mixture. Beat hard for 2 minutes. Add the remaining flour ½ cup at a time to form a soft dough that just clears the sides of the bowl, switching to a wooden spoon when necessary if mixing by hand.
4. Turn the dough out onto a lightly floured work surface and knead until springy and smooth, about 2 minutes,

adding flour 1 tablespoon at a time as necessary to prevent sticking. Place in a greased deep container, turn once to coat the top, and cover with plastic wrap. Let rise at room temperature until doubled, about 1 hour.
5. Turn the dough out onto the work surface and divide into 4 equal portions. Divide each portion into 5 to make 20 pieces. Shape as desired (see page 92), and place 1 inch apart, seam-side down, on a greased or parchment-lined baking sheet. Brush the tops lightly with extra olive oil. Cover loosely with 2 layers of plastic wrap, taking care to secure the edges. Immediately refrigerate for 2 to 24 hours.
6. When ready to bake, let the rolls stand at room temperature for no longer than 20 minutes. Meanwhile, preheat the oven to 400°. Dust the tops of the rolls with flour. Bake in the center of the preheated oven until evenly brown, about 12 to 15 minutes. Serve immediately.

Champagne Hard Rolls

Despite its sophisticated name, this is a rustic little French-style roll. It is formed into an oval pinched in at the ends to create the traditional *navette,* or weaver's-shuttle, shape that I am so fond of. Using a baking stone helps give these rolls a nice crunchy crust. Served warm from the oven, they are fragrant with the combined flavors of natural grain and wine. This is a good way to use leftover champagne.

Yield: 24 small rolls

1 tablespoon (1 package) active dry yeast
Pinch sugar
1½ cups warm water (105° to 115°)
¾ cup warm dry champagne (105° to 115°)
1 tablespoon sugar
1 tablespoon olive oil
1 tablespoon salt
About 6 cups unbleached all-purpose or
*   bread flour*
½ cup coarse white cornmeal for dusting

1. In a small bowl, sprinkle the yeast and sugar over ½ cup of the warm water. Stir to dissolve and let stand for 10 minutes, or until foamy.
2. In a large bowl, using a whisk, or in the workbowl of a heavy-duty electric mixer fitted with the paddle attachment, combine the remaining water, champagne, sugar, olive oil, and salt. Add 2 cups of the flour and the yeast mixture. Beat hard for 2 minutes. Add the remaining flour ½ cup at a time to form a soft dough that just clears the sides of the bowl, switching to a wooden spoon when necessary if mixing by hand.
3. Turn the dough out onto a lightly floured work surface and knead until the dough is smooth and resilient, about 3 minutes, adding 1 tablespoon of flour as necessary to prevent sticking. Place the dough in a greased deep container and turn it once to coat the top. Cover with plastic wrap and let rise in warm place for about 1 hour, or until tripled in bulk.
4. Turn the dough out onto a very lightly floured work surface. Divide the dough into 4 equal portions. Further divide each quarter into 6 equal portions to make 24 small rolls. Form each into a round or oval, pinching the ends firmly to form a spindle shape. Dust the rolls lightly all over with flour. With a serrated knife, quickly make a slash down the middle of each roll.
5. Place the rolls about 2 inches apart on 2 greased or parchment-lined baking sheets dusted with cornmeal. Cover loosely with plastic wrap and let rest for no longer than 20 minutes. Meanwhile, preheat the oven to 450° with a baking stone, or to 400° without a stone. Pinch the ends of the rolls again to define the oval shape.
6. Place one baking sheet directly on the baking stone, if used, or directly on the oven rack. If the oven is set at 450°, immediately reduce heat to 400°. Bake the rolls for 12 to 15 minutes, or until golden brown. Remove from the oven and bake the second sheet. Cool on a rack or immediately pile into a basket to serve.

Maple Brown Buns

Wheat is cultivated all over the world, except in cold tundra regions and humid tropical zones. A member of the vast Gramineae, or grass, family along with corn and oats, it is the basis for all yeast-bread making. Here is a whole-grain and maple-sweet roll that is as unpretentious as it is delicious. Serve warm with a thick spinach or vegetable soup, roast poultry or meats, or cheeses.

Yield: 2 dozen rolls

½ cup cornmeal
½ cup rolled oats
½ cup maple syrup
1 tablespoon salt
½ cup (1 stick) unsalted butter, cut into
*   pieces*
2½ cups boiling water
1½ tablespoons (1½ packages) active
*   dry yeast*
About 5½ cups unbleached all-purpose or
*   bread flour*
⅔ cup wheat bran or wheat germ

1. In a large bowl, using a whisk, or in the workbowl of a heavy-duty electric mixer fitted with the paddle attachment, combine the cornmeal, oats, maple syrup, salt, and unsalted butter. Pour the boiling water over, and mix until the butter is melted. Let cool to warm (105° to 115°), about 20 to 30 minutes.
2. Add the yeast and 2 cups of flour. Beat until evenly combined, about 1 minute. Cover with plastic wrap and let stand for 15 minutes at room temperature. Add the remaining flour ½ cup at a time to form a soft dough that just clears the

sides of the bowl, switching to a wooden spoon when necessary if mixing by hand.

3. Turn the dough out onto a lightly floured work surface and knead until a course-textured, but mildly tacky dough is formed, about 3 minutes, adding flour 1 tablespoon at a time as necessary to prevent sticking. Place the dough in a greased deep container and turn once to coat the top. Cover with plastic wrap and let rise at room temperature until doubled in bulk, about 1½ to 2 hours.

4. Turn the dough out onto the work surface and divide into 2 equal portions. Divide each portion into 12 portions and form each into small, tight round balls, or divide each portion into 6 portions to make larger rounds. Roll the top surface of each in bran or wheat germ. Place the rolls about 1 inch apart on 2 greased or parchment-lined baking sheets. Press with your palm to flatten. Cover loosely with plastic wrap and let rise at room temperature until doubled, about 45 minutes. Preheat oven to 375°.

5. With a serrated knife, slash an X onto the top of each roll to allow for expansion during baking. Place in the preheated oven and bake until brown and crusty, 20 to 25 minutes. Serve immediately, or let cool to reheat later or to freeze.

Whole-Wheat Ricotta Rolls with Toasted Quinoa

Although quinoa (pronounced KEEN-wa) is indigenous to the Andes Mountains of South America, it is now grown in Colorado. Delicate in flavor, it looks and tastes like millet and has a 16 percent protein content, the highest of any grain. It adds a delightful crunchy texture to these chewy whole-wheat rolls, which can rise overnight in the refrigerator. Serve with fresh sweet butter.

Yield: 12 small rolls

2½ teaspoons active dry yeast
2 tablespoons brown sugar
1½ teaspoons salt
2¼ to 2¾ cups whole-wheat pastry flour
½ cup hot water (120°)
1 cup whole-milk ricotta cheese
3 tablespoons olive oil
1 egg
½ cup toasted quinoa (following)

1. In a large bowl or the workbowl of a heavy-duty electric mixer fitted with the paddle attachment, place the yeast, sugar, salt, and 1 cup of the flour. Stir in the hot water, ricotta, oil, and egg with a whisk or the mixer. Beat hard for 2 minutes, or until smooth. Add the quinoa and remaining flour ½ cup at a time to form a soft dough that just clears the sides of the bowl, switching to a wooden spoon when necessary if mixing by hand.

2. Turn the dough out onto a lightly floured work surface and knead gently until the dough is smooth and springy, about 3 minutes, adding flour 1 tablespoon at a time as necessary to prevent sticking. The dough should retain a slightly tacky, soft quality. Place in a greased deep container, turn once to coat the top, and cover with plastic wrap. Let rise at room temperature until doubled, about 1 hour.

3. Turn the dough out onto the work surface and divide into 12 equal portions. Roll each into a ball or an oval and place 1 inch apart and seam-side down on a greased or parchment-lined baking sheet. Brush the tops lightly with extra olive oil and cover loosely with 2 layers of plastic wrap, taking care to secure the edges. Immediately refrigerate for 2 to 24 hours. When ready to bake, let stand at room temperature for no longer than 20 minutes. Meanwhile, preheat the oven to 375°. Using scissors positioned at a 45-degree angle, make three ½-inch-deep snips into the center of each roll to create triangular peaks.

4. Bake in the center of the preheated oven until the bottoms are evenly browned and hollow sounding when tapped, about 20 to 25 minutes. Serve immediately.

Toasted Quinoa
Place ½ cup quinoa in a fine strainer. Rinse under cold running water to remove the bitter coating. Place in a large skillet or sauté pan over medium heat. Shake the pan to evenly brown the grains, about 5 minutes. Remove from the pan to cool completely before adding to other ingredients. Toasted quinoa may be stored airtight at room temperature for 1 month.

Country Rolls with Shallots and Pecans

Reminiscent of the hearty and excellent *cuisine bourgeoise* of southern Burgundy, these flavorful, savory French rolls are superb dinner breads to break open and butter lavishly. Serve with soups, salads, roast meats, and rustic red wines. They are also excellent with fresh goat cheese and fruit.

Yield: 1 dozen rolls

1 cup pecans
2½ teaspoons active dry yeast
Pinch sugar or honey
½ cup warm water (105° to 115°)
2 large shallots, chopped
4 tablespoons unsalted butter or nut oil
1 teaspoon salt
¼ cup bran
¼ cup whole-wheat flour
About 2 to 2½ cups unbleached all-purpose or
    bread flour
½ cup warm milk (105° to 115°)

1. Preheat the oven to 325°. Place the pecans on an ungreased baking sheet and toast for 10 minutes in the preheated oven. Let cool and coarsely chop.
2. In a small bowl, sprinkle the yeast and sugar or honey over the warm water. Stir to dissolve and let stand until foamy, about 10 minutes.
3. In a small skillet or sauté pan, sauté the shallots in butter or oil until just soft and translucent, about 5 minutes. Remove from heat and set aside.
4. In a large bowl, using a whisk, or in the workbowl of a heavy-duty electric mixer fitted with paddle attachment, combine the salt, bran, whole-wheat flour, and 1 cup of the unbleached flour. Add the yeast mixture, milk, pecans, and shallots. Beat for 1 minute to mix thoroughly. Add the remaining unbleached flour ¼ cup at a time to form a soft dough that just clears the sides of the bowl, switching to a wooden spoon when necessary if mixing by hand.
5. Turn the dough out onto a lightly floured work surface and knead until a smooth, springy, soft dough is formed, about 1 minute, adding 1 tablespoon flour at a time as necessary to prevent sticking. The dough will retain a slight stickiness due to the whole-grain flour. Place in a greased deep container and turn once to coat the top. Cover with plastic wrap and let rise in a warm place until doubled in bulk, about 1 to 1½ hours.
6. Turn the dough out onto the work surface and divide into 12 equal portions. Form into tight, round balls and place about 2 inches apart, seam-side down, on a greased or parchment-lined baking sheet. Cover loosely with plastic wrap and let rise in a warm place until doubled in bulk, about 40 minutes. Twenty minutes before baking, preheat the oven to 400°.
7. With a serrated knife, slash the tops of the rolls no more than ¼ inch deep, and bake on the center rack of the preheated oven until brown and crusty, about 20 to 25 minutes. Cool on racks or serve warm.

Pine Nut and Mozzarella Cheese Rolls

Italian yeast rolls are called *panini,* or "little breads." These nut and cheese rolls are a crusty and savory culinary inspiration. The pine nuts are toasted lightly to bring out their delicate perfume before being added to the dough. These are best eaten the same day they are baked, and they disappear fast. Eat plain with antipasto, roast poultry, and crisp salads.

Yield: 16 rolls

Sponge
1 tablespoon (1 package) active dry yeast
2½ cups warm water (105° to 115°)
⅓ cup wheat bran
3 cups unbleached all-purpose or bread flour

Dough
1½ to 2 cups unbleached all-purpose or
    bread flour
¼ cup fruity olive oil
2 teaspoons salt
Sponge, above
1 cup pine nuts
8 ounces whole-milk mozzarella cheese, cut
    into ½-inch cubes

1. To prepare the sponge: In a large bowl or the workbowl of a heavy-duty electric mixer fitted with the paddle attachment, sprinkle the yeast over the warm water. Stir to dissolve. Add the bran and flour. Beat with a whisk or the mixer until smooth. Cover loosely with plastic wrap and let stand at room temperature for 4 hours to overnight. The sponge will be

bubbly. It can be stored for 3 days in the refrigerator before using, if necessary.

2. To prepare the dough: Add 1 cup of the unbleached flour, olive oil, and salt to the sponge and beat hard with the whisk or the mixer on medium speed until elastic, about 1 minute. Continue to add the remaining flour ¼ cup at a time to form a dough that just pulls away from the sides of the bowl, switching to a wooden spoon when necessary if mixing by hand.

3. Turn the dough out onto a lightly floured work surface and knead vigorously until elastic, yet still moist and slightly tacky, about 1 to 2 minutes. This is important for a light texture. Add 1 tablespoon of flour at a time as necessary to prevent sticking. Place in a greased deep container, turn once to coat the top, and cover with plastic wrap. Let stand at room temperature until tripled in volume, about 2 to 2½ hours.

4. Preheat the oven to 325°. Place the pine nuts on a baking sheet and toast to a light golden color, about 8 to 10 minutes. Let cool.

5. Turn the dough onto the work surface. Pat into a large, thick rectangle. Sprinkle with the cheese cubes and pine nuts. Press the cheese and nuts firmly into the dough, fold it over, and knead gently to evenly distribute. Divide the dough into 16 equal pieces. Shape each piece into a tight round. Place about 1 inch apart on greased or parchment-lined baking sheets. Cover loosely with plastic wrap and let stand at room temperature until doubled in bulk, about 45 minutes. Twenty minutes before baking, preheat the oven to 450° with a baking stone, or to 400° without a stone.

6. With floured kitchen shears, snip the top of each roll. Reduce the oven to 400°, if using a baking stone, and bake the rolls in the preheated oven until browned and hollow sounding when tapped, about 20 to 25 minutes. Serve immediately.

Yeasted Sopaipillas

With Southwestern food all the rage, the sopaipilla, a staple bread served as a dinner roll, is experiencing a renaissance. These light little "pillows" of fried dough are similar to Navajo fry bread. Most recipes use baking powder, but this is a yeast-risen version. It is important to spoon hot oil over them while frying, so that they puff evenly. Traditionally eaten split, drizzled with local saguaro or sage blossom honey, they may also be stuffed with chili beans, lettuce, and tomatoes, or eaten plain. Replace an equal amount of flour with ½ cup white, yellow, or blue fine-ground cornmeal for a delicious untraditional variation.

Yield: 24 little breads

1 tablespoon (1 package) active dry yeast
Pinch sugar
¼ cup warm water (105° to 115°)
About 3 cups unbleached all-purpose flour
1 teaspoon salt
2 tablespoons sugar
¾ cup milk
1 egg
2 tablespoons solid vegetable shortening or
   unsalted butter, melted
Vegetable oil for deep frying

1. In a small bowl, sprinkle the yeast and pinch of sugar over the warm water. Stir to dissolve and let stand for 10 minutes, or until bubbly.

2. In a large bowl, place 2¾ cups of the flour, salt, and sugar. Add the yeast, milk, egg, and melted shortening or butter. With a wooden spoon, beat hard until smooth, about 1 minute. The mixing may also be done in a heavy-duty electric mixer.

3. Turn the dough out onto a lightly floured work surface and knead gently just until smooth, about 10 kneads, adding flour 1 tablespoon at a time as necessary to prevent sticking. The dough must remain *very* soft. Place in a greased deep container, turn once to grease the top, cover with plastic wrap, and let rise at room temperature about 45 minutes or in the refrigerator for about 2 hours. The dough may be refrigerated at this point for up to 3 days, but it should be punched down daily.

4. Place the dough on a lightly floured work surface and divide it into quarters. Gently roll each section of dough out to a ⅛- to ¼-inch thickness. Fold the dough in half and gently re-roll it twice, in the same manner as for biscuits. Let the dough rest for a few minutes if it becomes too springy or hard to handle. With a dough wheel or a very sharp knife, cut each section of dough into 6 equal squares, oblongs, triangles, or diamonds. The shapes can be irregular, but they should be about 3 by 4 inches. Place on a lightly floured baking sheet and cover lightly with plastic wrap. The dough can stay at room temperature for up to 5 minutes; otherwise refrigerate it (up to overnight) until ready to fry.

5. In a deep, heavy saucepan, Dutch oven, electric frying pan, or deep-fat fryer, pour the vegetable oil to a depth of 1 to 2 inches and heat to 400°. Test the oil by dropping in a scrap of dough; the oil is hot enough when it puffs immediately. Place 2 or 3 pieces of dough in the oil. It is important not to crowd the sopaipillas. When the puffs begin to swell, gently push the portion where the bubble is forming down into the hot oil with a pancake turner or slotted spoon several times to help it puff evenly, or spoon oil over the top. Turn several times as needed; cook until just pale gold and hollow looking, about 45 to 60 seconds per side. Drain on several layers of paper towels and keep warm in a 350° oven while cooking the remaining dough. Serve warm.

Buckwheat Yeast Waffles

The down-home tastes of buckwheat and brown sugar give these waffles their rich, wholesome flavor. Serve for breakfast with sweet butter, real maple syrup, and hot applesauce. Or, for a luxurious brunch or a light savory supper dish, serve with Creamed Wild Mushrooms, page 164. Buckwheat and mushrooms are one of the classic culinary food pairs.

Yield: 6 servings

1½ cups milk
2 tablespoons brown sugar
3 tablespoons unsalted butter
2 teaspoons active dry yeast
Pinch of brown sugar
¼ cup warm water (105° to 115°)
1 large egg
1¼ cups unsifted unbleached all-purpose flour
¼ cup unsifted buckwheat flour
½ teaspoon salt

1. In a 1-quart saucepan, heat the milk just until bubbles form around the edge of the pan. Remove from heat and stir in the brown sugar and butter. Let cool to lukewarm. In a medium bowl, sprinkle the yeast and pinch of brown sugar over the warm water. Stir to dissolve and let stand until foamy, about 10 minutes.
2. Beat the egg into the yeast mixture. Add the flours and salt alternately with the warm milk mixture, stirring with wire whisk until well blended. Cover the batter loosely with plastic wrap and let rise in a warm place until doubled in bulk, about 45 minutes.
3. Heat a waffle iron according to the manufacturer's directions. Stir down the waffle batter.
4. Ladle or pour enough batter over the hot waffle iron to cover two thirds of the grid. With a metal spatula, spread the batter to the edges of the grid. Close the lid and cook until the steam stops, about 5 minutes. Keep the waffles warm in a low oven while cooking the remaining batter.

SWEET BREADS

Sweet Yeast Dough

Most baking is an act of sustenance, but sweet-bread baking moves into the realm of the artistic. Higher in fat and sugar than everyday loaves, sweet breads are refined and luxurious in both taste and texture. They sport mysterious luscious fillings, splashes of wine and liqueurs, glistening dried fruits, dashes of exotic spices, and buttery nuts. They can be fashioned into a myriad of shapes, from rolls to braids. A good all-purpose sweet dough has a place in every baker's repertoire, as all sweet doughs are minor variations of the same basic proportions, though the fillings and shapes will vary. As this bread bakes, the kitchen will fill with a delicate perfume. The dough is good enough to be baked as a simple loaf: Form it into two 3-strand braids, drizzle it with a liqueur-spiked glaze, and decorate with silver-coated almonds, dragées, bits of angelica, chocolate coffee beans, or glazed nut halves for a spectacular presentation. Serve with hot coffee, tea, or fresh juices.

Yield: 2 free-form braids

Sponge
*1½ tablespoons (1½ packages) active
    dry yeast*
1 tablespoon sugar
¼ cup warm water (105° to 115°)
1¼ cups warm milk (105° to 115°)
2 cups unbleached all-purpose or bread flour

Dough
2 large eggs
Finely grated zest of 1 lemon or orange
2 teaspoons salt
⅓ cup sugar

*2½ to 3 cups unbleached all-purpose or
    bread flour*
Sponge, above
*¾ cup (1½ sticks) unsalted butter at room
    temperature, cut into small pieces*

Rich Egg Glaze, page 155

1. To prepare the sponge: In a large bowl, using a whisk, or in the workbowl of a heavy-duty electric mixer fitted with the paddle attachment, combine the yeast, sugar, water, milk, and 2 cups of the flour. Beat hard until smooth, about 1 minute. Cover with plastic wrap and let rest at room temperature 30 minutes, until bubbly.

2. Add the eggs, zest, salt, sugar, and 1 cup more of the flour to the sponge. Beat until smooth. Add the butter a few pieces at a time, and beat until incorporated. Add the remaining flour ¼ cup at a time to form a soft dough that just clears the sides of the bowl, switching to a wooden spoon when necessary if mixing by hand. It is important that this dough be very soft.

3. Turn the dough out onto a lightly floured work surface and knead until smooth, shiny, and soft, about 2 minutes, adding 1 tablespoon of flour at a time as necessary to prevent sticking. It is important that this dough remain very soft and pliable. Place in a greased deep container, turn once to coat the top, and cover with plastic wrap. Let rise at room temperature until doubled in bulk, about 1½ to 2 hours. Gently deflate the dough, re-cover, and refrigerate for 12 to 24 hours.

4. Turn the dough out onto the lightly floured work surface and divide into 6 equal portions. Roll each section into a strip with your palms and lay 3 strips side by side. Braid from the middle to taper the ends. Pinch the ends and tuck them under. Place on a greased or parchment-lined baking sheet. Cover loosely with plastic wrap and let rise at room temperature until *almost* doubled in bulk, about 40 minutes. Because of the eggs, this loaf should not completely double during rising, as it will rise a lot in the oven. Twenty minutes before baking, preheat the oven to 350°.

5. Brush with Rich Egg Glaze for a shiny brown crust. Bake in the center of the preheated oven until deep golden brown and hollow sounding when tapped, 35 to 40 minutes. Carefully lift the braids off the baking sheet with a large spatula to cool completely on a wire rack.

Lemon-Ricotta Coffee Cake

The lemon tree has the ability to bear blossoms and ripe fruit all at the same time year round, making lemons available as both winter and summer additions to all types of baking. Lemon cultivation began in India before recorded history and came to Rome via merchant trading. Lemons proliferated commercially in California during the Gold Rush, when they cost $1 apiece and were eaten to combat scurvy. Today California and Italy produce the bulk of the world's lemons. Look for heavy fruits with some give to the touch, as they are the juiciest.

Yield: 2 braids

One recipe Sweet Yeast Dough, page 107, risen overnight in the refrigerator

Filling
2 cups whole-milk ricotta cheese
2 whole large eggs
1/3 cup sugar
2 tablespoons all-purpose flour
Grated zest of 1 lemon
2 tablespoons fresh lemon juice
2 tablespoons dried currants

Lemon Glaze
1/4 cup sugar
2 teaspoons milk
1 teaspoon fresh lemon juice

1. To prepare the filling: In a medium bowl, combine the ricotta, eggs, sugar, flour, zest, and lemon juice. Beat by hand or with an electric mixer until fluffy and smooth. Stir in the currants until evenly distributed.

2. Divide the Sweet Yeast Dough into 2 equal portions. On a lightly floured work surface, roll out each portion with a rolling pin to a 9-by-16-inch rectangle. Transfer to a greased or parchment-lined baking sheet and even out to a rectangular shape. Spread the ricotta filling down the center third, leaving a 1-inch border on the top and bottom edges. With a sharp knife, cut diagonal strips 2 inches apart almost through to the filling. Starting at the top, fold the strips alternately over the filling. If there is any excess dough at the end, tuck it under. Cover loosely with plastic wrap and let rise at room temperature until almost doubled, about 50 minutes. Twenty minutes before baking, preheat the oven to 350°.

3. To prepare the glaze: In a small bowl, whisk the sugar, milk, and lemon juice until smooth. Brush gently over the surface of the bread with a pastry brush. Bake in the preheated oven until the bread is golden brown and the filling is set, 25 to 30 minutes. Remove from the pan carefully to cool completely on a rack.

Amaretto Roulade

Grown throughout the Mediterranean, the delicious almond is an important commercial food crop along with the olive and the grape. Almonds are a traditional "fruit of the earth" christening gift in Catholic countries, symbolizing purity. It is the first blossom to herald the coming of spring, and that is a good time to prepare this elegant and rich roulade for special occasions.

Yield: 2 long loaves

One recipe Sweet Yeast Dough, with 1/2 cup Amaretto liqueur added to the dough in place of 1/2 cup milk and risen overnight in the refrigerator

Almond Filling
1 1/2 cups almonds
1/2 cup (1 stick) unsalted butter at room temperature
1/2 cup sugar
Grated zest of 1 orange
1 egg
2 tablespoons Amaretto liqueur
1/2 cup golden raisins

Rich Egg Glaze, page 155

1. To prepare the filling: Chop the almonds fine and set them aside. In a medium bowl, cream the butter with the sugar, zest, and egg until smooth. Add the liqueur. Fold in the almonds and raisins.

2. Turn the Sweet Yeast Dough out onto a lightly floured work surface and divide into 2 equal portions. Roll out each portion to a 9-by-12-inch rectangle. Using a metal spatula, spread half the almond filling evenly over the surface of the dough, leaving a 1-inch border on all sides. Beginning with the long edge, roll up the dough jelly-roll fashion. Pinch to close the seam. Leave the ends of the roll open. Repeat with the second roll. Place seam-side down on a greased or parchment-lined baking sheet and cover loosely with plastic wrap. Let rise at room temperature until doubled in bulk, about 40 minutes. Twenty minutes before baking, preheat the oven to 350°.

3. Brush the surface with Rich Egg Glaze and bake in the center of the preheated oven for 20 minutes. Brush again with glaze, return to the oven, and bake another 15 to 20 minutes. The loaves

should be golden brown and the filling set. Remove from the baking sheet to cool on racks before slicing.

Ciambella di Fichi

(Fig Wreath)

Ciambella is Italian for "wreath," the shape of this fig-and-hazelnut-filled tea ring. Dried fruits stewed in good red wine add an ambrosial sweetness to this winter yeast bread filling. Use white Calimyrna or deep purple Black Mission figs, both grown in California. The fig, a member of the mulberry family, is botanically not a fruit, but a fleshy container that flowers on the inside; what we think of as its seeds are really miniature fruits. In some versions of the story of Eden, the fig tree is the mystical Tree of Knowledge, replacing the apple.

Yield: 2 tea rings

One recipe Sweet Yeast Dough, page 107, risen overnight in the refrigerator

Fig Filling
3 cups dried figs, stemmed and chopped
6 dried pears, cored and cut into ½-inch pieces
⅓ cup good red wine
¼ cup water
¼ cup honey
3 tablespoons unsalted butter
Juice and zest of 1 lemon
1 teaspoon ground cinnamon
½ cup whole hazelnuts, lightly toasted and skinned (following)

Lemon Powdered Sugar Glaze, page 155

1. To make the filling: In a medium saucepan, combine the fruits, wine, water, honey, butter, juice, and lemon zest. Let stand 1 hour. Partially cover and simmer over low heat until very thick, about 15 minutes. The fruit will be soft but not mushy. Remove from heat and stir in the cinnamon and hazelnuts. Set aside to cool. The filling may be made the day ahead and refrigerated.

2. Turn the Sweet Yeast Dough out onto a lightly floured work surface and divide into 2 equal portions. Roll out each portion with a rolling pin to a 9-by-12-inch rectangle. Spread half the filling evenly over each rectangle, leaving a ½-inch border around the edges. Roll each rectangle up jelly-roll fashion from the long end. Pinch the seams to seal. Place on a greased or parchment-lined baking sheet and form into a circle by connecting the two open ends. Seal by pinching. Cover loosely with plastic wrap and let rise at room temperature until doubled in bulk, about 45 minutes. Twenty minutes before baking, preheat the oven to 350°.

3. With floured kitchen shears or a sharp knife, snip the dough two thirds of the way from the outer edge towards the center at 3-inch intervals. Twist each section slightly to one side, so the cut side is facing up. Bake in the center of the preheated oven until browned and a cake tester inserted into the center comes out clean, about 30 to 35 minutes. Remove from the baking pan and place on wire racks. Combine the ingredients for the Lemon Glaze and drizzle over the warm ciambella. Let cool completely before serving.

To Toast and Skin Hazelnuts:
Place hazelnuts in a single layer on an ungreased baking sheet. Toast in a preheated 350° oven for 10 to 15 minutes, or until they are lightly golden and the skins blister. Wrap the nuts in a clean dish towel and let them stand 1 minute. In small batches, rub the hazelnuts briskly in the towel to remove the skins. Let cool before using.

Raspberry Braid

The tart, tasty, and refreshing raspberry has the same vitamin and mineral content as citrus fruits. Rich in its own natural pectin, it cooks into a thick, luscious filling. Raspberry Braid can be baked easily in the dead of winter from summer's bounty of frozen unsweetened berries. This shape is known as a "false plait," and it is one of my favorite methods of forming yeast breads to showcase colorful, delectable fillings.

Yield: Two 8-inch loaves

One recipe Sweet Yeast Dough, page 107, risen overnight in the refrigerator

Raspberry Filling
2 cups fresh or unthawed frozen unsweetened raspberries
¼ cup sugar
¼ cup cornstarch
2 tablespoons fresh lemon juice or fruit liqueur, such as framboise

Streusel

1/2 cup granulated sugar
Grated zest of 1 lemon
1 teaspoon ground cinnamon
1/3 cup unbleached all-purpose flour
4 tablespoons cold unsalted butter, cut into
    pieces

1. To prepare the filling: In a medium saucepan, combine all the filling ingredients and bring to a boil. Lower the heat and simmer until the fruit juices are thick, stirring occasionally and gently to keep the berries as whole as possible. Remove from heat and set aside to cool.
2. To prepare the streusel: In a small bowl, combine the sugar, zest, cinnamon, and flour. Cut in the butter pieces with your fingers, pastry cutter, or food processor until coarse crumbs are formed. Set aside.
3. Turn the Sweet Yeast Dough out onto a lightly floured work surface and divide into 2 equal portions. Roll out each portion of the dough with a rolling pin into an 8-by-12-inch rectangle. Transfer to a greased or parchment-lined baking sheet and even out the rectangular shape. Spread half the raspberry filling down the center third of each rectangle. With a sharp knife, cut diagonal strips at 2-inch intervals down the outside portions of the dough, almost through to the filling. Starting at the top, fold the strips alternately from each side at a slight angle. If there is any excess at the end, tuck it under. Cover loosely with plastic wrap and let rise at room temperature until doubled in bulk, about 45 minutes. Twenty minutes before baking, preheat oven to 350°.

4. Sprinkle the surface of the plaits with the streusel. Bake in the center of the preheated oven until the filling is bubbly and the crust is golden brown, about 35 to 40 minutes. Remove from the pan to cool completely on a rack.

Prune Swirl with Amaretti Crumbs

Plums have been called the "fruit of Venus," probably because of their succulent nature. Any plum may be dried to become a prune, but some species keep better dried than others. Grown mostly on the West Coast, plums vary in color and shape, and range in size from that of a small cherry to a large egg. Prunes make a superior sweet filling that is almost black in color and strongly flavored. Imported amaretti cookies (Italian almond-kernel macaroons) are sold in attractive red tins at good supermarket delis and specialty foods stores.

Yield: 2 coffee cakes

One recipe Sweet Yeast Dough, page 107,
    risen overnight in the refrigerator

Prune Filling

3 cups pitted prunes
1 cinnamon stick
4 whole cloves
1/2 cup sugar
4 tablespoons unsalted butter
2 tablespoons fresh lemon juice

Amaretti Streusel

12 pairs amaretti cookies
1/4 cup unbleached all-purpose flour
1/4 cup sugar
Dash salt
1/2 teaspoon ground cinnamon
5 tablespoons cold unsalted butter, cut into
    10 pieces

1. In a small saucepan, place the prunes, cinnamon stick, cloves, and water to cover. Bring to a boil and simmer uncovered until tender, about 15 minutes. Drain, and remove the whole spices. Puree until smooth and fluffy by hand, in a food mill, or food processor. Beat in the sugar, butter, and lemon juice until just combined. This filling may be made the day before.
2. To make the streusel: In a blender or food processor, combine the cookies, flour, sugar, salt, and cinnamon. Process until the cookies are coarsely broken into crumbs. Add the butter pieces and process until a crumbly mixture is formed. Set aside.
3. Turn the Sweet Yeast Dough out onto a lightly floured surface and divide into 2 equal portions. Roll each portion of the dough into a 10-by-16-inch rectangle with a rolling pin. Spread one half of the prune filling over the surface of each rectangle, leaving a 1/2-inch margin around the edges. Roll up each rectangle jelly-roll fashion from the long end and pinch the seam to seal. Place each roll into a greased 6-cup miniature tube pan, seam side down, filling the pan half full. Cover loosely with plastic wrap and let rise at room temperature until even with the top of the pans, about 40 minutes. Twenty minutes before baking, preheat the oven to 350°.

4. With scissors, snip the center of the dough surface ½ inch deep to make a cut that runs completely around the top. Sprinkle each cake evenly with Amaretti Streusel. Bake in the center of the preheated oven until browned and a cake tester inserted into the center comes out clean, about 35 to 40 minutes. Let sit in the pans for 15 minutes before turning out onto racks, with the crumb top up, to cool completely before slicing.

Winter Fruit Torte

Winter Fruit Torte is constructed like a deep-dish fruit pie with a rich yeast crust. The filling is an aromatic combination of winter apples, pears, and old-fashioned quinces. Quinces are a hard, acidy fruit with a short season, appearing in early fall. When cooked and sweetened, the golden-yellow flesh is transformed to a stunning crimson. Use a good French or a domestic apple brandy from Oregon, New England applejack, or sweet cider to complement the fruits and spice. Cut into wedges for a late-season outdoor brunch. This recipe is an adaptation from a wonderful book, *The Picnic Gourmet,* by Rocky Mountaineers Joan Hemingway and Connie Maricich (Random House, 1975).

Yield: One 9-inch fruit torte

One-half recipe Sweet Yeast Dough, page 107, risen overnight in the refrigerator

Winter Fruit Filling

4 large green apples, such as pippin or Granny Smith, peeled, cored, and sliced ¼ inch thick
3 small quince, peeled and cut into eighths
½ cup (1 stick) unsalted butter
½ cup sugar
2 teaspoons ground cinnamon
¼ cup apple brandy or cider
3 under-ripe medium pears such as Bosc, Bartlett, or Comice, peeled, cored, and quartered
One 16-ounce can sour cherries, drained

Rich Egg Glaze, page 155
2 tablespoons granulated sugar mixed with 1 teaspoon ground cinnamon for sprinkling

1. To make the Winter Fruit Filling: In a large 12-inch sauté pan or skillet, cook the apples and quince with the butter over medium heat. As the fruits begin to soften, sprinkle with the sugar and cinnamon. Add the apple brandy or cider and cook until evaporated by half. Add the pears and cherries. Stir the fruits together for 1 minute and remove from heat. Let cool to room temperature.

2. To assemble the torte: Place the Sweet Yeast Dough on a lightly floured surface and divide into 2 uneven portions of about two thirds and one third of the whole. Roll the larger portion out into a thin 12-inch round. Fit the round into the bottom and 3 to 4 inches up the sides of a greased 9-inch springform pan. Fill with the Winter Fruit Filling, mounding slightly in the center. Roll out the smaller portion of dough to a 9-inch round, dust with flour, and fold gently in half. With miniature biscuit cutters, cut a few shapes, such as half-moons, diamonds, or hearts, through both layers. Unfold and place the dough over the top of the fruit. Crimp the edges to seal decoratively. Cover loosely with plastic wrap and let rise at room temperature for 15 minutes while preheating the oven to 375°.

3. Gently brush the dough surface with Rich Egg Glaze and sprinkle the top with cinnamon sugar. Bake in the preheated oven for 45 to 50 minutes, or until the crust is golden brown and the filling is bubbly. Let cool in the pan for 20 minutes before removing the sides. Let stand on a rack until completely cool before serving.

Golden Italian Coffee Cake

A humble name for a beautiful sweet bread redolent of lemon, orange, and vanilla. Reminiscent of *pandoro*, or "golden bread," which is baked in a geometric fluted mold, this bread is baked in 6-cup mini-bundt pans. To serve, fill the center with fresh berries and dust the bread with the powdered sugar.

Yield: Two 8-inch bundt cakes

1½ tablespoons (1½ packages) active
   dry yeast
½ cup sugar
½ cup warm water (105° to 115°)
5 cups unbleached all-purpose flour
1 tablespoon each grated lemon and
   orange zest
2 teaspoons salt
½ cup warm milk (105° to 115°)
4 eggs at room temperature
1 teaspoon pure vanilla extract
½ cup (1 stick) unsalted butter at
   room temperature
About ⅓ cup Vanilla Powdered Sugar for
   dusting (following)

1. In a small bowl, sprinkle the yeast and a pinch of sugar over the warm water. Stir to dissolve and let stand until foamy, about 10 minutes.
2. In a large bowl, using a whisk, or in the workbowl of a heavy-duty electric mixer fitted with the paddle attachment, combine 2 cups of the flour, remaining sugar, zests, and salt. Add the milk, eggs, vanilla, and yeast mixture. Beat until smooth, about 1 minute. Add the butter

in 4 pieces and 1 cup more of the flour. Beat until smooth, about 1 minute. Add the remaining flour ½ cup at a time, stopping at exactly 5 cups, switching to a wooden spoon when necessary if mixing by hand. The dough will be shaggy.

3. Turn the dough out onto an unfloured work surface and knead for about 1 minute, adding no more flour. Transfer to a greased deep container, turn once to coat the top, and cover with plastic wrap. Let rise at room temperature until doubled in bulk, about 1½ hours.
4. Turn the dough out onto the work surface. Divide the dough into 2 equal portions. Roll the halves into 2 fat cylinders with the palms of your hands. Place each in a greased 6-cup bundt pan, filling each about half full. Cover loosely with plastic wrap and let rise at room temperature until 1 inch above the rim of the pan, about 45 minutes to 1 hour. Twenty minutes before baking, preheat the oven to 350°.
5. Bake in the center of the preheated oven until golden and hollow sounding when tapped, 35 to 40 minutes. A cake tester will come out clean when inserted into the center. Let stand for 5 minutes in the pans, then turn out onto racks to cool. Dust with Vanilla Powdered Sugar before serving.

Vanilla Powdered Sugar

Place a piece of a whole or split vanilla bean into 2 cups sifted powdered sugar in an airtight container. Let stand at room temperature for 4 days to 1 week, or until scented as desired.

Graham-Granola Bread

Whole wheat can be substituted for the graham flour in this recipe, but the latter is far more nutty and sweet when baked. This is a glorious morning bread for toast. Its character is built on the quality of granola used, so make your own, page 166, or use a favorite commercial brand. Serve with fresh orange juice, sweet butter, and sliced fresh pears.

Yield: Three 8-by-4-inch loaves

1½ tablespoons (1½ packages) active
   dry yeast
Pinch sugar
1½ cups warm water (105° to 115°)
2 cups granola
1 cup buttermilk at room temperature
4 tablespoons unsalted butter, melted
1 egg
2½ teaspoons salt
1¼ cups graham flour
3½ to 4 cups unbleached all-purpose or
   bread flour

1. In a small bowl, sprinkle the yeast and sugar over ½ cup of the warm water. Stir to dissolve and let stand until foamy, about 10 minutes.
2. Place 1 cup of the granola in a blender or food processor and process until finely ground; set aside.
3. In a large bowl, using a whisk, or in the workbowl of a heavy-duty electric mixer fitted with the paddle attachment, combine the remaining 1 cup of water, buttermilk, and butter. Add the egg, salt, ground granola, ½ cup of the remaining

whole granola, graham flour, and 1 cup of the unbleached flour. Beat until smooth. Add the yeast mixture and 1 cup more flour. Beat 1 minute. Add unbleached flour ½ cup at a time to form a soft dough that just clears the sides of the bowl, switching to a wooden spoon when necessary if mixing by hand.

4. Turn the dough out onto a lightly floured work surface and knead until smooth and springy, about 3 minutes, adding 1 tablespoon of flour at a time as necessary to prevent sticking. The dough should be soft and a bit sticky, so do not add too much flour or the bread will be dry. Place in a greased deep container, turn once to coat the top, and cover with plastic wrap. Let rise at room temperature until doubled in bulk, about 1½ hours.

5. Turn the dough out onto a lightly floured work surface and divide into 3 equal portions. Divide each portion in half and form each into a fat cylinder with your palms, about 10 inches long. Wrap 2 cylinders around each other to form a simple twist; repeat to make 3 loaves. Grease three 8-by-4-inch loaf pans and sprinkle each with one third of the remaining ½ cup whole granola, shaking pans to coat all surfaces. Lay each twist in a pan, tucking the ends under. Cover loosely with plastic wrap and let rise to 1 inch above the rim of the pans, about 45 minutes. Twenty minutes before baking, preheat the oven to 375°.

6. Bake in the center of the preheated oven until browned and hollow sounding when tapped, about 35 to 40 minutes. Turn out of the pans to cool completely on racks.

Orange Raisin Bread with Golden Rum Glaze

Orange Raisin Bread is a loaf that drives homemade-bread lovers wild. It is perfect during the winter or holiday season, as it is absolutely delicious, yet easy enough for the most timid novice to make. Bake in standard loaves or in two small *kugelhopf* molds for entertaining, or form into 12 beautiful mini-bundt molds for individual servings.

Yield: Two 9-by-5-inch loaves

1½ cups golden raisins
1 cup chopped candied orange peel, preferably homemade
½ cup golden rum
5½ to 6 cups unbleached all-purpose or bread flour
¼ cup dried buttermilk
1 tablespoon (1 package) active dry yeast
1 tablespoon salt
2 cups hot water (120°)
¼ cup nut oil, such as walnut or almond
1 egg

Golden Rum Glaze, page 156

1. In a small bowl, combine the golden raisins and candied orange peel. Add the rum and cover with plastic wrap. Let stand for 1 to 4 hours at room temperature to macerate.

2. In a large mixing bowl, using a whisk, or in the workbowl of a heavy-duty electric mixer fitted with the paddle attachment, combine 2 cups of the flour, dried buttermilk, yeast, and salt. Mix in the hot water and oil. Beat until creamy, about 1 minute. Add the egg and soaked fruits. Add the remaining flour ½ cup at a time to form a soft dough that just clears the sides of the bowl, switching to a wooden spoon when necessary if mixing by hand.

3. Turn the dough out onto a lightly floured work surface and knead until smooth and springy, about 3 minutes, adding 1 tablespoon flour at a time as necessary to prevent sticking. Push back any fruits that fall out. Place in a greased deep container, turn once to coat the top, and cover with plastic wrap. Let rise at room temperature until doubled in bulk, about 1½ hours.

4. Turn the dough out onto the work surface and divide into 6 equal portions. Roll each section into a 10-inch strip and lay 3 strips side by side. Braid tightly. Pinch the ends and tuck them under. Place in 2 greased 9-by-5-inch loaf pans. Cover loosely with plastic wrap and let rise until 1 inch above the rim of the pans, about 45 minutes. Twenty minutes before baking, preheat the oven to 375°.

5. Bake in the center of the preheated oven until brown and hollow sounding when tapped, about 40 to 45 minutes. Turn out of the pans to place on racks over plates to catch drips. While warm, drizzle with Golden Rum Glaze. Let stand until the bread is cool and the glaze is set.

Marzipan Brioche with Apricot Brandy Glaze

"Stunning" is the best description of this rich cake-bread swirled with the popular filling French and Germans call *marzipan* and Italians call *marzapane*. The marzipan in this recipe is a creamy, sweet almond filling in the European tradition, rather than the "marchpane" molded candies from Elizabethan times. This bread freezes well when cooled, but wait until ready to serve before gilding with the apricot-hued glaze.

Yield: One 10-inch coffee cake serving 10 to 12

1 recipe Brioche dough, page 51, risen overnight in the refrigerator

Almond Crème
½ cup currants or dried apricots
3 tablespoons brandy
½ cup (1 stick) unsalted butter at room temperature
½ cup sugar
1 egg
1 cup almonds, ground
1 teaspoon almond extract

Apricot Brandy Glaze, page 156

1. Prepare the Almond Crème: In a small bowl, combine the dried fruit and brandy. Let stand at room temperature for 1 hour to macerate. Cream the butter and sugar until fluffy with a wooden spoon, an electric mixer, or a food processor. Add the egg and beat until smooth. Stir in the almonds and extract until just combined. Set aside at room temperature if using immediately. If made the day before, bring to room temperature before using.

2. Place the chilled Brioche dough on a lightly floured surface and divide in half. Roll out one half into a 14-inch round, like a pie crust. Place in an ungreased 10-inch springform pan, nonstick preferred. Press into the bottom and all the way up the sides. Trim any overhang even with the pan rim.

3. Roll out the other half of the dough into a large 12-by-18-inch rectangle. Spread evenly with Almond Crème, leaving a ½-inch margin around the edges. Roll up jelly-roll fashion from the long end. Cut into 8 equal portions with a serrated knife. Lay the rolls cut-side up in the dough-lined pan, placing 7 around the edges and 1 in the middle, all barely touching. Cover loosely with plastic wrap and let rise at a cool room temperature until doubled and puffy, about 1½ hours. Twenty minutes before baking, preheat the oven to 350°.

4. Bake in the preheated oven, 65 to 75 minutes, until golden and a cake tester comes out clean when inserted into the center. Just before the cake is done, prepare the Apricot Brandy Glaze; keep warm. Remove the cake from the oven and immediately pour the glaze over the hot cake in the pan. Let stand for 15 minutes before removing the sides of the pan. Place on a rack to cool completely before cutting into wedges to serve.

Vanilla Date Bread

California dates grow exclusively in the desert oasis of Coachella Valley, an area that spans from Palm Springs to the Salton Sea. Date groves flourish when the palms have their "feet in water and heads in the fire of heaven." Although a date looks like a dried fruit, actually it is sold fresh. Use a soft date for this bread, such as the exquisite sugary Barhi or the velvety Medjool. The common commercial variety, the amber Deglet Noor, also known as the "date of light," is also fine to use. Vanilla Date Bread uses very little sugar, because the honey-like taste of the dates makes it sweet. Serve for brunch with a bowl of Vanilla Butter, page 159, for spreading.

Yield: 3 round loaves

Sponge
1¼ cups warm milk (105° to 115°)
½ cup warm water (105° to 115°)
¼ cup sugar
1 tablespoon (1 package) active dry yeast
2 cups unbleached all-purpose or bread flour

Dough
Sponge, above
5 to 5½ cups unbleached all-purpose or bread flour
4 tablespoons unsalted butter, melted
2½ teaspoons salt
1½ tablespoons pure vanilla extract
2 eggs
2 cups pitted dates, chopped

1. To make the sponge: In a large bowl or deep plastic container, whisk together the milk, water, sugar, yeast, and 2 cups of flour. When smooth, scrape down the sides with a spatula and cover with plas-

tic wrap. Let stand at room temperature for 1 hour, or until bubbly. Stir down.

2. To make the dough: Place the sponge in a large bowl or the workbowl of a heavy-duty electric mixer fitted with the paddle attachment. Mix in 1 cup of the flour, butter, salt, vanilla, and eggs with a whisk or the mixer. Beat until smooth, about 1 minute. Add the remaining flour ½ cup at a time to form a soft dough that just clears the sides of the bowl, switching to a wooden spoon when necessary if mixing by hand.

3. Turn the dough out onto a lightly floured work surface and knead until just smooth and springy, about 3 minutes, adding 1 tablespoon of flour at a time as necessary to prevent sticking. The dough should be soft, but hold its own shape. Place in a greased deep container, turn once to coat the top, and cover with plastic wrap. Let rise at room temperature until doubled in bulk, about 1½ hours.

4. Turn the dough out onto the work surface and pat into a large, thick rectangle. Sprinkle with the chopped dates and fold the dough. Knead gently to evenly distribute the fruit. Divide into 3 equal portions. Form into tight round loaves and place at least 3 inches apart seam-side down, on a greased or parchment-lined baking sheet. Cover loosely with plastic wrap and let rise at room temperature until doubled in bulk, about 45 minutes. Twenty minutes before baking, preheat the oven to 350°.

5. With a serrated knife, decoratively slash the tops not more than ¼ inch deep. Bake in the center of the preheated oven until golden and a cake tester inserted into the center comes out clean, about 35 to 40 minutes. Remove from the pan to cool completely on racks.

Whole-Wheat Maple Blueberry Bread

Plump, sweet blueberries are sold in the familiar pint box, which weighs about 14 ounces and yields about 2 cups. Our commercial berry is the North American native high-bush variety, which is grown in Oregon, Washington, North Carolina, and Florida. Blueberry bushes are so prolific that they were not cultivated commercially until this century. The smaller, intensely flavored low-bush varieties grow wild throughout the United States and parts of Canada. It is important to wash blueberries right before using, as they will absorb water if they sit. Make this bread at the height of the blueberry season, mid- to late summer, or during the winter using frozen berries.

Yield: 2 large loaves about 15 inches long

Whole-Wheat Sweet Yeast Dough
1½ tablespoons (1½ packages) active dry yeast
Pinch sugar
Pinch ground ginger
¼ cup warm water (105° to 115°)
1 cup warm milk (105° to 115°)
6 tablespoons unsalted butter, melted
⅓ cup pure maple syrup
2 teaspoons salt
2 eggs
Grated zest of 1 lemon
2 cups whole-wheat flour
About 2½ to 3 cups unbleached all-purpose or bread flour

Filling
1 pint (2 cups) fresh blueberries, or one 16-ounce package unsweetened frozen blueberries, unthawed
¼ cup pure maple syrup
¼ cup cornstarch
2 tablespoons fresh lemon juice

Lemon Streusel
½ cup sugar
Grated zest of 1 lemon
1 teaspoon ground cinnamon
⅓ cup unbleached all-purpose flour
4 tablespoons cold unsalted butter, cut into 8 pieces

1. To make the dough: In a small bowl, sprinkle the yeast, sugar, and ginger, over the warm water. Stir to dissolve and let stand until foamy, about 10 minutes.

2. In a large bowl, using a whisk, or in the workbowl of a heavy-duty electric mixer fitted with the paddle attachment, combine the milk, butter, maple syrup, salt, eggs, zest, and whole-wheat flour. Beat until creamy, about 1 minute. Add the yeast mixture and 1 cup of the unbleached flour. Beat for 1 minute. Gradually add the remaining flour ¼ cup at a time to form a soft dough that just clears the sides of the bowl, switching to a wooden spoon when necessary if mixing by hand.

3. Turn the dough out onto a lightly floured work surface and knead until smooth, firm, and elastic, about 3 minutes, adding 1 tablespoon of flour at a time as necessary to prevent sticking. Do not add too much flour. The dough should hold its own shape, but be soft and pliable. Place in a greased deep container, turn once to coat the top, and cover with plastic wrap. Let rise at room

temperature until doubled in bulk, about 1 to 1½ hours.

4. While the dough is rising, prepare the Blueberry Filling: In a medium saucepan, combine all the ingredients and bring to a boil. Lower heat and simmer until the blueberry juices are thick, stirring occasionally and gently to keep as many berries whole as possible. Remove from heat and let cool to room temperature.

5. To make the Lemon Streusel: In a small bowl, combine the sugar, zest, cinnamon, and flour. Cut in the cold butter pieces using your fingers, a pastry cutter, or a food processor, until coarse crumbs are formed. Set aside.

6. Turn the dough out onto the work surface and divide into 2 equal portions. With a rolling pin, roll each portion into a 9-by-15-inch rectangle. Transfer to a greased or parchment-lined baking sheet and even the edges. Spread the blueberry filling down the center third of a rectangle. With a sharp knife, cut strips at 2-inch intervals diagonally on both sides of the filling, cutting almost through to the filling. Starting at the top, fold the strips alternately from each side at a slight angle to make a criss-cross braid. Tuck under any excess dough at the end. Repeat to make the second loaf. Cover loosely with plastic wrap and let rise at room temperature until doubled in bulk, about 45 minutes. Twenty minutes before baking, preheat the oven to 350°.

7. Sprinkle the tops evenly with lemon streusel. Bake in the preheated oven 40–45 minutes or until an even golden brown and a cake tester inserted into the center comes out clean. Transfer gently to racks to cool completely before serving.

Orange Cinnamon Swirl

What would a bread book be without a recipe for a sugar and spice swirl? This dough is delicately orange-flavored from the addition of fresh or frozen juice. Use commercial or home-grown sweet oranges such as Valencias or navels, ruby blood oranges, tangerines, or mandarins to vary the flavor and color. This bread has a fabulous taste and texture, and makes very special toast.

Yield: Two 9-by-5-inch loaves

1 tablespoon (1 package) active dry yeast
Pinch sugar
¼ cup warm water (105° to 115°)
1 cup warm milk (105° to 115°)
1 cup orange juice
½ cup sugar
4 tablespoons unsalted butter, melted
2 eggs
Grated zest of 2 oranges
6½ to 7½ cups unbleached all-purpose or bread flour
⅔ cup granulated sugar mixed with 1½ tablespoons ground cinnamon
2 tablespoons unsalted butter, melted, for brushing
Ground cinnamon for dusting (optional)

1. In a small bowl, sprinkle the yeast and the pinch of sugar over the warm water. Stir to dissolve and let stand until foamy, about 10 minutes.

2. In a large bowl, using a whisk, or in the workbowl of a heavy-duty electric mixer fitted with the paddle attachment, combine the milk, juice, sugar, butter, eggs, zest, and 2 cups of the unbleached flour. Beat until smooth, about 1 minute. Add the yeast mixture and 1 cup more flour. Beat 1 minute more. Add the remaining flour ½ cup at a time to form a soft dough that just clears the sides of the bowl, switching to a wooden spoon when necessary if mixing by hand.

3. Turn the dough out onto a lightly floured work surface and knead until smooth and springy, about 3 minutes, adding 1 tablespoon of flour at a time as necessary to prevent sticking. Place in a greased deep container, turn once to coat the top, and cover with plastic wrap. Let rise at room temperature until doubled in bulk, about 1 to 1½ hours.

4. Turn the dough out onto the work surface and divide into 2 equal portions. Roll or pat each portion into a thick rectangle about 8 by 12 inches. Brush the surface of each rectangle lightly with melted butter and sprinkle with half of the cinnamon sugar, leaving a 1-inch border all around the edges. Roll up jelly-roll fashion from the narrow end to form a fat loaf shape. Pinch all the seams to completely seal. Place each loaf seam-side down in a greased 9-by-5-inch loaf pan. Lightly dust with plain ground cinnamon for decoration, if desired. Cover loosely with plastic wrap and let rise at room temperature until 1 inch above the rims of the pans, about 45 minutes. Twenty minutes before baking, preheat the oven to 350°.

5. Bake in the center of the preheated oven until the bread is golden brown, hollow sounding when tapped, and a cake tester inserted into the center of a loaf comes out clean, about 40 to 45 minutes. Remove from the pans to cool completely on racks before slicing.

Almond Butter Coffee Cake

Similar to German and Austrian *kuchens,* this coffee cake can take center stage at brunches and teas. It is baked into a flat round cake and then cut into wedges. This recipe utilizes the folding technique used to form the flaky layers of croissants. The flavor and light texture of this coffee cake are sensational, so don't let the folding of the dough intimidate you. It is easy to do and the cake freezes perfectly.

Yield: One 12-inch coffee cake

1 tablespoon (1 package) active dry yeast
Pinch sugar
¼ cup warm water (105° to 115°)
⅓ cup sugar
¾ cup (1½ sticks) unsalted butter at room temperature, cut into 12 pieces
2 eggs
½ cup warm milk (105° to 115°)
1 teaspoon pure vanilla extract
1 teaspoon salt
2½ to 2¾ cups unbleached all-purpose flour

Almond Butter Topping
½ cup (1 stick) unsalted butter at room temperature
½ cup granulated sugar
1 teaspoon pure almond extract
½ teaspoon pure vanilla extract

¾ cup sliced almonds for sprinkling

1. In a small bowl, sprinkle the yeast and pinch of sugar over the warm water. Stir to dissolve and let stand until foamy, about 10 minutes.

2. In a large bowl, using a wooden spoon, or in the workbowl of a heavy-duty electric mixer fitted with the paddle attachment, cream the sugar and 6 tablespoons of the butter until fluffy. Add the eggs one at a time until incorporated, using a whisk if mixing by hand. Add the milk, vanilla, salt, yeast mixture, and 1 cup of the flour. Beat until smooth, 1 minute. Add the remaining flour ½ cup at a time to form a soft dough that just pulls away from the sides of the bowl, switching to a wooden spoon when necessary if mixing by hand.

3. Turn the dough out onto a lightly floured work surface and knead 4 or 5 times to form a soft, smooth round dough ball. It should hold its shape gently and not be sticky, but it will definitely be softer than any bread dough. Place in a greased deep container, turn once to coat the top, and cover with plastic wrap. Let rise at room temperature until doubled in bulk, about 45 minutes.

4. Place the dough on a lightly floured work surface and pat or roll it out into an 8-by-12-inch rectangle. Spread 3 tablespoons of the remaining 6 tablespoons soft butter evenly over the center third of the dough. Pull one third of the dough from the side to cover the buttered area. Spread the last 3 tablespoons of butter evenly over the top of the dough. Fold over the remaining third side of the dough and pinch all edges to seal. With a rolling pin, roll out the dough into the same size of rectangle again. Fold in thirds again. Cover tightly with plastic wrap and refrigerate for 25 minutes, just to gently firm the butter and chill the dough for easier handling.

5. Gently roll the dough out into a 12-inch round. Pat into a greased 12-inch springform or deep-dish pizza pan. Press the dough about 1 inch up the sides to form a low border. Cover loosely with plastic wrap and let rise at room temperature exactly 30 minutes. Meanwhile, preheat the oven to 375° and make the topping.

6. To make the almond butter topping: With a wooden spoon, an electric mixer, or a food processor, cream the butter with the sugar and extracts until fluffy and smooth.

7. Gently press your thumb all over the top of the cake to make evenly spaced depressions. Drop the almond butter topping by tablespoonfuls into the depressions on the top of the cake, using up all the topping. Sprinkle evenly with the sliced almonds. Bake in the center of the preheated oven until the edges are golden brown and a cake tester comes out clean when inserted into the center, 30 to 35 minutes. Let stand for 10 minutes before removing the springform sides, if your pan has them. Place on a rack to cool and allow the butter topping to be reabsorbed into the cake. Serve warm from the pan in wedges.

Walnut-Banana Bread

The banana is an archaic fruit, predating even rice, and there is a Hindu legend calling bananas the forbidden fruit in Paradise. The unique flavor and fragrance of the canary-yellow banana makes for a rich and satisfying addition to yeast bread. Use either the familiar Grand Nain or the Valery imported commerical variety, or an organically grown domestic such as a fragrant Manzano, a triangular Cardabas, or the rich, sweet Cavendish from Seaside Banana Gardens in Southern California (see Source Directory). Walnut-Banana Bread has an especially moist texture that makes wonderful toast.

Yield: Two 9-by-5-inch loaves

1 tablespoon (1 package) active dry yeast
Pinch brown sugar
1 cup warm water (105° to 115°)
1 cup warm milk (105° to 115°)
2 medium bananas, pureed to make 1 cup
1 cup walnuts, coarsely chopped
¼ cup walnut oil
2 tablespoons brown sugar
1½ tablespoons ground cinnamon
1 tablespoon salt
Grated zest of 1 orange
*5½ to 6 cups unbleached all-purpose or
    bread flour*

1. In a small bowl, sprinkle the yeast and pinch of brown sugar over ½ cup of the warm water. Stir to dissolve and let stand until foamy, about 10 minutes.

2. In a large bowl, using a whisk, or in the workbowl of a heavy-duty electric mixer fitted with the paddle attachment, combine the remaining ½ cup water, milk, banana puree, walnuts, oil, brown sugar, cinnamon, salt, zest, and 2 cups of flour. Beat for 1 minute. Add the yeast mixture and 1 cup more flour. Beat 2 minutes more, or until creamy. Add the remaining flour ½ cup at a time to form a soft dough that just clears the sides of the bowl, switching to a wooden spoon when necessary if mixing by hand.

3. Turn the dough out onto a lightly floured work surface and knead until smooth and springy, about 3 minutes, adding 1 tablespoon of flour at a time as necessary to prevent sticking. Place in a greased deep container, turn once to coat the top, and cover with plastic wrap. Let rise at room temperature until doubled in bulk, about 1½ hours.

4. Turn the dough out onto the work surface and divide into 6 equal portions. Roll each portion into a fat strip and lay 3 strips side by side. Braid the 3 strips and taper the ends. Pinch the ends and tuck them under. Repeat to make a second loaf. Place the loaves in greased 9-by-5-inch loaf pans. Cover loosely with plastic wrap and let rise again at room temperature until 1 inch above the rim of the pans, about 40 minutes. Twenty minutes before baking, preheat the oven to 350°.

5. Bake in the center of the preheated oven until browned and hollow sounding when tapped, about 40 to 45 minutes. Remove from the pans immediately and cool on racks.

LITTLE SWEET BREADS

Rum-Raisin Milk Buns

My photographer, Joyce, has fond memories of rich yeasted raisin buns, which are a bakery staple in her native Amsterdam. Here is my interpretation of her mother's home recipe. Serve as tea cakes with Sweet Orange Butter, page 159, and cups of Earl Grey tea.

Yield: 1 dozen 4-inch buns

1½ cups dark raisins
½ cup dried currants
½ cup golden rum
1 tablespoon (1 package) active dry yeast
¼ cup sugar
¼ cup warm water (105° to 115°)
1 cup warm milk (105° to 115°)
2 teaspoons salt
1 egg
3¼ to 3¾ cups unbleached all-purpose or bread flour
5 tablespoons unsalted butter at room temperature
3 tablespoons milk mixed with 1 tablespoon sugar for glaze

1. In a small bowl, combine the raisins, currants, and rum and let stand at room temperature for 2 hours.
2. In a small bowl, sprinkle the yeast and a pinch of the sugar over the warm water. Stir to dissolve and let stand at room temperature until foamy, about 10 minutes.
3. In a large bowl, using a whisk, or in the workbowl of a heavy-duty electric mixer fitted with the paddle attachment, combine the remaining sugar, milk, salt, egg, and 1 cup of the flour. Add the yeast mixture and beat until smooth, about 1 minute. Add 1 cup more flour and the butter and beat. Add the remaining flour ½ cup at a time to form a soft dough that just clears the sides of the bowl, switching to a wooden spoon as necessary if mixing by hand.
4. Turn the dough out onto a lightly floured work surface and knead until soft and springy, about 3 minutes, adding 1 tablespoon of flour at a time as necessary to prevent sticking. Place in a greased deep container, turn once to coat the top, and cover with plastic wrap. Let rise at room temperature until doubled in bulk, 1 to 1½ hours.
5. Turn the dough out onto the work surface and pat into a large rectangle. Sprinkle the undrained rum-raisin mixture over the surface. Knead and fold over several times to evenly incorporate. Divide into 12 equal portions and shape into smooth rounds by forming each portion into a ball, pulling the dough together at the bottom to give each ball a taut surface. Press each round with a rolling pin to form a flat round 3 to 4 inches in diameter. Place about 2 inches apart, seam-side down, on a greased or parchment-lined baking sheet. Let rise at room temperature until doubled in bulk, about 45 minutes. Twenty minutes before baking, preheat the oven to 375°, with a baking stone if you like.
6. Brush the surface of each round with glaze and bake in the preheated oven until browned, about 20 to 25 minutes. If using 2 baking sheets, reverse the position of the pans halfway through the baking time. Remove the buns from the pans to racks. Serve warm or at room temperature.

Cornmeal Buns with Sambuca Glaze

Sambuca is a popular Italian liqueur with a delightful licorice flavor, sometimes sold in an enticing giraffe-neck bottle. Made from a combination of aniseed and the leaves of an elderberry bush known as *Sambucus nigra,* it flavors the unique glaze on these pale yellow cornmeal egg buns. Serve with Sambuca's natural flavor accompaniment, coffee, in the form of steaming hot espresso with lemon zest garnishes.

Yield: Sixteen 3½-inch buns

One recipe Cornmeal Brioche, page 49, chilled overnight

Glaze
¼ cup granulated sugar
¼ cup Sambuca liqueur
1 tablespoon water

1. Gently turn the chilled dough out onto a lightly floured work surface and divide into 16 equal portions. Form each into a tight round and place in each of 16 greased fluted baby brioche tins or standard muffin cups. Place individual tins on a baking sheet for easier handling. Cover loosely with plastic wrap and let stand at a cool room temperature until doubled in bulk, about 1 hour. Twenty minutes before baking, preheat the oven to 400°.
2. With sharp scissors, snip an X on the top of each bun and place on the center rack of the preheated oven. Immediately combine the glaze ingredients in a small bowl with a whisk. The glaze will have a grainy consistency. After 10 minutes,

remove the buns from the oven and gently brush the surface of each bun with the glaze. Return to the oven for 5 to 7 minutes longer, or until the buns are golden and a cake tester inserted in the center of one comes out clean. Remove from the oven and brush immediately with a second coating of glaze. Let stand for 5 minutes before turning out onto racks to cool.

Pumpkin Brioche with Macadamia Nut Butter

The pumpkin is really a large, brightly colored berry with a tough skin. These large annual plants with curling tendrils and vine-like shoots are popular with home gardeners for food as well as for ornamental uses. This is one of my favorite little sweet breads for fall; the rolls are pale orange in color and melt-in-the-mouth tender. Serve with Macadamia Nut Butter, page 159.

Yield: 18 individual rolls

1 tablespoon (1 package) active dry yeast
Pinch sugar
3 tablespoons warm water (105° to 115°)
1 cup fresh or canned pumpkin puree at room temperature (see page 99)
3¾ cups unbleached all-purpose flour
¼ cup brown sugar
1 teaspoon salt
½ teaspoon each ground cinnamon and nutmeg
¼ teaspoon ground cloves

4 eggs
1 cup (2 sticks) unsalted butter at room temperature, cut into pieces

1. In a small bowl, sprinkle the yeast and sugar over the warm water. Stir to dissolve and let stand until foamy, about 10 minutes.
2. In a large bowl, using a whisk, or in the workbowl of a heavy-duty electric mixer fitted with the paddle attachment, combine the pumpkin, 1 cup of the flour, sugar, salt, and spices. Add the yeast mixture and beat until smooth.
3. Add the eggs one at a time, beating well after each addition. Gradually add 2 cups more of the flour, switching to a wooden spoon when necessary if mixing by hand. Add the butter a few pieces at a time and beat until incorporated. Add *exactly* ¾ cup more flour and beat until creamy. The dough will be soft, sticky, and batter-like.
4. Scrape the dough into a greased deep container, cover with plastic wrap, and let rise at a cool room temperature until doubled or tripled in bulk, about 3 hours. Gently deflate the dough and cover it tightly with plastic. Refrigerate overnight.
5. Turn the chilled dough out onto a lightly floured work surface and divide into 3 equal portions. Divide each portion into 6 equal portions. With floured fingers, form each portion into a small ball and place in a greased 3½-inch fluted brioche tin or standard muffin cup. Using kitchen shears dipped in flour, snip the top of each with an X. Place individual tins on a baking sheet for easier handling. Let rise at a cool room temperature until doubled in bulk, about 1 to 1½

hours. Twenty minutes before baking, preheat the oven to 400°.
6. Bake in the center of the preheated oven for 10 minutes. Reduce heat to 350° and bake 5 to 7 minutes more, or until the buns are golden and a cake tester inserted in the center of a bun comes out clean. Remove from the tins immediately to cool on wire racks before serving. These buns are best served reheated.

Honey-Cinnamon Walnut Rolls

Giant cinnamon rolls are an irresistible homey morning treat. An easy-to-handle dough is risen only once before being used to encase the sweet filling and formed into spirals. The spiral is a symbol from Paleolithic times, reminiscent of the whorl of seashells, coiled serpents, and unfurling fern fronds. This simple shape is well suited to yeast baking, as it retains its form perfectly. The smooth Orange Frangelico Frosting is nothing short of sensational.

Yield: About 18 to 20 large rolls

Dough
4 large eggs
1½ cups warm water (105° to 110°)
¼ cup mild honey
2 tablespoons (2 packages) active dry yeast
7½ to 8 cups unbleached all-purpose flour
2 teaspoons salt
2 tablespoons ground cinnamon
1½ cups (3 sticks) unsalted butter at room temperature, cut into pieces

Filling

1½ cups light brown sugar
2 cups chopped walnuts
½ teaspoon salt
⅓ cup ground cinnamon
½ cup (1 stick) unsalted butter, melted
1 cup dark raisins

Orange Frangelico Frosting

1 cup (2 sticks) unsalted butter at room
temperature
4 cups sifted powdered sugar
1 teaspoon ground cinnamon
1½ teaspoons salt
Grated zest and juice from 1 orange
2 to 3 tablespoons hazelnut liqueur, such as
Frangelico

1. In a medium bowl, beat the eggs with a whisk until light and foamy. Add the water and honey. Stir to dissolve. Sprinkle with the yeast, stir to dissolve, and let stand until foamy, about 15 minutes.

2. Into a large bowl, sift together 7½ cups of the flour, salt, and cinnamon. Cut in the butter with a pastry cutter or 2 knives until a coarse meal is formed. This may also be done in a heavy-duty electric mixer. Make a well in the center and pour in the yeast mixture. Stir with a wooden spoon until the dough clears the sides of the bowl.

3. Turn the dough out onto a lightly floured work surface and knead until smooth and springy, about 3 minutes, adding flour 1 tablespoon at a time as necessary to prevent sticking. Cover with a towel and let rest 10 minutes on the work surface.

4. To make the filling: In a medium bowl, combine the sugar, walnuts, salt, and cinnamon. Divide the dough into 2 equal portions, if desired, for easier

handling. Roll each portion out to a large rectangle ½ inch thick. Brush the surface with the melted butter and spread evenly with the walnut filling. Sprinkle with the raisins. Roll up from the long side jelly-roll fashion. Pinch all seams to seal. With a serrated knife, slice into eighteen to twenty 1-inch slices. Place at least 2 inches apart on 2 greased or parchment-lined baking sheets. Cover loosely with plastic wrap. Let rise at room temperature until doubled in bulk, about 1 hour. Twenty minutes before baking, preheat the oven to 350°.

5. Bake in the center of the preheated oven for 15 to 20 minutes. The rolls should be a bit underdone, as they dry out easily during reheating.

6. While the rolls are baking, make the Orange Frangelico frosting: In a large bowl, using a wooden spoon, or in the workbowl of a heavy-duty electric mixer fitted with the paddle attachment, cream the butter together with the sugar, spice, and salt. When crumbly, add the orange zest, juice, and liqueur. Beat hard by hand or on high speed until light and fluffy, about 1 minute. The glaze should be the spreading consistency of a soft buttercream frosting.

7. Remove the rolls from the oven and, using a metal spatula, immediately frost each one. Let cool completely on the pans. Eat immediately, or place each roll in a sandwich-size plastic freezer bag and freeze for up to 1 month.

8. To reheat: Remove from the freezer and let thaw in the bag at room temperature. Remove the roll from the bag, place on a heatproof plate, and microwave for no more than 30 seconds or bake at 350° for about 7 minutes in a preheated oven. Serve immediately.

Butter-Pecan Caramel Rolls

I have been making these rolls for years at home and in my cooking classes. They are incredibly easy to prepare, considering how delicious they taste and how exotic they look. Don't expect them to last long after they come out of the oven.

Yield: 12 rolls

1 recipe Sweet Yeast Dough, page 107, or
¼ recipe Farmhouse White Bread with
Cardamom, page 60

Caramel

½ cup (1 stick) unsalted butter
1 cup brown sugar
¼ cup light corn syrup
2 tablespoons water

Pecan Filling

5 tablespoons unsalted butter, melted
¾ cup light brown sugar
2 tablespoons ground cinnamon
1½ cups chopped pecans
1 cup pecan halves

1. To make the caramel: In the bottom of a 9-by-13-inch baking dish, two 8-inch cake or springform pans, or one 12-inch ovenproof skillet, melt the butter, brown sugar, corn syrup, and water over low heat, stirring constantly. When melted, remove from heat. Set aside.

2. Turn the dough out onto a lightly floured work surface and roll or pat into a 12-by-15-inch rectangle. To fill: Leaving a 1-inch border all around the edges of the rectangle, brush the surface with melted butter, then sprinkle evenly with

brown sugar, cinnamon, and chopped nuts. Roll up jelly-roll fashion from the long end and pinch the seam to seal. With a serrated knife, cut into 12 equal portions, 1 to 1½ inches thick.

3. In the bottom of the caramel pan, sprinkle the pecan halves evenly and set the slices close together, spiral-side down. Cover loosely with plastic wrap and let the rolls rise at room temperature for 30 minutes, or until puffy and even with the rim of the pan. Meanwhile, preheat the oven to 350°.

4. Bake in the center of the preheated oven until the tops are brown, 30 to 35 minutes. Remove from the oven and let stand 5 minutes. Place a cooling rack on top of the pan and, holding the hot pan with oven mitts, invert rack and pan on a plate or baking sheet. Take care not to touch the hot caramel. Let cool for at least 20 minutes and pull apart to serve.

Orange Brioche with Golden Raisins and Dried Cherries

When I saw this on the menu at the Sonoma Mission Inn, I was excited by the idea of raisins combined with tart dried cherries in an eggy brioche dough. Of course, there wasn't enough dried fruit for my palate, so when I got home, I developed this recipe with fruit in every bite and a spicy topping. This recipe also makes a beautiful flatbread.

Yield: 16 *petites brioches,* one 14-inch round, or one 12-by-18-inch rectangle

One recipe Brioche dough, page 51, with the ¼ cup sugar whirled in a food processor or blender with the zest of 2 oranges until finely ground, then refrigerated overnight

1 cup dried sour cherries
1 cup golden raisins
Rich Egg Glaze, page 155
¼ cup granulated sugar combined with 1½ teaspoons coarsely crushed aniseed

1. Turn the chilled dough out onto a lightly floured work surface. Roll out to a large, thick rectangle and sprinkle with the dried fruits. Fold the dough into thirds, roll out, and fold again to distribute the fruits evenly. Divide into 16 equal portions and roll each into a tight ball. Place in 16 greased 3½-inch fluted molds or 16 greased standard muffin cups for individual buns. For flatbread, roll the dough out into a 14-inch round or a 12-by-18-inch rectangle, depending on the shape desired. Place in a greased round deep-dish pizza pan or on a greased baking sheet with a 1-inch rim. Cover loosely with plastic wrap and let rise at a cool room temperature until doubled in bulk, about 45 minutes to 1½ hours. Twenty minutes before baking, preheat the oven to 375°.

2. Brush the dough with Rich Egg Glaze and sprinkle the surface with anise sugar. Bake in the preheated oven until puffy and browned, about 15 to 20 minutes for individual buns and 35 to 40 minutes for flatbread. Remove from molds to cool on a rack completely before serving.

Brioche Pastry with Goat Cheese and Fruit

A fruit-encased pastry served hot in a pool of colorful fresh fruit puree is a show-stopper for brunch or a filling dessert. Suggestions for fruit combinations are given at the end of the recipe, but always let the seasons and your own palate be your guide. This recipe is adapted from a dessert served in a popular East Bay restaurant.

Yield: 12 large individual pastries

One recipe Brioche dough, page 51, risen overnight in the refrigerator
24 ounces goat cheese, such as French Montrachet or domestic Chabi
1 pound fresh fruit, stemmed, peeled, and sliced, for filling (see Note)
1 pound fresh fruit, stemmed, peeled, and sliced, for puree (see Note)
Juice from 1 lemon, lime, or orange
¼ cup sugar, or to taste
2 tablespoons fruit liqueur, such as black raspberry, pear, cherry, or orange

Rich Egg Glaze, page 155
Fresh fruit for garnish

1. Place the cold dough on a lightly floured work surface and divide into 12 equal portions, reserving a small amount of dough for decorative cutouts, if desired. Roll or pat each portion into a 5-inch square. Place about 2 ounces of goat cheese and a layer of fresh fruit on top of the cheese in the middle of each dough square. Fold 2 opposite sides of the dough over the fruit and brush with water to adhere. Slightly elongate the remaining 2 sides to pull and wrap the

dough tightly. Fill the remaining portions of dough. Place at least 2 inches apart on a greased or parchment-lined baking sheet. Cover with plastic wrap and refrigerate until ready to bake, as long as overnight.

2. To make the puree: Place the fruit to be pureed and the citrus juice in a blender or food processor with the sugar and liqueur; puree. Cover and chill. The sauce will keep for 2 days in the refrigerator and about 1 month in the freezer.

3. Let the pastries stand at room temperature for about 40 minutes, or until puffy. Meanwhile, chill 12 dessert plates. Twenty minutes before baking, preheat the oven to 400°. Roll out any reserved dough and cut out small decorations, if desired. Brush the pastries with Rich Egg Glaze and affix the cutouts. Apply another layer of glaze. Bake in the center of the preheated oven until puffy and golden brown, 15 to 20 minutes.

4. To serve, cover the bottom of each chilled plate with ¼ cup of fruit puree. Place the hot pastry on top of the puree and garnish with a few pieces of fresh fruit. Serve at once.

Note: Try these fruit combinations:
• Mangos with strawberry puree • Blueberries with papaya puree • Pears with blueberry puree • Peaches with blackberry puree • Cherries with apricot puree • Figs with raspberry puree • Plums with pineapple puree • Apples with cranberry-orange puree

Cider-glazed Apple Schnecken

Schnecken is the German word for "snail." It describes the spiral shape of this irresistible filled, rolled, sliced, and baked pastry, which is similar to our American cinnamon roll. Use a firm cooking apple, such as Rome Beauty, Golden Delicious, pippin, or Granny Smith. Of course, apples from a local orchard or home-grown heirloom apple would be a very special touch.

Yield: 2 dozen snails

One recipe Sweet Yeast Dough, page 107, risen overnight in the refrigerator

Apple Filling
2 to 3 large apples, peeled, cored, and diced (2 to 2½ cups)
¾ cup dried apricots, chopped
¼ cup currants
Grated zest and juice of 1 lemon
2 tablespoons unbleached all-purpose flour
1 cup brown sugar
1 tablespoon ground cinnamon
⅛ teaspoon ground cardamom
½ cup (1 stick) unsalted butter, melted
Cider Powdered Sugar Glaze, page 156

1. To make the apple filling: In a medium bowl, combine the apples, apricots, and currants. Toss with the lemon zest and juice, flour, sugar, and spices. Set aside at room temperature.
2. Turn the dough out onto a lightly floured work surface and divide into 2 equal portions. Roll out to a 12-by-14-inch rectangle. Brush the dough heavily with the melted butter. Sprinkle with half the apple filling, leaving a 1-inch

border all around the edges. From the long end, roll up tightly, jelly-roll fashion, to form a smooth log. Pinch the seams to close. Cut with a serrated knife to make 12 equal portions 1 to 1¼ inch thick.

3. Place each roll in a well-greased standard muffin cup with the spiral pattern facing up and down. Cover loosely with plastic wrap and let rise at room temperature until puffy, about 30 minutes. The rolls may also rise in the refrigerator for 12 to 24 hours. Twenty minutes before baking, preheat the oven to 375°.

4. Bake on the center rack of the preheated oven until the tops are golden brown and a cake tester inserted into the center of a roll comes out clean, 18 to 22 minutes. Let stand for 10 minutes before removing to racks. Place a sheet of waxed paper under the racks to catch drips, and drizzle the warm rolls with cider glaze. Let stand to cool and firm glaze.

Chocolate Breakfast Rolls

Quick to prepare and very tasty, chocolate-filled rolls are an American variation of the French delicacy *pain au chocolat,* but are ready to eat within 2 hours. Keep a few imported chocolate bars such as Tobler, Perugina, or Lindt on the pantry shelf for the special ingredient in these rolls. If you can find raspberry-, apricot-, or nut-filled bars, they are even better.

Yield: 16 crescents

1 tablespoon (1 package) active dry yeast
Pinch sugar
1/3 cup warm water (105° to 115°)
1 cup warm milk(105° to 115°)
1/4 cup sugar
4 tablespoons unsalted butter, melted
1 egg
1 teaspoon pure vanilla extract
1 teaspoon salt
2 1/2 to 3 cups unbleached all-purpose flour
Two 3 1/2-ounce bars imported bittersweet,
   white, or milk chocolate

Rich Egg Glaze, page 155

1. In a small bowl, sprinkle the yeast and
   pinch sugar over warm water. Stir to dissolve and let stand until foamy, about
   10 minutes.
2. In a medium mixing bowl, using a
   whisk, or in the workbowl of a heavy-
   duty electric mixer fitted with the paddle
   attachment, combine the milk, sugar,
   butter, egg, vanilla, salt, and 1 cup of the
   flour. Beat hard for 1 minute. Add the
   yeast mixture and 1/2 cup more flour.
   Beat again for 1 minute. Add the remaining flour 1/4 cup at a time to form a soft
   dough that just clears the sides of the
   bowl, switching to a wooden spoon
   when necessary if mixing by hand.
3. Turn the dough out onto a lightly
   floured work surface and knead until
   smooth and elastic, about 1 to 2 minutes, adding flour 1 tablespoon at a time
   as necessary to prevent sticking. Cover
   the dough with a towel and let rest for
   20 minutes on the work surface.
4. Divide the dough in half. Roll out each
   portion to a 12-inch round. Cut each
   round into 8 wedges with a pastry wheel
   or sharp knife. Break the chocolate bar
   into its scored sections. Set a section on

the base of each wedge. Roll up from the
base to the point and form into a crescent. Arrange about 2 inches apart on a
greased or parchment-lined baking
sheet. Cover loosely with plastic wrap
and let rise at room temperature until
puffy, about 30 minutes. The pastries
may also rise overnight in the refrigerator. Twenty minutes before baking, preheat the oven to 375°.
5. Brush the tops with Rich Egg Glaze.
   Bake in the center of the preheated oven
   until golden brown on top and bottom,
   12 to 15 minutes. Let cool for 10 minutes before eating.

Traditional English Muffins

English muffins really should be named
American muffins, as they are the pure Yan-
kee offshoot of the griddle-baked Celtic
crumpet and bannock. A distant relative of
the pancake, they are an unusual but traditional home-baked yeasted little bread.
Store muffins, wrapped tightly in plastic, in
the refrigerator or freezer after baking. To
serve, pull them apart with a fork and toast.
Serve with lots of sweet butter and Citrus
Curd, page 164.

Yield: 1 dozen 3-inch muffins

1 tablespoon (1 package) active dry yeast
Pinch sugar
1/4 cup warm water (105° to 115°)
4 to 4 1/2 cups unbleached all-purpose flour
2 teaspoons salt
1 egg
1 1/4 cups warm milk (105° to 115°)

2 tablespoons unsalted butter, melted
1/2 cup dried currants (optional)
1/4 cup cornmeal or coarse semolina for
   sprinkling

1. In a small bowl, sprinkle the yeast and
   pinch of sugar over the warm water. Stir
   to dissolve and let stand until foamy,
   about 10 minutes.
2. Place 2 cups of the flour and salt in a
   large bowl or the workbowl of a heavy-
   duty electric mixer fitted with the paddle
   attachment, and make a well. Add the
   egg, milk, butter, and yeast mixture.
   Beat with a whisk or the mixer until
   creamy, about 2 minutes. Add the
   remaining flour 1/2 cup at a time, and
   the currants, if desired, to form a soft
   dough that just clears the sides of the
   bowl, switching to a wooden spoon
   when necessary if mixing by hand.
3. Turn the dough out onto a lightly
   floured surface and knead until smooth
   and springy, about 3 minutes, adding 1
   tablespoon of flour at a time as necessary
   to prevent sticking. *Note:* The softer you
   leave the dough, the lighter the muffin.
   Place in a greased deep container, turn
   once to coat the top, and cover with
   plastic wrap. Let rise at room temperature until doubled in bulk, about 1 1/2
   hours.
4. Lightly sprinkle the work surface with
   cornmeal or semolina. Turn the dough
   out onto the surface and roll into a
   rectangle about 1/2 inch thick. Sprinkle
   the top with cornmeal or semolina to
   prevent sticking while rolling. Cut out
   the muffins with a 2 1/2- or 3-inch biscuit
   cutter or a drinking glass. Roll out the
   trimmings and cut out the remaining
   muffins.

5. Preheat an electric griddle to 350° or 375°, or heat a cast-iron stovetop griddle over medium heat until a drop of water sprinkled on the griddle dances across the surface. Lightly grease the surface.

6. Immediately place several muffins on the hot griddle. Cook for about 10 minutes on each side, turning them when they are quite brown. English muffins take time to bake all the way through, and they will swell and be very puffy while baking. Cover the uncooked muffins with a towel or place them in the refrigerator if they are rising too fast while the others are baking. Cool the baked muffins on a rack.

Whole-Wheat Croissants

Long the domain of the professional baker, croissants are made by following a logical set of simple instructions to create a dough with over 150 layers. The crescent symbol was first recorded in Neolithic cave paintings and later in the paintings of bull horns in ancient Mediterranean temples. But croissants themselves were created in the shape of the crescent moon motif on the Turkish flag to commemorate a seventeenth-century military victory over the Turks by the Austro-Hungarian Empire.

Use unsalted butter for your *croissants au beurre,* as it has a superior flavor and stays cold longer than salted butter, which contains a higher percentage of moisture. The most important advice in working with a folded dough is to keep the dough and butter cold every step of the way. The nuttiness of whole-wheat pastry flour gives these croissants a dense, chewy texture and a rich flavor. Serve for breakfast with café au lait, as a dinner or sandwich roll, or with a sweet filling.

Yield: 18 large or 28 small croissants

1½ tablespoons (1½ packages) active dry yeast
¼ cup brown sugar
⅓ cup warm water (105° to 115°)
¼ cup vegetable oil
2 teaspoons salt
1 cup cold milk
1 egg
1 cup whole-wheat pastry flour
4 cups unbleached all-purpose flour
2 cups (4 sticks) cold unsalted butter

Rich Egg Glaze, page 155

1. In a small bowl, sprinkle the yeast and a pinch of the brown sugar over the warm water. Stir to dissolve and let stand until foamy, about 10 minutes.

2. In a large bowl, using a whisk, or in the workbowl of a heavy-duty electric mixer fitted with the paddle attachment, mix together the oil, remaining brown sugar, salt, milk, egg, and whole-wheat flour until smooth. Add the yeast mixture and *exactly* 3¼ cups of the unbleached flour. Switching to a wooden spoon if making by hand, mix until the dough comes together into a shaggy mass and the flour is just absorbed with no dry patches. *Do not knead.* Add 1 tablespoon of flour at a time as necessary to prevent stickiness, but do not add more than a total of 4 tablespoons; this dough should be *very* soft.

3. Lightly dust an ungreased baking sheet with flour. Place the dough on the sheet and, with your fingers, spread the dough to lie flat in a large free-form rectangle about 1 inch thick. Cover tightly with plastic wrap, making certain all the dough is covered to avoid forming dry patches. Refrigerate in the coldest part of the refrigerator until thoroughly chilled, about 45 minutes.

4. Using an electric mixer, quickly combine the cold butter with ½ cup of the flour until smooth with no hard lumps. Or, to make by hand: With a spatula, smear the butter on a work surface, dump the flour on top, and use a chopping motion to combine; knead quickly until the flour is absorbed into the butter. Form the butter into a rough block shape on the work surface. Pat or roll quickly into a fat rectangle. Wrap in plastic and refrigerate if at all soft or sticky. The butter should be chilled, but pliable.

5. Place the dough on a lightly floured work surface. Roll into a 10-by-20-inch rectangle about ½ inch thick. Divide the butter into 2 equal portions and roll each into a 6-by-8-inch rectangle. Place half the butter in the middle third of the dough. Pull one third over from the side to cover. Seal the edges to encase the butter. Place the remaining butter on top and fold over the remaining third of the dough. Pinch the edges to seal completely. Place the folded edge of dough at 12 o'clock.

6. First Turn: Roll the dough into another large rectangle using firm strokes. Fold again into thirds. Replace on a baking sheet and cover with plastic wrap. Refrigerate for 20 to no longer than 30 minutes to chill. (If chilled longer than 30 minutes, the butter may harden too

much. The chilling period rests the gluten and firms the butter to allow continued rolling to create a layered effect.)

7. Repeat the process of rolling out and folding into thirds 2 more times. Take care not to tear the dough or allow the butter to get too soft. Remember to adjust the corners as you are working, to keep the dough square, and to move the dough constantly to avoid sticking. Use a soft brush to dust off any excess flour. These are the second and third turns. Chill the dough at any point that it becomes sticky, and remember to keep the folded edge at 12 o'clock.

8. Wrap the dough tightly in plastic wrap, replace on the baking sheet, and refrigerate overnight or up to 48 hours. At this point, the dough also may be frozen for up to 1 month.

9. Gently press the dough to deflate it, and cut it in half. Place one half back in refrigerator. Place the other half on a lightly floured work surface and roll it out into a rectangle about 15 by 26 inches. The dough will be about ¼ inch thick. Keep lifting and moving the dough to prevent sticking or tearing. Roll the dough on a diagonal to achieve an even width.

10. With a large knife or pastry wheel, cut lengthwise to create 2 long strips. Cut triangles of desired size, taking care to cut cleanly and not pull on the dough. Guide to Sizing: For small croissants, cut 3-by-6-inch triangles, for medium cut 4-by-8-inch triangles, and for large cut 5-by-10-inch triangles. Slash a cut no more than 1 inch deep into the center of the base of each triangle.

11. To shape, pull the points of the triangles to correct their dimensions, if neces-sary. With the base of a triangle facing you, spread the slit and tightly roll the base up towards the point with one hand, while holding the point and stretching it slightly. Place each croissant on a nonstick, greased, or parchment-lined baking sheet with the tip on the bottom, and bend it into a crescent shape by curving the tapered ends towards the center until they are about 2 inches apart. Do not crowd the croissants on the baking sheet. Formed croissants may be frozen at this point for up to 1 week. Repeat with the second half of the dough.

12. Let rise, uncovered, at room temperature until doubled in bulk, about 1½ hours. Twenty minutes before baking, preheat the oven to 425°. When light and springy to the touch, brush with Rich Egg Glaze. Place another baking sheet of the same dimensions under the pan with the croissants to "double pan" and protect the bottoms from burning. Bake in the center of the preheated oven for 15 to 18 minutes. Remove to cool on racks for 15 minutes before eating.

To Freeze Baked Croissants: Freeze in plastic bags as soon as completely cooled. To serve, heat frozen croissants in a preheated 400° oven for about 10 minutes to thaw, warm, and restore flakiness.

To Bake Frozen Raw Formed Croissants: Remove from the freezer and place on a greased or parchment-lined baking sheet. Cover with plastic wrap and let defrost in the refrigerator for 12 to 18 hours, or overnight. Let stand, uncovered, at room temperature for about 1 hour, and bake in a preheated oven as directed in the recipe.

Cornmeal Croissants
Substitute ⅔ cup fine-ground yellow cornmeal and ⅓ cup unbleached flour for the whole-wheat pastry flour in Step 2. Proceed to mix, fold, form, and bake as for Whole-Wheat Croissants.

Croissant Fillings

MORNING ROLLS
Roll out one half of the croissant pastry to a rectangle about 18 by 12 inches. Sprinkle the entire surface with 1 cup granulated sugar mixed with 1 tablespoon ground cinnamon and press in gently with a rolling pin. Cut 16 long triangles, each with a 1-inch-wide blunt end at the top point and a 2½-inch wide base at the bottom, across the surface of the dough. Roll up from the bottom, keeping one side of the base flush, to form a gradated pointed cone shape on the other end. Place the flat end into a very lightly greased *nonstick* standard muffin cup. Repeat to make about 16 rolls. Let rise, uncovered, until doubled in bulk, about 1 hour. Bake in a preheated 400° oven for about 15 minutes, or until brown and puffed over the edge of the cups. Let stand 5 minutes, then turn out of the muffin cups to cool on racks before eating.

PAIN AU CHOCOLAT (Bread with Chocolate)
Cut the rolled dough into rectangles instead of triangles. Place 1 tablespoon grated bittersweet chocolate or semisweet chocolate chips on the lower third of the

dough. Roll up to form a 3-by-5-inch rectangle and pinch the end seams. Place seam down on a greased or parchment-lined baking sheet. Make 2 or 3 diagonal slashes across the top of the dough with a sharp knife. Repeat to make about 18 rolls. Let rise and bake as for croissants.

PAIN D'AMANDE (Almond Bread)

Almond Filling
½ cup (1 stick) unsalted butter at room temperature
1 cup (8 ounces) almond paste at room temperature
2 eggs
¼ teaspoon each vanilla and almond extract
1 tablespoon flour
Sifted powdered sugar for dusting

In a medium bowl, cream the butter and almond paste with a wooden spoon until smooth. Add the remaining ingredients and beat until light and fluffy. Place 1 tablespoon in the center of the base of each triangle before rolling. Roll, let rise, and bake as for croissants. Dust with powdered sugar before serving. Store unused filling in the refrigerator up to 1 month.

RASPBERRY OR BLUEBERRY CROISSANTS
Place 2 teaspoons high-quality raspberry or blueberry preserves at the base of each triangle before rolling, and add 3 or 4 fresh or frozen berries, if desired. Let rise and bake as for croissants.

GOAT CHEESE CROISSANTS
Place 1 tablespoon imported or domestic soft fresh goat cheese or Goat Cheese with Sun-Dried Tomatoes and Herbs, page 162, at the base of each triangle before rolling. Roll, glaze, and sprinkle with poppy or ses-

ame seeds. Let rise and bake as for croissants. These are also especially good with 1 teaspoon of olive paste or sun-dried tomato pesto added along with the plain goat cheese. Serve with soups, salads, or as a smashing hors d'oeuvre.

HAM, CHEESE, AND OLIVE CROISSANTS
Roll out the dough and cut into eighteen 6-inch squares. Combine 1 cup shredded ham, 1 cup shredded cheddar, Jarlsberg, or Swiss or chopped Brie, and ¼ cup chopped black olives of choice. Spread 1 teaspoon Dijon or honey mustard on half of the square to form a center triangle with a full 1-inch border. Place 3 tablespoons of filling over the mustard. Form, let rise, glaze, and bake as for croissants. Yield: About 18 turnovers.

Yeasted Buttermilk Waffles

The crisp, deeply indented *gaufre,* or "waffle," is a beloved breakfast food and one of the most versatile batter breads. This recipe is suitable for either a regular hinged waffle iron or an oversized Belgian waffle maker. Yeast adds a dimension of flavor by allowing the batter to develop overnight before baking. Remember that a high temperature tends to make a crisp waffle, while a lower temperature produces a waffle that is moist and tender. Serve with your choice of a dazzling array of accompaniments: raspberry puree and crème fraîche, a fruit butter, sliced bananas or fresh berries and vanilla yogurt, sautéed apples, or lots of pure maple syrup and sweet butter.

Yield: About 14 medium waffles

1 tablespoon (1 package) active dry yeast
2 tablespoons sugar
4 cups (1 quart) buttermilk
¾ cup (1½ sticks) unsalted butter, melted
2 teaspoons salt
5 cups unbleached all-purpose flour
4 eggs, beaten
1½ teaspoons baking soda

1. The night before serving, begin the waffle batter: In a large bowl or plastic container, combine the yeast, sugar, buttermilk, butter, salt, and flour with a whisk. Beat hard until smooth, about 1 minute. Cover with plastic wrap and let rest in the refrigerator overnight.
2. When ready to serve, preheat the oven to 250°. Heat a waffle iron to medium-high heat and brush with oil to prevent sticking. Beat the eggs and baking soda into the batter with a whisk until evenly incorporated. Ladle ½ cup batter into the center of the iron, close the lid, and cook until crisp and golden, about 2 minutes. Place each waffle in the warm oven in a single layer until the rest of the waffles are baked. Serve warm with one or more of the accompaniments suggested above.
3. To store, cool the waffles completely on a wire rack, wrap in plastic and then aluminum foil or plastic freezer bags, and freeze for up to 1 month. Reheat frozen waffles in a toaster without thawing.

Cornmeal Yeast Waffles with Blueberries

Substitute 2 cups yellow or blue cornmeal for 2 cups of the unbleached flour and add 2 cups fresh or frozen blueberries to the batter before baking. Proceed to bake as above. Serve with Spiked Maple Syrup, page 165.

Buttermilk-Nut Waffles

Add 1 to 2 cups raw or toasted sunflower seeds or chopped pecans or ground hazelnuts and 1 tablespoon vanilla extract to the batter before baking. Proceed to bake as above. Serve with hot applesauce, maple syrup, and butter.

Whole-Wheat Yeast Waffles with Sesame Seeds

Substitute 2½ cups whole-wheat pastry flour for an equal amount of unbleached flour during the mixing. After ladling the batter onto the hot griddle, sprinkle with 1 tablespoon raw sesame seeds before closing the lid. Proceed to bake as above. Serve with Strawberry Butter, page 159.

Rice-Buttermilk Waffles

Add 1½ cups cool cooked wild, brown, or white rice to the batter before baking. Proceed to bake as above. Serve with Maple Stewed Blueberries, page 165.

Oatmeal Yeast Waffles with Dried Fruit

Substitute 2 cups rolled oats for 2 cups of the unbleached flour during mixing. Add 1 cup chopped dried prunes, apricots, pears, or apples and ¼ cup golden raisins before baking. Proceed to bake as above. Serve with Orange Syrup, page 165.

Egg Bagels

Viennese in origin, bagels are immersed in boiling water before baking; this gives them their characteristic hairline crust and firm, chewy interior. Homemade bagels will never be as evenly shaped as commercial ones, so don't dispair at uneven rounds. Despite the initial boiling process, bagels are faster to make than many yeast breads. Split, toast, and serve bagels with butter and jam or lox and cream cheese. Bagel bread, formed and baked in a traditional yeast loaf shape, is also delicious.

Yield: 28 to 32 bagels, or two 9-by-5-inch loaves

1 large russet potato (about ¾ pound)
2½ cups water
2 tablespoons (2 packages) active dry yeast
1½ tablespoons sugar
1½ tablespoons salt
7 to 7½ cups unbleached all-purpose or
*   bread flour*
¼ cup corn oil
4 eggs
3 to 4 quarts of water
2 tablespoons salt or sugar

Egg Glaze, page 155
Sesame or poppy seeds

1. Peel the potato and cut into large chunks. Place in a small saucepan and cover with the 2½ cups water. Bring to a boil, reduce heat, and simmer uncovered until the potato is soft. Drain the potato (use for other purposes), reserving 2 cups of the potato water. Let cool to 120°.

2. In a large bowl, using a whisk, or in the workbowl of a heavy-duty electric mixer fitted with the paddle attachment, combine the yeast, sugar, salt, and 2 cups of the flour.

3. Add the potato water and oil. Beat on medium speed for 2 minutes. Add 1 cup of the flour and the eggs. Beat again for 2 minutes. Add the remaining flour ½ cup at a time to form a soft dough that just clears the sides of the bowl, switching to a wooden spoon when necessary if mixing by hand.

4. Turn the dough out onto a lightly floured work surface and knead until a smooth, firm, and springy dough is formed, about 3 minutes, adding flour 1 tablespoon at a time as necessary to prevent sticking. Place in a greased deep container, turn once to coat the top, and cover with plastic wrap. Let rise at room temperature until doubled in bulk, about 1 hour.

5. Turn the dough out onto a lightly floured work surface and divide it into quarters. Divide each quarter into 6 to 8 equal portions. To form bagels: Shape each ball of dough into a smooth round, tucking the excess dough underneath. Flatten with your palm. Poke a floured finger through the middle of the ball. Stretch the hole with your fingers to make it about 1 inch in diameter. Spin the dough around your finger. The hole will be quite large as you spin, but will shrink slightly when you stop. Set aside on a lightly floured surface while forming the other bagels. The bagels will need no further rising at this point.

6. Preheat the oven to 425° and grease or line 2 baking sheets with parchment. Meanwhile, in a large pot, bring 3 to 4 quarts of water to a boil. Add 2 tablespoons salt or sugar to the boiling water, depending on the flavor you want the crust to have. Reduce heat to maintain a gentle low boil over medium heat.

7. With a slotted spatula, lower 3 to 4 bagels at a time into the gently boiling water. They will drop to the bottom and then rise to the surface. As they come to the surface, turn each bagel and boil it 3 minutes on the other side. This goes very quickly; if you are making the entire batch of bagels, I suggest a second pot of boiling water.

8. Remove from the boiling water with a slotted spoon and place 1 inch apart on the prepared baking sheet. When all the bagels have been boiled, brush with Egg Glaze and sprinkle with seeds. Bake in the preheated oven for 25 to 30 minutes, or until deep golden. Remove from the baking sheets to cool on racks.

Whole-Wheat Bagels
Substitute 3 cups whole-wheat flour for an equal portion of the unbleached flour.

Orange-Oatmeal Bagels
Substitute 1½ cups oatmeal for an equal portion of the unbleached flour. Add 1 tablespoon grated orange zest and 2 tablespoons honey to recipe.

Cinnamon-Raisin Bagels
Increase the sugar to ¼ cup. Add 1 tablespoon ground cinnamon, 1 teaspoon ground mace or nutmeg, and ½ teaspoon ground cardamom with the flour in the initial mixing. Add 1½ cups golden or dark raisins during mixing. Formed into a loaf and topped with sesame seeds, this makes a wonderful bread for toasting.

Pumpernickel Bagels
Substitute 2 cups medium or dark rye flour for an equal portion of unbleached flour. Add ¼ cup molasses, 1 tablespoon unsweetened cocoa, and 1 tablespoon powdered instant coffee. Sprinkle the tops with caraway seeds.

Onion Bagels
Sauté 1 medium onion, chopped fine, in 4 tablespoons unsalted butter until limp. Set aside. Halfway through baking, brush the bagel tops with egg glaze and spread 2 teaspoons onion mixture over each bagel. Finish baking.

CELEBRATION BREADS

The American baking tradition combines old-world religion, folk art, history, culture, and fantasy. Ceremonial breads are symbolic of archaic celebrations in honor of harvest time, fertility rites, seasonal changes, birth, death, and gratitude to the gods. Ancient cultures linked humanity, agriculture, and religion directly to the animate and inanimate natural world. Along with the elements of water, fire, earth, and air, various foods, such as the fig, represented the archetypes of renewal, transformation, fecundity, and the universal life force. Grains were regarded as sacred seeds of life, and reverent ceremonies throughout the year were performed to ensure communities their most important food for survival. Ancient bakers were regarded as highly as priests in Egypt, and many temples contained ovens. The Bread Church of Eleusis worshipped the Greek goddess of agriculture, Demeter, with ceremonies honoring the planting of the autumn grains. During the Middle Ages, both domestic and consecrated baking was kept alive by the monastic orders.

Daily bread was made from the simple alchemy of flour, salt, water, and leavening. The flour was most often coarse and dark from primitive milling techniques and dirt. But ceremonial baking utilized the purest and rarest ingredients: bolted wheat flour, eggs, rare sweetenings, and precious spices hoarded for the occasion.

Over the centuries, sweet bread recipes, along with specific directions for shaping and decorating, have been handed down within families and communities. With recipes updated for today's ingredients, baking these breads is easy and satisfying, and gives bakers an opportunity to showcase their art. These festive creations never go out of style, because they are based on simple formulas and result in visually stunning loaves that taste fabulous. The fragrant, yeasty aroma and silky texture of celebration breads have universal appeal. Avoid the disillusionment of dry and tasteless commercial versions of these classic breads. As with all handmade foods, you have control over your ingredients when you make special breads at home. These festive creations are not only perfect for traditional holidays such as Christmas and Easter, but for christenings, birthdays, wedding feasts, and anniversaries as well.

The passionate baker can choose from an array of recipes for fluted, nut-studded, and sweet-encrusted loaves. The special fascination of celebration breads is due in part to the myriad of shapes: tall cylinders, wreaths, sheaves of wheat, swollen grapes, braids, twists, domes, and various doll and animal forms, all finished with whimsical, eye-catching decorations.

The flavors are varied, including spices, nuts, citrus, the bold essences of spirits, and glistening dried and homemade candied fruits. Mouth-watering fillings are encased in delicate egg doughs to create beautiful patterns when sliced. Glazing is an important finishing touch, a lively accent of concentrated sweetness and glossy visual appeal. Yeasted celebration breads are the jewels of the season, a baker's personal creative statement.

Hints for Perfect Celebration Breads

- Avoid commercial brands of candied fruit peels. They are laced with preservatives and artificial colors, and lack the intense bittersweet flavor and texture of homemade. Make your own candied peels, or substitute dried fruits. You can keep a variety of dried fruits on hand in the freezer for up to 1 year.

- Rework the dough if you are not satisfied with the shapes you have formed: Allow the dough to rest on the work surface, covered with a towel or plastic wrap, for about 10 minutes to relax, then re-form. Bread dough is both sturdy and forgiving, so experiment until you get the shape you want.

- The dough will rise double in the last rise and then again in the oven, so fussy details in shaping and decorating will not remain distinct. Over years of baking, I have found the classic simple shapes to be the most successful.

- Bake loaves well ahead of the holiday rush and freeze them for up to 1 month. Defrost on the day needed, adding the final glazing and decorative touches at that time. The loaf will taste and slice as though freshly baked.

Italian Sweet Bread with Fennel, Fruit, and Nuts

Here is a slightly sweet country egg bread rich with the combination of almonds, walnuts, dried figs, and raisins known in the sun-drenched Mediterranean cuisine since medieval times as *quatre mendiants*, or the "four beggars." It needs a long initial rise to create its delicate texture and complex, yeasty flavor, so don't rush it. Serve with Goat Cheese Spread, page 162, drizzled with warm honey for special gatherings.

Yield: 1 large loaf

Sponge
2 teaspoons active dry yeast
1 tablespoon sugar
1 cup unbleached all-purpose or bread flour
1 cup warm water (105° to 115°)

Dough
Sponge, above
1 teaspoon active dry yeast
2/3 cup sugar
3 large eggs
3½ to 3¾ cups unbleached all-purpose or bread flour
2 teaspoons salt
1 teaspoon crushed fennel seed
1 teaspoon pure vanilla extract
Grated zest of 1 orange and 1 lemon
¾ cup (1½ sticks) unsalted butter at room temperature, cut into 10 pieces

Fruit and Nut Mixture
1 cup slivered blanched almonds
1 cup walnut pieces
¾ cup dried figs, such as Mission or Calimyrna, stemmed and coarsely chopped
¾ cup dark raisins, such as muscat
1 tablespoon all-purpose or bread flour
1 tablespoon brown sugar

1. To make the sponge: In a medium bowl or plastic container, whisk together the yeast, sugar, flour, and water until smooth. Cover with plastic wrap and let rise at room temperature for 1 hour, or until bubbly.
2. To make the dough: In a large bowl, using a whisk, or in the workbowl of a heavy-duty electric mixer fitted with the paddle attachment, mix the sponge, yeast, sugar, eggs, and 1 cup of the flour until smooth. Add the salt, fennel, vanilla, zests, butter pieces, and 1 cup of the flour. Beat on low speed for 1 minute. Continue to add flour ½ cup at a time until a very soft dough is formed, switching to a wooden spoon when necessary if mixing by hand. The dough will be very sticky and have the consistency of a soft batter.
3. With a dough scraper, turn the dough out onto a lightly floured work surface and knead 4 or 5 times to just form a cohesive, yet soft, uneven mass. Place in a greased deep container and cover with plastic wrap. Let rise in a warm place for about 2 hours, or until doubled in bulk. Meanwhile, make the fruit and nut mixture: Preheat the oven to 350°. Spread the almonds and walnuts over the surface of a jelly-roll pan and bake until lightly toasted, about 8 minutes. Let cool. In a large bowl, toss together all the ingredients to combine; set aside.
4. Turn the dough out onto a lightly floured work surface and gently pat into a rectangle. Sprinkle with fruit and nuts. Fold the edges over and knead to evenly distribute. The dough will remain very soft and almost sticky. Form into a long, fat log with your palms and place in a 10-inch fluted or plain ring mold, filling it half full. Cover with plastic wrap and let rise in a warm place until even with the rim of the pan, about 1 to 1½ hours. Twenty minutes before baking, preheat the oven to 350°.
5. Bake in the center of the preheated oven for 50 to 55 minutes, or until a cake tester inserted in the center of the loaf comes out clean and the top is firm when pressed. Unmold onto a rack to cool before slicing.

Portuguese Sweet Bread with Honey

From the Azores to Cape Cod to the Hawaiian Islands—the beloved Portuguese Sweet Bread appears on Easter tables and in bakeries halfway around the world from its place of origin. A simple egg bread traditionally topped with hard-cooked eggs and a cross made of dough, it is just as appealing plain. Serve fresh or toasted, spread with Fruit Butter, page 161, and accompanied with steaming cups of China tea. Slice thick to make fabulous French toast.

Yield: 2 round loaves

Sponge

1½ tablespoons (1½ packages) active
dry yeast
½ cup warm water (105° to 115°)
1 cup warm milk (105° to 115°)
¼ cup sugar
2 cups unbleached all-purpose or bread flour

Dough

Sponge, above
½ cup (1 stick) unsalted butter at room
temperature, cut into small pieces
½ cup local honey
2 teaspoons salt
3 eggs
3½ to 4 cups unbleached all-purpose or
bread flour

Rich Egg Glaze, page 155

1. To make the sponge: In a large bowl or plastic container, whisk together the yeast, water, milk, sugar, and the flour until smooth. Scrape down the sides and cover with plastic wrap. Let stand at room temperature for 1 hour, or until bubbly.

2. To make the dough: Stir down the sponge and add the butter, honey, salt, eggs, and 1 cup of the flour. Beat hard with a whisk until creamy, about 1 minute. Continue to add flour ½ cup at a time to form a soft dough that just clears the sides of the bowl, switching to a wooden spoon when necessary.

3. Turn the dough out onto a lightly floured work surface and knead for about 2 to 3 minutes, or until a soft, smooth, and springy dough is formed, adding flour 1 tablespoon at a time as necessary to prevent sticking. Place in a greased deep container, turn once to coat the top, and cover with plastic wrap.

Let rise at room temperature until doubled in bulk, about 1½ hours.

4. Turn the dough out onto the work surface and divide into 2 equal portions. Form into 2 tight, round loaves and place on a greased or parchment-lined baking sheet. Cover loosely with plastic and let rise at room temperature until puffy, but not quite doubled in bulk, about 30 minutes. Meanwhile, preheat the oven to 375°.

5. Brush the loaves gently with the egg glaze and bake on the center rack of the preheated oven for 35–40 minutes or until golden brown and hollow sounding when tapped. Remove from the pan to cool on a rack before slicing.

Saffron Bread with Scented-Geranium Sugar

Tinted marigold yellow with saffron threads, this loaf is part of the repertoire of both English and Scandinavian bakers, who added it to dough to make up for the lack of egg yolks. Saffron breads appear in culinary records from the seventeenth and eighteenth centuries. To gild the lily, dust this barely sweet baked *Safranbröd* with your own Scented-Geranium Powdered Sugar. Serve with sherry or freshly brewed coffee. It is wonderful toasted and is perfect for Easter brunch spread with rich, creamy Dried Fruit Pahska, page 163.

Yield: 1 large braided or round wreath

1 cup dried currants
¼ cup cream sherry
½ teaspoon saffron threads, crumbled
⅓ cup water
1 tablespoon (1 package) active dry yeast
Pinch sugar
1 cup warm milk (105° to 115°)
2 eggs
¼ cup sugar
2 teaspoons salt
4 to 4½ cups unbleached all-purpose or
bread flour
½ cup (1 stick) unsalted butter at room
temperature, cut into 8 pieces
Scented-Geranium Powdered Sugar,
following

1. In a small bowl, toss the currants with the sherry. Set aside and let macerate for about 1 hour. In a small saucepan, sprinkle the saffron over the water, bring to a simmer, and remove from heat. Let stand at room temperature for 30 minutes.

2. In a large bowl, or the workbowl of a heavy-duty electric mixer fitted with the paddle attachment, sprinkle the yeast and sugar over the milk. Stir to dissolve and let stand until foamy, about 10 minutes.

3. Add the eggs, sugar, salt, and 1 cup of the flour to the yeast mixture and beat with a whisk or the mixer until creamy. Add the saffron water, currants and sherry, and 1 cup more of the flour. Beat for 1 minute. Add the butter a few pieces at a time, beating well after each addition to incorporate. Add the remaining flour ½ cup at a time to form a soft dough that just clears the sides of the bowl, switching to a wooden spoon when necessary if mixing by hand.

4. Turn the dough out onto a lightly floured work surface and knead until smooth and springy, about 3 minutes, adding 1 tablespoon of flour at a time as necessary to prevent sticking. Place in a greased deep container, turn once to coat the top, and cover with plastic wrap. Let rise at room temperature until doubled in bulk, about 1½ hours.

5. Turn the dough out onto the work surface and divide into 3 equal portions. Form each into a 14-inch-long fat rope. Lay the ropes parallel on a greased or parchment-lined baking sheet. Braid gently but tightly, interweaving the ropes without stretching the dough. Pinch the ends together and tuck them under. The dough may also be connected at both ends to form a round braid. It may also be formed without braiding by forming it into one thick log and connecting both ends to make a circle. With floured kitchen shears, make 2-inch-deep parallel cuts at 1-inch intervals on the top of the loaf. Cover loosely with plastic wrap and let rise at room temperature until doubled in bulk, about 45 minutes. Twenty minutes before baking, preheat the oven to 375°.

6. Bake in the center of the preheated oven until browned and hollow sounding when tapped, about 35 to 40 minutes. Remove from the pan to cool on a rack. Just before serving, dust with Scented-Geranium Powdered Sugar.

Scented-Geranium Powdered Sugar

2 cups sifted powdered sugar
6 scented geranium leaves of one variety, rinsed and dried on paper towels

In an airtight container, place a bottom layer of about ½ cup of the powdered sugar. Lay 2 of the geranium leaves on top of the sugar. Continue to layer sugar and leaves 2 more times, ending with a layer of sugar. Cover tightly and let stand at room temperature 1 week before using. This will keep for 3 months.

Note: Scented geraniums are members of the genus *Pelargonium*. The variety of scents include lemon, rose, cinnamon, nutmeg, peppermint, apple, lime, and even strawberry.

Dried Cherry and Pineapple Stollen

The stollen is a Germanic holiday bread whose large, tapered shape symbolizes the Christ child in swaddling clothes. When forming, please note that the traditional flat loaf is best, as the dough is rich in butter and dried fruits with a rather firm, dry texture. Stollen will keep perfectly for 2 weeks at room temperature wrapped in plastic. Cut into thin slices to serve with hot coffee with liqueurs, eggnog, or hot mulled cider.

Yield: 2 large flat loaves

½ cup dried cherries
½ cup dried currants
½ cup dried pineapple
½ cup golden raisins

Sponge
1 cup warm milk (105° to 115°)
½ cup sugar
1 tablespoon (1 package) active dry yeast
1 cup unbleached all-purpose flour

Dough
2 large eggs
2 tablespoons Cognac
Grated zest of 1 lemon
½ teaspoon fresh-ground nutmeg
1 teaspoon salt
3½ to 4 cups unbleached all-purpose flour
¾ cup (1½ sticks) unsalted butter at room temperature, cut into 12 pieces
Sponge, above

4 tablespoons unsalted butter, melted
2 tablespoons sugar mixed with ½ teaspoon ground cinnamon
Sifted powdered sugar for dusting

1. Place the dried fruit in a medium bowl, and cover with boiling water to plump. Set aside to cool.

2. To make the sponge: In a large bowl, using a whisk, or in the workbowl of a heavy-duty electric mixer fitted with the paddle attachment, combine the milk and sugar. Sprinkle with the yeast and stir to dissolve. Let stand for 5 minutes. Sprinkle with 1 cup of the flour and beat until smooth. Scrape down the sides and cover with plastic wrap. Let stand 1 hour at room temperature, or until bubbly.

3. To make the dough: Add the eggs, Cognac, lemon zest, nutmeg, salt, well-drained dried fruit, and 1 cup of the flour to the sponge. Beat until combined. Add the butter a few pieces at a time, beating after each addition. Continue to add the flour ½ cup at a time to form a dough that just clears the sides of the bowl, switching to a wooden spoon when necessary if mixing by hand.

4. Turn the dough out onto a lightly floured work surface and knead until smooth and springy, about 2 to 3 minutes, adding 1 tablespoon of flour at a

time as necessary to prevent sticking. Press back any fruits that fall out of the dough while kneading. Cover the dough with a towel and let rest for 10 minutes on the work surface.

5. Divide the dough into 2 equal portions. Roll or pat the dough into a 12-by-8-inch oval about ½ inch thick. Use only enough flour on the work surface to keep the dough from sticking. Brush each oval with melted butter and sprinkle each with half of the cinnamon sugar. Make a crease down the center of the oval and, without stretching it, fold the long side over to within ¾ inch of the opposite side, forming a long, narrow loaf with tapered ends. Press the top edge lightly to seal. Repeat to form the second stollen Place the stollens on a greased or parchment-lined baking sheet and cover loosely with plastic wrap. Let rise again in a warm place until almost doubled in bulk, about 1 hour. Twenty minutes before baking, preheat the oven to 375°.

6. Bake on the center rack of the preheated oven for 35 to 40 minutes, or until lightly browned. If the tops are browning too fast, cover loosely with aluminum foil. Take care not to overbake. Remove from the baking sheet and cool on a rack. Dust with powdered sugar before serving.

Pernod Panettone

A Mediterranean specialty, good panettone can be bought during the holidays in a *pan-etteria*. Although traditionally made with candied fruits, this version of panettone is full of sun-dried fruits and flavored with anise liqueur. It can be formed into a round or a tall cylindrical loaf to serve as a celebration bread or to slice for Sunday toast. Day-old panettone is good sliced into thick fingers and baked in a single layer on an ungreased baking sheet at 300° for 45 minutes to 1 hour, or until pale golden and crisp. Similiar to biscotti, these dry toasts can be served with tea or as an accompaniment to fresh fruits, sorbets, and gelatos.

Yield: 2 medium round loaves, or 1 tall loaf baked in a panettone mold or a 2-pound coffee can

½ cup golden raisins
½ cup snipped dried apricots
½ cup Pernod liqueur
1 tablespoon (1 package) active dry yeast
Pinch sugar
¼ cup warm water (105° to 115°)
1 cup warm milk (105° to 115°)
½ cup (1 stick) unsalted butter, melted
⅓ cup sugar
1 teaspoon salt
2 eggs
2 tablespoons Pernod liqueur
About 4 cups unbleached all-purpose flour
¼ cup pine nuts
¼ cup slivered blanched almonds
3 tablespoons sugar for glaze

1. In a small bowl, combine the dried fruits and liqueur. Let stand for 1 hour to soften.

2. In a small bowl, sprinkle the yeast and sugar over the water. Stir to dissolve and let stand until foamy, about 10 minutes.

3. In a large bowl, using a whisk, or in the workbowl of a heavy-duty electric mixer fitted with the paddle attachment, combine the milk, butter, sugar, and salt. Add the eggs, liqueur, and 1 cup of the flour, beating until smooth and creamy, about 1 minute. Add the yeast mixture and 1 cup more of the flour. Beat 1 minute more. Drain the fruits and set aside the drained liqueur for the glaze. Add the fruits and nuts to the batter. Continue to add the remaining flour ½ cup at a time until a soft dough is formed that just clears the sides of the bowl and the embellishments are evenly distributed, switching to a wooden spoon when necessary if mixing by hand.

4. Turn the dough out onto a lightly floured work surface and knead until smooth and springy, about 3 minutes, adding flour 1 tablespoon at a time as necessary to prevent sticking. Push back any fruits that fall out of the dough during kneading. The dough should remain soft. Place the dough in a greased deep container, turn once to coat the top, and cover with plastic wrap. Let rise in a warm place until doubled in bulk, about 2 hours.

5. Turn the dough out onto the work surface and divide into 2 equal portions for round loaves, or leave in one piece for a cylindrical loaf. Form each of the 2 portions into a tight, round ball and place at least 3 inches apart on a greased or parchment-lined baking sheet. With a serrated knife, cut a ½-inch deep X into the top of each loaf. To make a cylindrical loaf, place the whole amount of dough in a greased panettone mold or 2-pound coffee can. Cover loosely with plastic wrap and let rise again at room temperature until doubled in bulk, about 35 to 40 minutes. Twenty minutes before baking, preheat the oven to 375°.

6. Bake in the preheated oven until browned and hollow sounding when tapped, 40 to 45 minutes. Remove from

the baking sheet or mold to cool on a rack. While warm, brush with the Pernod glaze: Combine the drained liqueur and water to equal ¼ cup. If all the liqueur has been absorbed, combine 2 tablespoons water with 2 tablespoons Pernod. Place in a small saucepan. Add the 3 tablespoons sugar and heat to just dissolve the sugar. Brush each warm loaf surface twice all over and let stand to dry completely.

Hungarian Poppy Seed Bread

This traditional Slavic holiday egg bread is swirled with a dark, delicious spiral design within. You can use a prepared poppy seed filling, but the homemade version is simple, and can be made up to 3 days before baking. Form the dough into braids, or bake in traditional loaf pans or in a dramatic fluted kugelhopf mold for special occasions. To serve as a coffee cake, slice and accompany with soft whipped sweet butter and pots of hot Darjeeling tea with lemon or milk.

Yield: Two 9-by-5-inch standard or braided loaves

1½ tablespoons (1½ packages) active
  dry yeast
⅓ cup brown sugar
Grated zest of 2 lemons
2 teaspoons salt
5 to 5½ cups unbleached all-purpose or
  bread flour
1 cup milk
½ cup water

6 tablespoons unsalted butter
3 eggs

Poppy Seed Almond Filling
¾ cup whole black poppy seeds, ground in a
  blender or food processor
1⅓ cups light cream or half-and-half
⅓ cup granulated sugar
1½ teaspoons pure almond extract
3 tablespoons cornstarch
1 egg yolk

1 cup golden raisins
¼ cup Amaretto liqueur
Sifted powdered sugar for dusting

1. In a large bowl, using a whisk, or in the workbowl of a heavy-duty electric mixer fitted with the paddle attachment, combine the yeast, sugar, lemon zest, salt, and 2 cups of the flour. In a small saucepan, combine the milk, water, and butter and heat until just warm. Stir to melt the butter. Let cool to 120°.
2. Add the milk and eggs into the dry mixture and beat hard for 1 minute, or until creamy. Add the remaining flour ½ cup at a time to form a soft dough that just clears the sides of the bowl, switching to a wooden spoon when necessary if mixing by hand.
3. Turn the dough out onto a lightly floured work surface and knead until smooth, springy, and soft, about 3 minutes, adding flour 1 tablespoon at a time as necessary to prevent sticking. Transfer to a greased deep container, turn once to coat the top, and cover with plastic wrap. Let rise in a warm place until doubled in bulk, about 1½ hours.
4. While the dough is rising, prepare the Poppy Seed Almond Filling: In a small saucepan, combine the poppy seeds and 1 cup of the cream. Bring to a boil.

Lower heat and simmer uncovered for 10 minutes, stirring occasionally, until slightly thickened. While the mixture is simmering, stir in the sugar and extract with a whisk. With a whisk or food processor, blend the cornstarch and yolk with the remaining ⅓ cup cream until smooth. With a whisk, gradually add the cornstarch mixture to the simmering poppy seed mixture, stirring constantly until very thick. When the whisk becomes clogged, switch to a wooden spoon. When filling clears the sides and bottom of the pan as it is being stirred, cook it 1 minute longer, stirring constantly. Remove from heat and, with a spatula, scrape into a small bowl to cool completely at room temperature before using. Cover tightly with plastic to refrigerate. This makes about 1½ cups.
5. Place the golden raisins and Amaretto in a small bowl and macerate for at least 30 minutes. Drain the raisins, reserving the liqueur. Turn the dough out onto the work surface and divide it in half. Pat or roll out each section into a 9-by-14-inch rectangle. Leaving a 1-inch border on all sides, spread each section evenly with half the poppy seed filling. Sprinkle with half the drained raisins. To form 2 standard loaves, roll each section up from the short end and pinch the seams to seal. Place each roll seam-side down in a greased 9-by-5-inch loaf pan. Press on the loaves, flattening them slightly to produce an oval swirl when baked. To form a braided loaf, roll up each rectangle from the long end and elongate with your palms. Cut in half. Place 2 rolls side by side and pinch the top ends together. Twist the rolls around each other into a 2-strand spiral. Place on a greased or

parchment-lined baking sheet. Brush the tops of the loaf or loaves with a bit of reserved liqueur to moisten. Loosely cover with plastic wrap and let rise until 1 inch above the rim of the pans, about 40 minutes. Twenty minutes before baking, preheat the oven to 350°.

6. Bake in the center of the preheated oven until browned and hollow sounding when tapped, 40 to 45 minutes. Remove from the pans to cool completely on racks before slicing. Dust with powdered sugar before serving.

Christmas Bread with Orange, Olive Oil, and Honey

The long winter holiday season provides an opportunity to create and serve a variety of celebration breads, including the Christopsomo, or "Christ's bread" (*psomi* translates to "bread" in Greek). In this adaptation by professional food writer and journalist Lou Pappas, the traditional ingredients of sugar, butter, bay leaf, and *mahleb* (a Greek spice ground from the seed of a wild cherry-like fruit) are replaced with honey, olive oil, and aniseed. Orange zest and juice enhance the adorned golden loaf. Cut the large round loaf in thirds, then slices for easy serving.

Yield: One large round loaf

Sponge
2 tablespoons (2 packages) active dry yeast
½ cup warm water (105° to 115°)
½ cup unbleached all-purpose or bread flour
¼ teaspoon sugar

Dough
3 eggs
⅓ cup fruity olive oil
⅓ cup strong-flavored honey such as sage, thyme, rosemary, or tupelo
1½ teaspoons salt
1 tablespoon aniseed
Zest of 1 orange, cut into thin julienne strips
1 cup warm milk (105° to 115°)
1 cup orange juice
5 to 5½ cups unbleached all-purpose or bread flour
Sponge, above

9 walnut or pecan halves

1. To make the sponge: In a medium bowl, sprinkle the yeast over the warm water. Whisk in ½ cup of the flour and sugar. Cover with plastic wrap and let stand at room temperature until tripled in volume, about 20 to 30 minutes.

2. To make the dough: In a large bowl, using a whisk, or in the workbowl of a heavy-duty electric mixer fitted with the paddle attachment, combine the eggs, oil, honey, salt, aniseed, orange zest, milk, juice, and 2 cups of the flour. Beat hard until smooth, about 1 minute. Add the sponge and 1 cup more flour. Beat 1 minute more. Continue to add the remaining flour ½ cup at a time, until a soft dough is formed that just clears the sides of the bowl, switching to a wooden spoon when necessary if mixing by hand.

3. Turn the dough out onto a lightly floured work surface and knead until soft, springy, and smooth, about 3 minutes, adding flour 1 tablespoon at a time as necessary to prevent sticking. Place in a greased deep container, turn once to coat the top, and cover with plastic wrap.

Let rise in a warm place until doubled in bulk, about 1½ hours.

4. Turn the dough out onto the work surface and cut off 2 pieces of dough, each about 3 inches in diameter. Set these aside. Shape the remaining dough into a tight, smooth round. Place on a greased or parchment-lined baking sheet or pizza pan. Flatten the dough into a cake 9 inches in diameter and about 2 inches thick. Roll each of the small balls into a 14-inch-long rope. Cut a 5-inch slash in the end of each. Lay the ropes over the surface of loaf, crossing at the center. Do not press down. Curl the slashed sections away from the center of each rope to form double circles at each end. Place a nut half in each circle and one in the center of the cross. Cover loosely with plastic wrap and set in a warm place to rise to almost doubled in bulk, about 45 minutes to 1 hour. Twenty minutes before baking, preheat the oven to 325°.

5. Bake in the center of the preheated oven for 50 to 55 minutes or until golden brown and hollow sounding when tapped. Do not underbake. Remove from pan to cool completely on a rack.

Crescia al Formaggio

Crescia is a savory Italian cheese bread that has been traditional Easter fare in Italy for hundreds of years. It is a dramatic and truly beautiful golden loaf of rich egg dough streaked with cheeses. The name crescia (from the Italian *crescere*, "to grow") decribes the puffy doming of the dough above its mold during baking, making a shape similar to the French *gannat*. Bake in any plain or fluted 12-cup tube mold, two clean coffee cans, or two 8-by-4-inch loaf pans. Serve at room temperature cut into thick wedges for brunch, or as part of a picnic with cold meats, cornichons and olives, fresh seasonal fruit, and of course, Chianti.

Yield: 1 large loaf serving 8 to 10

1 tablespoon (1 package) active dry yeast
Pinch sugar
¾ cup warm water (105° to 115°)
½ teaspoon salt
¾ cup grated Parmesan cheese
About 3½ cups unbleached all-purpose flour
5 eggs
½ cup (1 stick) unsalted butter at room temperature, cut into small pieces
3 cups (12 ounces) Swiss or Gruyère cheese, coarsely shredded

1. In a large bowl, or the workbowl of a heavy-duty electric mixer fitted with the paddle attachment, sprinkle the yeast and sugar over the warm water. Stir until dissolved and let stand until foamy, about 10 minutes.
2. Add the salt, Parmesan, and 1 cup of the flour to the yeast mixture. Beat with a whisk or the mixer on low speed until creamy, about 1 minute. Add 4 of the eggs one at a time. Add the remaining flour ½ cup at a time to form a soft dough that just clears the sides of the bowl, switching to a wooden spoon when necessary if mixing by hand.
3. Turn the dough out onto a lightly floured work surface and knead gently until a springy, satiny dough is formed, about 2 minutes, adding flour 1 tablespoon at a time as necessary to prevent sticking. The dough will have a slightly gritty feel from the cheese. Place in a greased deep container and dot all over with the pieces of butter. Cover with plastic wrap and let rise at room temperature until doubled in bulk, about 1½ hours.
4. With a wooden spoon or an electric mixer, beat the butter into the dough. Turn the dough out onto the work surface and pat into a 10-by-4-inch rectangle. In a small bowl, beat the remaining egg and toss with the shredded cheese. Spread the cheese mixture evenly over the dough surface, leaving a 1-inch border all around the edges. Starting from the long end, roll up jelly-roll fashion and pinch the seams to seal. Place the rope in a greased 12-cup mold with a center funnel; the mold should be no more than half full. Cover with plastic wrap and let rise at room temperature until fully doubled in bulk, about 45 minutes. Twenty minutes before baking, preheat the oven to 375°.
5. Bake on the lowest rack of the preheated oven until domed and golden brown, 40 to 45 minutes. Loosely place a piece of foil over the top if it is becoming too brown. Remove from the oven and let stand 15 minutes before turning out of the mold onto a rack to cool completely.

Alpine Easter Bread

Baked into a round loaf, this Easter bread is light, rich, and delicate in texture as well as flavor. Egg breads represent a garden of ancient myth and metaphor, and, as symbols of rebirth, they are the perfect offering for the spring equinox. The round shape represents the sun and the rhythm of the seasons. The aroma of this loaf is so intoxicating that legend says it has healing powers. Use a nut liqueur for a beautiful glazing effect that complements the vanilla and lemon. Serve Alpine Easter Bread as a coffee cake spread with Pahska (page 163), or Coeur à la Crème (page 163) and Spiced Honey (page 165).

Yield: One 10-inch round loaf

½ cup milk
½ cup (1 stick) unsalted butter
1½ tablespoons (1½ packages) active dry yeast
Pinch sugar
½ cup warm water (105° to 115°)
4 to 4½ cups unbleached all-purpose flour
⅔ cup sugar
2 teaspoons grated lemon zest
1½ teaspoons salt
3 eggs
1½ teaspoons pure vanilla extract, or 1 vanilla bean, split and scraped
½ teaspoon lemon extract

Nut Liqueur Glaze, page 156
10 whole toasted, chocolate, or silver-coated almonds

1. In a small saucepan, combine the milk and butter. Heat until the butter is melted. Let cool to 105° to 115°, about 20 minutes.

2. In a small bowl, sprinkle the yeast and sugar over the warm water. Stir to dissolve and let stand until foamy, about 10 minutes.

3. In a large bowl, using a whisk, or in the workbowl of a heavy-duty electric mixer fitted with the paddle attachment, combine 1½ cups of the flour, sugar, lemon zest, and salt. Add the yeast and milk mixtures, eggs, and extracts. Beat until creamy, about 2 minutes. Add the remaining flour ½ cup at a time on low speed until a soft dough is formed that just clears the sides of the bowl, switching to a wooden spoon when necessary if mixing by hand.

4. Turn the dough out onto a lightly floured work surface and knead until the dough is soft and springy, about 3 minutes, adding flour 1 tablespoon at a time as necessary to prevent sticking. The dough should not be dry. Place in a greased deep container, turn once to coat the top, and cover with plastic wrap. Let rise at warm room temperature until doubled in bulk, about 2 hours. Do not rush this dough, as the full rising time is important to develop flavor and texture.

5. Turn the dough out onto the work surface and shape into a smooth, round loaf. Place in a greased 10-inch springform or 4-inch-deep 10-inch cake pan. Loosely cover with plastic wrap and let rise at a warm room temperature until doubled in bulk, about 1 hour. Twenty minutes before baking, preheat the oven to 350°.

6. Bake in the center of the preheated oven until brown and a cake tester comes out clean when inserted into the center, about 50 to 60 minutes. Remove from the oven and let stand 15 minutes before removing from the mold to a rack. Place the rack over a plate or sheet of waxed paper to catch drips. Prepare the Nut Liqueur Glaze and drizzle the warm loaf with all of the glaze, letting it drip down the sides. Stud the outer edge with whole almonds, if desired. The glaze will set as the loaf cools.

Hot Cross Buns with Dried Fruit and Two Glazes

Little Celtic breads decorated with a Greek-style cross are a very old tradition, as this mystic symbol once was used to ward off evil spirits. Decorate with Lemon Icing over a shiny sugar glaze for Easter, and serve with Honeyed Ricotta, page 162. Or use a Molasses Glaze, page 156, and serve any time of year for breakfast.

Yield: 18 buns

1 tablespoon (1 package) active dry yeast
Pinch sugar
¾ cup warm water (105° to 115°)
1 cup warm milk (105° to 115°)
½ cup (1 stick) unsalted butter, melted
⅓ cup sugar
1 teaspoon salt
3 eggs
3½ to 4 cups unbleached all-purpose flour
1 cup dried currants
½ cup chopped dried apricots
½ teaspoon ground mace
½ teaspoon pure vanilla extract

Sugar Glaze
¼ cup granulated sugar
½ cup water

Lemon Icing
1 cup sifted powdered sugar
1 teaspoon fresh lemon juice
1 teaspoon grated lemon zest
1½ tablespoons milk

1. In a small bowl, sprinkle the yeast and sugar over the warm water. Stir to dissolve and let stand until foamy, about 10 minutes.

2. In a large bowl, combine the milk, butter, sugar, salt, eggs, and 1 cup of the flour. Whisk hard for 1 minute to combine. Add the yeast mixture, dried fruits, spice, vanilla, and 1 cup more flour. Beat hard with a wooden spoon for 1 minute, or until well mixed. Add the remaining flour ½ cup at a time to form a soft dough that just clears the sides of the bowl, switching to a wooden spoon when necessary if mixing by hand. The dough may also be mixed in a heavy-duty electric mixer fitted with the paddle attachment.

3. Turn the dough out onto a lightly floured work surface and knead until soft, smooth, and springy, about 3 minutes, pushing back any fruits that might fall out during kneading, and adding 1 tablespoon of flour at a time as necessary to prevent sticking. Place in a greased deep container, turn once to coat the top, and cover with plastic wrap. Let rise at room temperature until doubled in bulk, about 1 to 1½ hours.

4. Turn the dough out onto the work surface and divide into 2 equal portions. Roll each portion into a 10-inch-long log and, with a sharp knife, cut into 9 equal portions. Form each portion into a round bun and place about 1½ inches apart on a greased or parchment-lined baking sheet. Let rise, uncovered, at

room temperature until doubled, about 30 minutes. Meanwhile, preheat the oven to 375°. With a sharp knife, cut a cross no deeper than ½ inch over the surface of each bun.

5. Bake in the center of the preheated oven for 15 to 20 minutes, or until browned. While baking, prepare the sugar glaze: In a heavy saucepan, combine the sugar and water. Boil uncovered for 5 minutes. Use immediately, or store in a covered jar in the refrigerator, then reheat to boiling before using. Remove the buns from the pan to a rack. Brush immediately with the sugar glaze. Let cool. Meanwhile, prepare the Lemon Icing: In a small bowl, combine the powdered sugar, lemon juice and zest, and milk. Beat hard with a whisk until smooth. The icing should be a bit firm for piping. When the glaze is dry, place the icing in a pastry bag fitted with a small, plain tip and pipe a square cross over the top of each bun. Let stand for at least 20 minutes to set.

Raisin and Lemon Egg Bread with Macadamias

Macadamias, ornamental evergreen trees native to eastern Australia, are now cultivated in the Hawaiian Islands. The shell is hard to break, but the reward inside is a creamy, buttery-flavored nut that is a gourmet's delight. Serve with sliced fresh pineapple, a selection of favorite cheeses, and mugs of Kona coffee for an Easter brunch.

Yield: One 9-inch round loaf

2 tablespoons (2 packages) active dry yeast
Pinch sugar
1⅓ cups warm milk (105° to 115°)
½ cup dark raisins
½ cup golden raisins
¼ cup dried currants
5 to 5½ cups unbleached all-purpose flour
⅓ cup sugar
4 eggs
¾ cup (1½ sticks) unsalted butter, melted
½ cup local honey
1 tablespoon salt
Grated zest of 2 lemons
1 cup unsalted macadamia nuts

Rich Egg Glaze, page 155

1. In a small bowl, sprinkle the yeast and sugar over ⅓ cup of the warm milk. Stir to dissolve and let stand until foamy, about 10 minutes. Place both kinds of raisins and currants in a medium bowl and cover with hot water. Set aside to plump for 10 minutes.

2. In a large bowl, using a whisk, or in the workbowl of a heavy-duty electric mixer fitted with the paddle attachment, place 2 cups of the flour and make a well in the center. Add the yeast mixture, remaining 1 cup milk, sugar, eggs, butter, honey, salt, and lemon zest. Beat until smooth, about 2 minutes. Drain the raisins and add to the batter. Continue to add the remaining flour ½ cup at a time to form a soft dough that just clears the sides of the bowl, switching to a wooden spoon when necessary if mixing by hand.

3. Turn the dough out onto a lightly floured work surface and knead until soft, smooth, and springy, about 3 minutes, adding 1 tablespoon of flour at a time as necessary to prevent sticking. Place in a greased deep container, turn

once to coat the top, and cover with plastic wrap. Let rise at room temperature until doubled in bulk, about 1½ hours. Meanwhile, toast the nuts: Preheat the oven to 350°. Spread the nuts on a jelly-roll pan and bake until lightly toasted, about 7 to 10 minutes. Let cool, then chop coarsely and set aside.

4. Turn the dough out onto the work surface and pat into a large rectangle. Sprinkle with nuts and, with your palms, roll up into a thick cylindrical rope 20 to 24 inches long. Wrap the dough around one end to form a spiral. Tuck the remaining end under. Place on a greased or parchment-lined baking sheet, or in a greased 9-inch springform pan with a 4-inch collar of aluminum foil to make a high, mushroom-shaped loaf. Cover loosely with plastic wrap and let rise at room temperature until doubled in bulk, about 45 minutes. Remove the plastic as the dough rises to prevent sticking, if necessary. Twenty minutes before baking, preheat the oven to 350°.

5. Brush the loaf with egg glaze and bake in the center of the preheated oven until browned and hollow sounding when tapped, 50 to 60 minutes. A cake tester inserted into the center should come out clean. Remove from the pan to cool completely on a rack before slicing.

Hungarian Sweet Cheese Bread

It's my Hungarian blood that makes me crave this delicate sour cream pastry, baked in grand old European style. American cream cheese was commercially developed in 1872 in New York State by a dairyman for the then Empire Cheese Company, which later changed its name to Philadelphia Brand Cream Cheese. Combined with fresh goat cheese, its flavor is hauntingly similar to the tangy curd cheese fillings of rural eastern Europe and Italy, made from sheep's milk curdled in a skin bag. Serve for a special brunch or picnic dessert.

Yield: 2 small bundt cakes, each serving 4 to 6

1½ tablespoons (1½ packages) active dry yeast
Pinch sugar
½ cup warm water (105° to 115°)
1 cup (2 sticks) unsalted butter, melted
½ cup sugar
4 large eggs
1 cup sour cream
1 teaspoon salt
Grated zest of 1 lemon
5½ to 6 cups unbleached all-purpose or bread flour

Sweet Cheese Filling
8 ounces (1 cup) natural cream cheese at room temperature
8 ounces (1 cup) fresh goat cheese at room temperature
1 cup sugar
4 large eggs
1 tablespoon fresh lemon juice

Apricot Brandy Glaze, page 156

1. In a small bowl, sprinkle the yeast and sugar over the warm water. Stir to dissolve and let stand until foamy, about 10 minutes.
2. In a large bowl, beat the butter with the sugar until smooth with a wooden spoon or an electric mixer. Add the eggs one at a time and beat until incorporated. Add the yeast mixture, sour cream, salt, lemon zest, and 2 cups of flour. Beat until a smooth batter is formed, about 2 minutes. Add the remaining flour ½ cup at a time to form a soft dough that just clears the sides of the bowl.
3. Turn the dough out onto a lightly floured work surface and knead until a very soft, springy dough is formed, about 2 minutes, adding flour 1 tablespoon at a time as necessary to prevent sticking. This dough is very rich and does not require a long kneading time, as it can easily absorb too much flour. Take care to keep the dough as soft as possible. Place in a greased deep container, turn once to coat the top, and cover with plastic wrap. Let rise at room temperature until doubled in bulk, about 1½ hours.
4. Meanwhile, prepare the sweet cheese filling: Beat the cheeses until smooth in a bowl with a wooden spoon or an electric mixer. Add the sugar and beat until fluffy. Add the eggs one at a time, beating well after each addition. Add the lemon juice. Refrigerate until needed.
5. Turn the dough out onto the work surface. Brush two 6-cup fluted mini-bundt pan molds with melted butter. Divide the dough in half. Roll the dough out into a 12-inch circle about ½ to ¾ inch thick. Fold in half and place over one half of the prepared pan. Unfold the dough and carefully fit into the bottom with 2 to 3 inches of dough hanging over the outside the mold. The center tube will be covered by the dough. Take care not to break the dough; if it does break, repair it by pinching it closed. Repeat with the other portion of the dough.
6. Divide the cheese filling equally between the 2 pans and spread evenly. Lift the overhanging dough back over the filling and place in overlapping folds to cover the filling around the pan. Press the folded edges against the inside tube to encase the filling. With kitchen shears, cut an X in the dough covering the center tube. Fold each triangle back over the folds of dough. Cover loosely with plastic wrap and set aside at room temperature to rise for about 30 minutes, or until the dough comes to ¼ inch below the top rim. Meanwhile, preheat the oven to 350°.
7. Bake in the center of the preheated oven for 35 to 40 minutes, or until quite brown and a cake tester inserted in the center comes out clean. Let cool in the pan for 10 minutes before turning out onto a wire rack. While the cake is warm, brush with hot Apricot Brandy Glaze. Let cool at least 1 hour before slicing. Store in the refrigerator.

PAIRING BREAD AND CHEESE

Crusty country-style home-baked breads, with their yeasty flavor and porous texture, are a natural complement to the pungent flavors and dense texture of cheeses. Choose a cheese with regard to its texture as well as taste when pairing it with your bread. Let the cheese come to room temperature, as the flavors are then at their best. Place unwrapped wedges on a leaf-lined flat basket, serving platter, wooden cutting board, or marble slab, accompanying each type with its own knife or spreader. Grape, citrus, magnolia, fig, and ti leaves are my favorites. Serve a mixture of breads with a variety of cheeses as finger foods before dinner or as a snack. The breads should be served at room temperature or warm from the oven.

To develop a refrigerated cheese's full taste, remove its wrapping and let sit at room temperature for about 1 hour before serving. Cut cheeses in thin wedges like a cake, or use a cheese slicer to make thin slices of low-moisture hard cheese. Eating the rind is a matter of personal taste, except, of course, for pungent, washed, or musty rinds, or dried leaves or rinds made of plastic. Natural rinds are usually gray, brown, or beige. Mass-produced cheeses are more likely to be finished with bright red or black plastic or wax rinds. Remember, a rind, even though inedible, is important in protecting the cheese, so keep it on during storage.

Food pairing is an art when done with care, and combining cheese with your homemade breads is a good way to develop it. Classic white and whole-wheat country breads are perfect balances to the acid bite and high butterfat of goat cheese, Sonoma jack with chilies, and fresh Camembert. More complicated loaves such as Country Rolls with Shallots and Pecans, and Potato and Rye Vienna Twist are good with soft-ripened cheeses such as moon-shaped rounds of Brie de Meaux and the under-rated French Reblochon. Coarse-cracked wheat and multi-grain loaves, such as Pain de Campagne, Miller's Hearth Bread, or Seven-Grain Honey Bread are good with a wedge of sweet, nutty mountain cheese such as imported Emmenthaler, Gruyère, Doux de Montagne with green peppercorns, and Italian Fontina d'Aosta. Five-Grain Country Bread and Wild Rice Oatmeal Bread are great with the Mozzarella Company's soft Crescenza and Ancho Chili Cheese. Italian White Bread and variations of French Bread pair well with a creamy Washington state Quillisascut Manchego goat cheese or a California pyramid chèvre.

The best sharp cheddars from Vermont, such as one from Shelbourne Farms, are outstanding with Whole-Wheat Bread with Apricots and Seeds. Flamboyant English Double Gloucester is good with oatmeal breads. Pumpkin–Blue Corn Rye is remarkable with Sugarbush Farm's hickory-and-maple-smoked cheddar. Italian Whole-Wheat Country Bread or Mixed Rice Bread is excellent with a young domestic Asiago or Bulk Farm's Gouda. Pumpernickels are always good with Yakima gold Goudas, Monterey jack, and French Boursin. Try rye bread with a fat layer of straw-colored English Somerset cheddar for a memorable lunch. Yogurt Pumpernickel, dense Squaw Bread, or bittersweet Wild Rice–Molasses bread is an absolute must with Saint-André, the king of the voluptuous French *triple-crèmes*. It has a mild tang melded with a buttery texture people find addictive.

Breads embellished with dried fruit are good with veined cheeses such as the assertive Italian Gorgonzola, Maytag Blue, Kendall's Chèvre Bleu, French Roquefort, or sweet Fourme d'Ambert. I am partial to intensely flavored whole-grain and nut breads spread with tangy *fromage de chèvre* or served with cubes of a variety of good Swiss cheeses. The hazelnut-flavored Emmenthaler, the cider-cured Appenzell, and the French Comté are outstanding in this theater. Serve the layered English cheddar and Stilton cheese known as Huntsman with whole-grain dinner rolls such as Maple Brown Buns.

Spread creamy fresh goat cheese on hearty breads such as Country Walnut and Raisin, Yam Country Bread with Sesame, Pecan Wheat-Berry Bread, or Dakota Bread with Ancient Grains. Goat cheeses are the darling of the gourmet cheese world; use the fresh variety as a spread, and cut the piquant aged varieties into shavings. The name of a goat cheese usually describes the enchanting shapes of both imported and domestic brands—*coeur:* heart; *taupinière:* dome; *boucheron:* cork; *bûche:* log; *crottin:* button; *pyramide:* flat-topped pyramid; *clochette:* little bell. On the West Coast,

147

chèvres from Cypress Grove Chèvre, Laura Chenel, Sadie Kendall, and Rachel's Goat Cheese are a must; on the East Coast, try Coach Farms, Goat Folks, and Sheepscot Valley. Common French varieties are Montrachet, Bucheron, Cabecou, St. Marcellin, and Chabi.

Pizzas and focaccia have a natural affinity for melting cheeses such as mozzarellas, Italian *caciocavallo,* Wisconsin or Italian fontinas, and provolone. California dry jack, with its cocoa-dusted rind, and Monterey jack are good substitutes for the traditional imported Italian cheeses. Spread Rosemary-Raisin Bread with a mild, smooth Italian Bel Paese, which is also a good cheese to introduce to children.

Cheese added to a bread dough creates a glorious loaf. To use it as a major or accent ingredient in a dough, shred it with a grater or cut it into small cubes for the most even incorporation. For the best flavor, use classical combinations when adding cheese to a dough, such as Gruyère and Parmesan in Crescia al Formaggio, or cheddar in Anadama Bread with Tillamook Cheddar. Sprinkle a layer of shredded cheese over a large piece of dough, roll up, and bake. When the loaf is sliced, a delicate swirl of moist cheese is revealed, as in Pancetta-Onion Gruyère Ring. A small hunk enclosed in dough and then baked is perfect for lunch or a picnic with fruit and salad: see Pumpernickel Rolls with a Tillamook Cheddar Heart and Brie in Brioche. Italian melting cheeses are alternately layered with vegetables within a savory crust for torta rusticas.

Use delicate, creamy-textured fresh cheeses as a basis for spreads. Cream cheese, ricotta, fromage blanc, cottage cheese, and queso fresco are interchangeable. These cheeses are excellent with sweet or savory seasonings such as black pepper, sun-dried tomatoes, chives, or even dried cherries, fresh berries, nuts, and liqueurs. Fresh cheeses also may be molded into different shapes such as logs, rounds, or hearts. Brie, Saint-André, Marscarpone, Montrachet, and a young Gorgonzola make exciting spreads to complement breads. Firmer cheeses such as cheddars or provolone need to be creamed with butter or layered in a terrine to create a spreadable consis-

tency. Cottage cheese, farmer's cheese, ricotta, and fromage blanc may be substituted for liquid in recipes. The result, as in Whole-Wheat Ricotta Rolls with Toasted Quinoa, is a moist, firm-textured roll. Lemon-Ricotta Coffee Cake uses this cheese as a subtle ingredient for the sweet filling.

Serve one or two cheeses and homemade bread alongside a salad of fresh seasonal greens dressed with a sharp vinaigrette for a meal in itself. Sandwiches of bread and cheese fit into any time of day, and are the perfect food for a picnic. The ubiquitous grilled cheese sandwich and its peasant cousins, bruschette and crostini, are excellent as lunch offerings, before-dinner appetizers, and snacks. Or, you can eat your cheese as the French do: after dinner with bread, as the last course before dessert.

To mellow the effect of a strong cheese, spread your bread first with a bit of soft unsalted butter. Fresh or dried fruit, nuts, crunchy crudités, marinated mushrooms, strips of roasted peppers, slices of red onion, roasted whole garlic, and cold meats are natural accompaniments. Have plenty of good wine, cold beer, cider, or mineral water on hand. A variety of olives, such as little pungent niçoises, cracked green Sicilians, mellow Ligurians, oval Kalamatas, minute Picholines, creamy Arbequinas, or black Gaetas, are a legendary combination with bread, cheese, and wine. Accent olives by dressing them with herbs, cracked black pepper, lemon or orange zest, crushed garlic, or hot peppers moistened with an assertive olive oil.

Bouchées de Chèvre

Small, plump rounds of goat cheese are lightly coated with a variety of flavors and textures to recreate the homespun diminutive fresh cheeses of rural France. Serve as a snack to four guests or as part of a selection of cheeses.

One or two 11-ounce logs of plain French Montrachet or fresh domestic goat cheese, such as Chabi
Selection of 4 coatings: chopped fresh or crumbled dried thyme, tarragon, dill, savory, or rosemary; coarse-cracked black or mixed peppercorns; crushed dried fines herbes; paprika; herb blossoms; small fresh grape leaves with strands of chives or raffia for tying; minced toasted walnuts, pistachios, or hazelnuts

Cut the cheese logs into 1-inch-thick slices. With your palms, quickly mold each piece into a smooth round ball. Roll each ball in 1 to 2 teaspoons of a desired coating. The balls may also be wrapped individually in a small fresh grape or fig leaf and tied with strands of chive or raffia after rolling. To serve, arrange about 4 varieties and a few plain balls on a slab of marble or a serving platter with sliced breads.

Grilled Mustard and Cheese Rolls

Serve these hot cheese rolls with cornichons and olives for a snack.

Yield: 6 servings

6 crusty French or Italian rolls, about 6 inches in length
¼ cup mustard, such as Dijon, coarse-grain, or sweet-hot
6 wedges French Brie or other double cream or semi-soft cheese, such as Italian Toma, Doux de Montagne, or Monterey jack

Make an incision on the side of each roll, not cutting through completely. Hollow out a bit of the soft insides. Spread the inside with a thin layer of mustard. Stuff each roll with a wedge of cheese. Press the two sides of the roll together and place on a grill over hot coals or on an aluminum-foil-lined baking sheet under a preheated broiler until crusty and melted, about 5 minutes, turning frequently.

CROSTINI AND BRUSCHETTE

What are crostini? Literally translated "little crusts," they are Italian-style appetizer croutons. Usually toasted slowly until golden and then spread with a variety of tasty savory toppings, they are a clever way to use up day-old bread. A relative of the French *pain grillé*, these small rounds of toast tend to be smaller and less filling than the heartier bruschette, grilled bread rubbed with garlic and drizzled with oil. These toasts are traditionally grilled over an open fire, but they adapt easily to an outdoor grill, oven, or broiler.

Cut small rounds of bread from day-old baguettes or heavy country breads, or cut triangles from chewy whole-grain slices. When baked in the oven, use an ungreased baking sheet or line it with foil or parchment for easier cleaning. Crostini may be made ahead in large quantities for cocktail parties, where they can serve as rustic canapés or as part of an antipasto platter. Store toasts in an airtight container and spread just before serving with anchovy or caper butter, cheeses, shellfish, a fat layer of roasted peppers, ricotta with chopped olives, or a chicken liver pâté. Crostini may also be floated in soups, served with wine, or tucked alongside a good salad for a light meal.

Cheddar and Olive Crostini

Yield: 16 to 20 crostini

*1½ cups (6 ounces) grated sharp cheddar
    cheese
½ cup black olives, pitted and chopped
¼ cup chopped green onion
¾ cup good mayonnaise
2 teaspoons good curry powder
One French baguette, cut into 16 to 20 thin
    slices*

Preheat the oven to 400°. In a medium bowl, combine the cheese, olives, green onion, mayonnaise, and curry until evenly blended. Refrigerate until needed. Mound atop the bread slices and place on a baking sheet. Bake until puffed and melted, about 10 minutes.

Crostini with Artichokes and Mozzarella

Yield: 16 to 20 crostini

*½ cup (1 stick) unsalted butter at room
    temperature
2 to 3 garlic cloves, pressed
One French baguette, cut into 16 to 20 thin
    slices
Two 4-ounce jars marinated artichoke
    hearts, drained and chopped
1 pound mozzarella cheese, cut into thin slices*

Preheat the oven to 375°. Cream the butter and garlic until smooth. Spread thinly on one side of each slice of bread and place on a baking sheet. On each slice, place 1 tablespoon chopped artichokes. Cover with 1 slice of mozzarella. Bake until the cheese is melted and the edges are brown, 10 to 15 minutes. Strips of sun-dried tomatoes or roasted peppers may be substituted for the artichokes. For large gatherings, cut the baguette in half lengthwise and spread the entire surface; cut into hunks to serve.

Herbed Crostini

Yield: About 16 crostini

*¾ cup (6 ounces) whole-milk ricotta cheese
1 egg yolk
1½ tablespoons olive oil
Salt and fresh-ground pepper to taste
2 tablespoons chopped fresh herbs such as
    tarragon, basil, opal basil, lemon thyme,
    savory, chives, or parsley
1 baguette, cut into ¼-inch slices and
    brushed with olive oil
Small handful of chopped black olives or thin
    slices sweet bell pepper, if desired*

Preheat the oven to 350°. In a food processor or by hand, mix the ricotta, egg yolk, olive oil, seasonings, and herbs. Place the bread slices on a baking sheet and bake until crisp, about 8 minutes. Just before serving, spread with the cheese. Broil until hot, lightly browned and bubbly. Sprinkle with olives.

Crostini with Gorgonzola and Pine Nuts

Yield: About 16 crostini

6 tablespoons unsalted butter at room
    temperature
6 ounces Gorgonzola cheese, cut into
    small pieces
2 tablespoons chopped fresh basil leaves
8 slices firm homemade bread
1/3 cup pine nuts
1 bunch arugula, broken into sprigs

Preheat the oven to 400°. Cream the butter,
cheese, and basil until smooth. Set aside.
Place the slices of bread on a baking sheet
and toast for 5 minutes. Remove from the
oven and spread with the cheese mixture,
leaving a little rim around the bread uncovered. Sprinkle each slice with the pine nuts.
Bake for 10 to 15 minutes, or until brown
around the edges. Cut large slices of bread
diagonally into 2 triangles. Top with
arugula sprigs.

Eggplant Caviar on Crostini

Yield: 16 crostini

2 medium eggplants
1 garlic clove, pressed
1 large shallot, minced
Salt and fresh-ground pepper to taste
1/4 teaspoon ground cinnamon
1/2 cup chopped fresh parsley

2 tablespoons red wine vinegar
6 tablespoons olive oil
Grated zest of 1 lemon
1 tablespoon fresh lemon juice
1 teaspoon chopped fresh mint or basil
16 slices Italian bread

Preheat the oven to 350°. Slit each whole
eggplant in several places so the steam can
escape. Bake the eggplants in a 350° oven
for 50 minutes to 1 hour, or until soft and
cooked through. Let cool. Peel and chop,
with the skin on. Place in a medium bowl
and add all the rest of the ingredients,
except the bread. Mix well to combine. Let
stand for several hours or covered overnight
in the refrigerator before using. To serve,
toast, broil, or grill the bread slices and
spread with eggplant caviar.

Goat Cheese Fondue on Country-style Bread

Yield: 6 servings

1/4 cup dry white wine
1 garlic clove, peeled
8 ounces French Montrachet or domestic goat
    cheese, crumbled
1 cup (4 ounces) shredded Gruyère or Swiss
    cheese
2 tablespoons Cognac or brandy
1 tablespoon unsalted butter
1 teaspoon Dijon mustard
6 thick slices white or wheat country-style
    bread
6 fresh thyme sprigs or basil leaves

In a deep saucepan, bring the wine and garlic to a boil over low heat and cook until
reduced by half. Remove the garlic clove.
Add the cheeses and melt over low heat,
stirring with a wooden spoon. Remove
from heat and stir in the Cognac or brandy,
butter, and mustard. The fondue may be
made 30 minutes in advance and kept warm
in a hot-water bath over low heat.

    Preheat the broiler. A few minutes before
serving, place the bread slices on a baking
sheet and lightly toast both sides, about 2
minutes each. Remove from the oven and
immediately spread each slice with the
warm fondue. Garnish with an herb sprig
or basil leaf and serve immediately.

Crostini with Two Pestos

Yield: 20 crostini

Sun-dried Tomato Pesto
3 ounces (1/3 cup) bulk-style sun-dried
    tomatoes (not oil packed), soaked in hot
    water for 1 hour and drained
1/4 cup grated Parmesan cheese
1/4 bunch Italian flat-leaf parsley, stemmed
3 tablespoons tomato paste
1 garlic clove, peeled
1/4 to 1/2 cup good-quality olive oil

Basil Pesto
2½ cups fresh basil leaves
2 garlic cloves, peeled
½ cup grated Parmesan cheese
¼ cup pine nuts
⅓ cup good olive oil

20 pieces thinly sliced and toasted baguette or
    country-style bread
1 pound fresh mozzarella or fontina cheese,
    sliced

To make the pestos: Combine all the ingredients, except the oil, for each pesto separately in a blender or food processor and pulse while adding the oil slowly to form slightly coarse purees. The pestos may also be made by hand using a mortar and pestle. Store, covered, in the refrigerator until ready to use.

Preheat the broiler. Place toasts on a baking sheet, top each with a slice of cheese, and broil until melted. Remove from the oven and top each crostini with a teaspoonful of each pesto. Serve immediately.

Bagel Chips

Yield: About 3 dozen chips

6 homemade bagels, sliced horizontally into
    ¼-inch-thick round slices
½ cup (1 stick) unsalted butter, melted

Preheat the oven to 350°. Arrange the round bagel slices in 1 layer on a baking sheet. Brush evenly with melted butter. Bake in the preheated oven for 10 to 15 minutes, or until crisp and golden around the edges. Serve warm or store in an airtight container for 3 days to serve at room temperature.

Maple Tea Toasts

Yield: 6 toasts

½ cup (1 stick) unsalted butter at room
    temperature
¼ cup pure maple syrup or maple sugar
6 thin slices homemade white or whole-wheat
    bread

Preheat the oven to 350°. In a small bowl, cream the butter and maple syrup or sugar until smooth and well blended. Spread evenly on the bread slices. Place in one layer on a baking sheet. Bake in the preheated oven until toasted, about 15 minutes. Serve immediately.

Country Cinnamon Toasts

Yield: 24 toasts

¾ cup granulated sugar
1½ tablespoons ground cinnamon
8 medium slices homemade white or whole-
    wheat bread, each slice cut into 3 strips
¾ cup (1½ sticks) unsalted butter, melted
Whole nutmeg for grating

Preheat the oven to 350°. Combine the sugar and cinnamon on a plate. Brush both sides of the bread with melted butter and dip into the cinnamon sugar. Place in one layer on a baking sheet. Bake in the preheated oven until crisp, about 15 to 20 minutes, turning once. Grate nutmeg over the surface and serve immediately.

Bruschette

The word *bruschette* comes from the root word *bruciare* ("to scorch or burn"). The original garlic bread, it is a thick slice of chewy day-old country or sourdough bread that is toasted or grilled over a wood or charcoal fire until crusty. A large clove of garlic is rubbed over the sandpaper-like surface of the slice until the clove disappears completely into the pores of the bread, which is then drizzled with pungent new olive oil, the fruitier the better. This earthy, modest delight utilizes simple ingredients enjoyed by all the lands bordering the Mediterranean. Bruschette might be eaten topped with chopped vine-ripened tomatoes in Spain; with roasted red peppers and artichokes in Italy; and in Greece, with rich black olives and capers. Often bruschette appears sprinkled with fresh herbs. It is good as an appetizer around the grill with red wine and a hard cheese, such as Asiago, or as an accompaniment to soup or salads. The following is a recipe developed for indoor entertaining.

Yield: 12 bruschette

¾ cup good olive oil
6 medium garlic cloves, squeezed through a
    press
Twelve 2-inch-thick slices country-style,
    French, sourdough, or whole-wheat
    Italian bread

In a small saucepan, heat the olive oil until just warm and add the garlic. Remove from heat and set aside to let cool until needed. The oil may sit for up to 2 days.

Place the bread slices in a toaster, under a preheated broiler, or on an oiled rack about

4 inches above glowing coals. Toast both sides until golden brown. Generously brush one side of each slice with the garlic oil and serve hot with extra olive oil for drizzling.

Bruschette with Mozzarella and Olive Pesto

Yield: 6 servings

Olive Pesto
One 6-ounce can California pitted black olives
¼ cup grated Parmesan cheese
¼ bunch flat-leaf parsley, stemmed
1 tablespoon capers, rinsed and drained
2 to 4 tablespoons fruity olive oil
1 tablespoon fresh lemon juice
Pinch fresh or dried thyme leaves
Freshly ground black pepper to taste

1 loaf or 6 rolls Italian-style Country Bread with Sesame Seeds (page 42)
1 pound mozzarella cheese, cut into ¼-inch-thick slices

Place all the ingredients for the olive pesto in a blender or food processor fitted with the metal blade and pulse on and off until a rough-textured puree is made. Store in the refrigerator for up to 5 days before using. Olive Pesto may also be made using a mortar and pestle.

Preheat the oven to 400°. Cut the loaf of bread or rolls into 1-inch-thick vertical slices without cutting through to the bottom. Stuff each cut with a slice of cheese spread with a bit of olive pesto. Place on a baking sheet and bake for about 15 minutes, or until the bread is crisp and the cheese is melted. Serve immediately.

Two Bruschette: Roasted Sweet Pepper and Marinated Eggplant

Roasted Sweet Pepper Topping
4 red or yellow bell peppers
2 to 3 garlic cloves, minced
½ cup chopped fresh flat-leaf parsley
½ cup good olive oil

Marinated Eggplant Topping
4 Japanese or baby Italian eggplants, each cut lengthwise into 4 to 8 thick slices
⅓ cup good olive oil
¼ cup chopped fresh basil leaves
¼ cup balsamic vinegar
3 garlic cloves, peeled and chopped

12 large slices of country bread or baguette
Olive oil for brushing

To make the roasted pepper topping: Roast the peppers on a long-handled fork over a gas flame, on a charcoal grill, or under a broiler until the skin is blackened. Place immediately in a paper bag, close tightly, and let sit until cool, about 20 minutes. Scrape off the skin with your fingers or a small knife. Core and lay flat in thick strips. Place on a serving platter. Sprinkle evenly with the garlic, parsley, and olive oil. Let stand at least 30 minutes at room temperature, or refrigerate overnight before serving.

To make the eggplant topping: Preheat the oven to 400°. Place the eggplants in a single layer in a baking pan and drizzle with the olive oil. Bake until browned, about 20 minutes. The slices may also be grilled on an oiled rack over glowing coals. In a shallow bowl, layer the eggplant with basil, vinegar, and garlic. Repeat layering and sprinkling, finishing with an herb and vinegar layer. Cover with plastic wrap and refrigerate overnight to meld the flavors.

To serve: Preheat the oven to 350°. Place the slices of country bread or baguette on a baking sheet, brush with olive oil, and bake in the preheated oven until lightly brown, about 15 minutes. Place in a serving basket and serve with a choice with roasted peppers and marinated eggplant as toppings.

THE ART OF GLAZING

A glaze is used when a loaf needs a "finishing touch." An optional embellishment, a glaze can be brushed onto an unbaked loaf to give a dark, glossy surface when appearance is a priority. Although most home-style breads look beautiful to me au naturel, there are appropriate glazes and embellishments for most every kind of loaf, including sprinkles of seeds or grains to reflect the ingredients inside, or a dusting of flour before rising for that "earthy look." Use a soft brush, reserved exclusively for glazing, to gently apply egg glazes to the risen loaf just before baking, or as directed in the recipe, and take care not to puncture or deflate the delicate loaf before baking.

An egg wash is typically used by bakers to produce a shiny crust and as a glue to hold on any solid embellishments such as nuts, seeds, herbs, grain flakes, and sautéed onions. The yolk alone produces a darker crust and is often used on breads rich in fat and sugar. The white alone makes a shiny finish for a lean dough such as French bread. Milk and cream give a dark shiny finished look. Fats such as melted butter and oils can be brushed on a loaf at any point before, during, or after baking to keep the crust soft and shiny. Using a warm oil infused with a sprig of fresh herbs or garlic gives added flavor.

Sweet doughs usually are brushed while hot with a clear gloss for sparkle or drizzled with a powdered sugar glaze as a flavor enhancer. These toppings are most dramatic when their flavors complement or match the ingredients used to create the individual loaf.

Egg Glaze

For French-style and country breads.

1 egg white
1 tablespoon water
Dash salt

Whisk all the ingredients together until combined and foamy. Use to glaze uncooked dough before sprinkling with seeds.

Rich Egg Glaze

For American-style loaf breads and for brioches.

1 yolk or 1 whole egg
1 tablespoon water, milk, or cream

Whisk all the ingredients together until combined. Use to brush uncooked dough before sprinkling with seeds.

Powdered Sugar Glaze for Sweet Doughs

A thin, shiny, creamy-colored icing for fresh-baked sweet breads and rolls. Choose a flavor complementary to the ingredients in your loaf. Top the loaf with fruit or whole and/or chopped nuts while the icing is moist. The glaze will set up and adhere any embellishments as it dries.

1 cup sifted powdered sugar
1 tablespoon unsalted butter, melted
2 to 3 tablespoons milk or cream, spirit or
    liqueur, or hot water

In a small bowl, combine the ingredients and whisk until smooth. Adjust the consistency of the glaze by adding milk a few drops at a time. Drizzle over warm or cool bread in the desired pattern.

Variations

Vanilla: Add ½ teaspoon pure vanilla extract.

Almond: Add ½ teaspoon pure almond extract.

Maple: Substitute pure maple syrup for the milk.

Citrus: Substitute fresh or thawed frozen concentrated lemon, orange, lime, or tangerine juice for the milk.

Chocolate: Add 1 tablespoon unsweetened cocoa.

Coffee: Add 1 teaspoon powdered instant espresso.

Spice: Add ½ teaspoon ground cinnamon, cardamom, or nutmeg.

Cranberry: Substitute cranberry juice for the milk.

Cider: Place ½ cup apple wine or hard or sweet apple cider in a saucepan and bring to a boil. Reduce to about 3 tablespoons and substitute for the milk.

Nut Liqueur: Substitute for the milk a nut liqueur such as Pistacha, Amaretto, Frangelico, Nocino, Macadamia Nut, Crème des Noyaux, or Noisette.

Golden Rum Glaze

Use as a finishing glaze for baked sweet breads containing fruits, nuts, or citrus juice, such as Orange Raisin Bread, page 114.

1 cup sifted powdered sugar
1 tablespoon unsalted butter, melted
3 to 4 tablespoons imported golden rum

In a small bowl, combine the ingredients and whisk until smooth. Adjust the consistency by adding rum a few drops at a time. Drizzle over the top of the bread and allow to drip down the sides.

Fresh Orange Glaze

Drizzle over baked sweet breads such as Orange Cinnamon Swirl, page 119.

1 cup sifted powdered sugar
1 tablespoon unsalted butter, melted
Grated zest of 1 orange
2 to 3 tablespoons fresh orange juice

In a small bowl, combine the ingredients and whisk until smooth. Adjust the consistency by adding more juice a few drops at a time. Drizzle over the top of the bread.

Apricot Brandy Glaze

Use to brush over warm baked sweet loaves such as Hungarian Sweet Cheese Bread, page 145, and Marzipan Brioche, page 116.

¾ cup good-quality apricot jam, whirled in a
    blender or food processor until smooth
3 tablespoons brandy, Cognac, or orange or
    apricot liqueur

In a small saucepan, combine the jam and brandy, Cognac, or liqueur and heat to boiling. Immediately brush over warm baked bread.

BUTTERS

Sweet and savory compound butters are excellent versatile spreads for enhancing a variety of fresh yeast and quick breads, toast, bagels, muffins, biscuits, and pancakes. They make wonderful gifts when packed into attractive containers. Although a butter is perfect just spread right out of the crock, a variety of shapes, such as butter curls, molded rounds, decorated pats, and butter balls made with a melon baller are attractive alternates when something special is in order. Cheese spreads are an extravagant touch for your homemade breads, and are suitable for hors d'oeuvres as well as an accompaniment to light meals or a dessert with fresh fruit. Unless noted, compound butters and cheese spreads will keep for about 5 days, covered tightly, in the refrigerator.

Whipped Honey Butter

Yield: ¾ cup

½ cup (1 stick) unsalted butter at room temperature
¼ cup honey, such as star thistle, orange, wildflower, sage, or Spiced Honey (page 165)
½ teaspoon finely grated lemon zest (optional)

Beat the butter until creamy with a wooden spoon, an electric mixer, or a food processor. Add the honey and zest. Beat just until combined. Store, covered, in the refrigerator, until ready to use. To serve: Let stand 30 minutes at room temperature to soften.

Nasturtium Butter

Yield: 1 cup

1 cup (2 sticks) unsalted butter at room temperature
5 fresh-picked unsprayed nasturtium flowers, rinsed and patted dry

Cream the butter with a wooden spoon, an electric mixer, or a food processor until fluffy. In a glass serving bowl that will comfortably hold 1 cup of butter, place 1 nasturtium flower, face up, on the bottom of the bowl.

Pack in one third of the butter. Arrange 3 blossoms facing out and evenly spaced around the sides of the bowl, using butter

to hold them in place. Fill with the remaining butter, pressing carefully to press and cover the flowers in place.

Smooth the top and press the remaining blossom, face up, on top. Cover and refrigerate for 24 hours before serving. The butter will take on the summer perfume of the flowers and taste very rich.

Macadamia Nut Butter

Yield: About ¾ cup

¼ cup unsalted macadamia nuts
½ cup (1 stick) unsalted butter at room temperature
2 teaspoons Cognac or macadamia nut liqueur

Preheat the oven to 350°. Spread the nuts on a baking sheet and bake until lightly toasted, about 7 to 10 minutes. Let cool.

Place the nuts in a blender or a food processor and process until finely ground. Add the butter and brandy or liqueur, if desired. Process until just combined. Do not over-process or the butter will heat up and separate. Form into a log or pack into a crock. Store covered in the refrigerator until serving.

Sweet Orange Butter

Yield: About ½ cup

½ cup (1 stick) unsalted butter at room temperature
1 tablespoon sifted powdered sugar

Grated zest of 1 orange
¼ teaspoon orange extract or orange liqueur

Beat the butter with a wooden spoon, an electric mixer, or a food processor until fluffy. Add the remaining ingredients and beat until just blended. Scrape into a 4-ounce mold or a serving bowl. Serve immediately or refrigerate covered. To serve, let stand for 15 minutes at room temperature to soften.

Strawberry Butter

Yield: About 1 cup

½ cup fresh strawberries, stemmed and mashed
1 to 2 tablespoons sugar
½ cup (1 stick) unsalted butter at room temperature

Sprinkle the berries with sugar and let stand for 5 minutes. Puree the berries and butter in a blender or food processor until just combined. Do not over-process. Shape into a thick log, using plastic wrap to protect your hands. Wrap in clean plastic and twist the ends. Refrigerate until firm and slice to serve.

Vanilla Butter

Yield: About ¾ cup

½ cup (1 stick) unsalted butter at room temperature
3 tablespoons sifted powdered sugar
1½ tablespoons pure vanilla extract

With a wooden spoon, an electric mixer, or a food processor, cream together the butter and sugar until light and fluffy. Gradually beat in the vanilla until smooth. Scrape into a decorative serving dish and chill, covered, in the refrigerator for up to 2 weeks. Let stand at room temperature for at least 15 minutes before serving.

Pesto Butter

This recipe makes much more pesto than is needed for the butter, but the extra can be used in any number of recipes, and it also freezes beautifully. Serve Pesto Butter with Italian country breads and Wild Rice Bread Sticks, page 94.

Yield: 1½ cups pesto, and ½ cup pesto butter

Pesto
2½ cups fresh basil leaves
½ cup grated Parmesan cheese
1 to 2 garlic cloves
1 tablespoon pine nuts
⅓ cup olive oil

½ cup (1 stick) unsalted butter at room temperature

To make the pesto: Combine the basil, Parmesan, garlic, and pine nuts in a blender or food processor. Pulse to finely chop. Add the olive oil and just slightly puree. Do not over-process. The pesto may be frozen for months or kept in the refrigerator for 3 days.

To make pesto butter: Cream 1 tablespoon pesto into the butter until smooth.

CHEESE SPREADS

Brie and Walnut Spread

Yield: About 1½ cups

¼ *cup walnuts*
4 ounces ripe unpeeled Brie, cut into pieces
4 ounces (½ cup) natural cream cheese at room temperature
1 tablespoon raspberry brandy or liqueur

Preheat the oven to 350°. Spread the walnuts in a baking pan and bake until lightly toasted, about 8 minutes. Let cool.

Place the cheeses in a blender or food processor. Add the walnuts and brandy. Process just until smooth. Place in a small crock, cover, and refrigerate overnight to meld flavors.

Red Pepper Cream Cheese

Yield: About 2 cups

1 small red bell pepper, roasted, seeded, and peeled (see page 154)
12 ounces (1½ cups) natural cream cheese
Juice of ½ fresh lemon
3 pecan halves

Puree the bell pepper in a blender or food processor; you should have ½ to ⅔ cup of puree. Blend the red pepper puree, cream cheese, and lemon juice until smooth and creamy by hand or in an electric mixer. Pack into a serving crock or bowl and smooth the top. Stud with pecan halves for decoration. Refrigerate until serving.

Gorgonzola Butter

Yield: About 1½ cups

¼ *cup pine nuts*
6 ounces Gorgonzola blue cheese at room temperature, cut into pieces
6 ounces natural cream cheese at room temperature, cut into pieces
6 tablespoons unsalted butter at room temperature, cut into pieces
2 tablespoons Pernod or Cognac

Preheat the oven to 350°. Spread the pine nuts on a baking pan and bake until lightly toasted, about 8 minutes. Let cool.

Blend the cheeses, butter, and liqueur or Cognac until fluffy with a wooden spoon, an electric mixer, or a food processor. Scrape with a spatula onto a large piece of plastic wrap. Using the wrap to protect your hands, quickly pack into a ball. If too soft, refrigerate for 15 minutes. Roll the cheese ball in pine nuts and rewrap it in clean plastic and refrigerate until firm. Let stand for 30 minutes before spreading on fresh bread.

Vegetable Cream Cheese

Yield: About 2½ cups

1 celery stalk, finely chopped
2 radishes, chopped
½ *medium carrot, peeled and finely grated*
½ *small summer squash, finely grated*
6 frozen artichoke heart halves, thawed and chopped
8 ounces natural cream cheese
½ *teaspoon white Worcestershire sauce*

Drain the chopped vegetables on a paper towel if very wet. Combine all the ingredients in a medium bowl with a wooden spoon or on low speed in an electric mixer. Transfer to a serving crock, cover, and refrigerate until ready to use. Serve on thin slices of fresh bread, crackers, pita, or bagels, or in lettuce leaves.

Fruit Butter

Yield: About 1½ cups

4 ounces (½ cup) natural cream cheese at room temperature
4 tablespoons unsalted butter at room temperature
½ *cup good fruit preserves or jam*
1 tablespoon spirits of choice (see suggestions below)

Beat the cream cheese and butter together with a wooden spoon, an electric mixer, or in a food processor until just creamy. Add the preserves or jam and spirits, beating until just blended. Transfer to a serving bowl, cover, and refrigerate until ready to use.

Suggestions: Apricot preserves with orange brandy; quince jelly with Calvados; blueberry preserves with Cognac; strawberry jam with Amaretto; raspberry jam with framboise; cherry preserves with cherry marnier; pineapple preserves with golden rum.

161

Honeyed Ricotta

Yield: About 1¼ cups

¼ cup mild local honey
1 cup whole-milk ricotta cheese

Heat the honey slightly until it reaches pouring consistency. In a small bowl, combine the cheese and honey and beat until smooth and fluffy. Scrape into a decorative serving bowl and refrigerate until serving.

Date Cream Cheese

Yield: About 1½ cups

4 ounces (about 18) pitted dates
8 ounces (1 cup) natural cream cheese at
    room temperature
1 teaspoon pure vanilla extract
1 teaspoon ground cinnamon

In a small saucepan, cover the dates with water. Cook uncovered over low heat until the dates are soft and the water is absorbed, about 10 minutes. When cool, puree the dates in a blender or food processor with the cream cheese, vanilla extract, and cinnamon. Process until just blended. Pack into a decorative crock and refrigerate, covered, until serving.

Cheddar Cheese Spread with Dates and Brandy

½ cup sliced almonds
½ cup (1 stick) unsalted butter at room
    temperature
2 cups (8 ounces) shredded sharp cheddar
    cheese
4 ounces (about 18) dates, pitted and snipped
1½ tablespoons good brandy

Preheat the oven to 350°. Spread the almonds in a baking pan and bake until lightly toasted, about 8 minutes. Let cool.

Cream the butter until fluffy with a wooden spoon, an electric mixer, or a food processor. Fold in the cheese, dates, and brandy until evenly incorporated. Scrape the cheese into a rough ball with a spatula. Sprinkle the almonds on a sheet of aluminum foil. Roll the cheese in the almonds to coat the surface, and shape into a log. Wrap in plastic and refrigerate until firm. Let stand at room temperature for about 30 minutes before serving. Note: This is best made 1 day ahead to meld the flavors.

Goat Cheese Spread

Yield: About 2 cups

6 ounces (¾ cup) natural cream cheese at
    room temperature
6 ounces fresh goat cheese, such as domestic
    Chabi or imported Montrachet, at room
    temperature
¼ cup extra-virgin olive oil

Beat the cheeses together until fluffy and well blended with a wooden spoon, an electric mixer, or a food processor. Scrape into a small crock, ceramic coeur à la crème mold, or bowl lined with 2 layers of damp cheesecloth. Pack down and fold the edges of the cheesecloth over the top to cover completely. Cover with plastic wrap. Store in the refrigerator for up to 2 days. To serve, remove the cheese from the mold and place on a serving plate. Remove the cheesecloth. Drizzle with olive oil to serve, or garnish with fresh fruit.

Goat Cheese with Sun-dried Tomatoes and Herbs

Yield: About 2 cups

6 slices sun-dried tomatoes (not packed in oil)
½ cup (1 stick) unsalted butter at room
    temperature
4 ounces fresh goat cheese, such as Chabi or
    Montrachet, at room temperature
4 ounces natural cream cheese at room
    temperature
1 tablespoon chopped fresh tarragon
1 tablespoon chopped fresh basil

In a small bowl, cover the sun-dried tomatoes with hot water. Let stand at room temperature for 15 minutes to soften. Drain well and chop coarsely. Set aside.

Blend the butter and cheeses with a wooden spoon, an electric mixer, or a food processor until just combined. Add the chopped tomatoes and herbs, folding them in carefully, as the tomatoes can bleed.

Spoon into a crock or small bowl. Cover and store in the refrigerator until ready to serve. Serve at room temperature.

Chèvre Coeur à la Crème with Thyme and Walnuts

Yield: Two 1-cup molds

This soft cheese is packed into a cheesecloth-lined, heart-shaped porcelain or straw mold, and allowed to sit overnight to drain off extra whey, leaving a dense, creamy spread that is perfect with fresh breads.

¼ cup walnuts
8 ounces domestic or imported fresh goat
*   cheese, such as Bucheron*
¼ cup crème fraîche or sour cream
¼ cup heavy cream, whipped
1 tablespoon apple brandy, such as Calvados
Leaves from 1 to 2 fresh thyme sprigs
Dash white pepper
2 bay leaves
4 walnut halves

1. Preheat the oven to 350°. Spread the walnuts in a baking pan and bake until lightly toasted, about 8 minutes. Let cool.
2. In a food processor or with an electric mixer, combine all the ingredients except the bay leaves and walnut halves. Beat until just smooth and evenly combined.
3. Line 2 individual heart molds with a double layer of damp cheesecloth. Place 2 walnut halves with a bay leaf in the

center for decoration in each mold. Scrape the cheese into both molds. Fold the cheesecloth completely over the cheese. Place the molds on a plate to drain in the refrigerator overnight.
4. To serve, unfold the cheesecloth and invert each mold onto a serving plate. Remove the cheesecloth carefully. Serve with heads of roasted garlic and country-style bread.

Dried Fruit Pahska

Yield: Serves about 16

Pahska is a creamy white cheese dessert embellished with bits of chopped fruit and traditionally served for Russian Orthodox Easter celebrations, along with a stately plain yeast cake similiar to a brioche. Molded into a tall, narrow pyramid, pahska is served cut into slices, as the consistency is similar to uncooked cheesecake. Its flavor is clean, slightly acid, and never runny or moldy. In lieu of a carved, truncated wooden pahska mold, a mesh or metal colander with the capacity of about 2½ quarts will do nicely. A cone-shaped chinois strainer is close to the traditional shape, right down to its planed tip. Pahska must sit in the refrigerator for 2 days, where it will drain off a surprising amount of liquid, so place the mold over a shallow bowl and cover it with plastic wrap to protect the delicate flavors.

Decorate the unmolded pahska with whole blanched almonds, placing them down the sides. Surround with whole, fresh strawberries and a few flowers, if desired, and sliced Easter breads.

1 cup heavy (whipping) cream
1½ teaspoons vanilla extract or finely minced
*   vanilla bean*
2 tablespoons fruit liqueur, such as apricot,
*   pear, or raspberry*
2½ pounds fresh farmer's cheese
1 cup (2 sticks) unsalted butter at room
*   temperature*
2 egg yolks
1 cup superfine sugar
Grated zest of 1 orange and 1 lemon
¼ cup dried currants
¼ cup golden raisins
¼ cup minced dried apricots
¼ cup minced dried pineapple
½ cup slivered blanched almonds

1. Whip the cream with the vanilla and liqueur until soft peaks form. Set aside. Combine the cheese and butter with a wooden spoon or an electric mixer, beating until fluffy and well blended. Add the yolks one at a time and beat in the sugar. Add the whipped cream mixture and the zests, fruits, and nuts. Mix just to combine evenly.
2. Line the mold with 2 layers of damp cheesecloth, with the excess hanging over the edge. Spoon the cheese mixture into the mold, filling it to the brim. Fold the edges of cloth over the cheese. Cover with plastic wrap and place a heavy object, such as a foil-wrapped brick, on the cheese. Place over a shallow bowl and refrigerate from overnight to 2 days.
3. To unmold, place a serving plate over the mold and invert. Gently lift off the mold and remove the cheesecloth. Stud the sides with the whole blanched almonds. Serve immediately or refrigerate until serving time. Refrigerate any leftovers immediately and store, tightly wrapped, for up to 4 days.

ACCOMPANIMENTS AND SAUCES

Citrus Curd

The perfect spread for toasted English muffins, waffles, and fresh scones.

Yield: About 2 cups

½ cup (1 stick) unsalted butter
⅔ cup fresh or frozen orange, tangerine, tangelo, mandarin, or blood orange juice
¼ cup fresh lemon juice
Grated zest of 2 oranges
Grated zest of 1 lemon
⅔ cup sugar
4 eggs
2 egg yolks

Melt the butter in the top section of a double boiler. Beat together the remaining ingredients with a whisk or in a blender or food processor. With the water at a simmer, slowly add the egg mixture to the butter, stirring constantly with a whisk. Cook over medium heat, stirring constantly, until thickened, a full 10 minutes. Pour into a jar and let cool before storing in the refrigerator for up to 3 weeks.

Lemon-Mustard Mayonnaise

Serve this classic *maionese al limone* with Vegetable and Mozzarella Torta Rustica, page 84.

Yield: 1¼ cups

1 egg
Grated zest of 1 large lemon

1 small garlic clove, pressed
2 teaspoons Dijon mustard
¼ teaspoon salt
⅛ teaspoon each paprika and ground white pepper
1 tablespoon each fresh lemon juice and white wine vinegar
¼ cup olive oil
¾ cup vegetable oil

Combine all the ingredients except the oils in a blender or a food processor fitted with the metal blade. While the machine is running, immediately begin pouring in the oils in a slow, steady stream. Process until thick. This sauce may also be made by hand with a whisk. Refrigerate until serving, for up to 1 week.

Creamed Wild Mushrooms

I serve this mushroom dish over Buckwheat Yeast Waffles, page 104, for dinner or brunch. It is also good served in individual *croustades* of French rolls. Try this recipe with 2 cups chopped cooked chicken in place of the mushrooms.

Yield: 6 servings

6 tablespoons unsalted butter
1 pound cultivated or wild fresh mushrooms (such as chanterelles, shiitake, oyster, or porcini), wiped clean with a damp paper towel and sliced
3 tablespoons dry sherry
6 tablespoons unbleached all-purpose flour
1½ cups homemade or canned chicken broth
1 cup heavy (whipping) cream

1 teaspoon salt or to taste
⅛ teaspoon ground white pepper
¼ cup chopped fresh parsley

1. In a large skillet or sauté pan, heat half of the butter over high heat until foamy and add the sliced mushrooms. Sauté until tender, stirring frequently. Add the sherry and cook until the liquid is just evaporated. Remove from heat and set aside.
2. In a large saucepan, melt the remaining butter over low heat. Whisk in the flour and stir with the whisk until well blended. Cook for 1 minute, or until bubbly. Remove from heat and stir in the broth and cream. Return to heat and bring to a boil. Cook, stirring constantly, until thick and smooth, about 1 minute.
3. Add the sautéed mushrooms and salt and pepper. Garnish with parsley and serve immediately.

Watercress-Dill Sauce

This is a luscious sauce to serve with Coulibiac in Buckwheat Brioche, page 86.

Yield: About 2½ cups

2 cups good mayonnaise or light sour cream
2 tablespoons fresh lemon juice
¼ cup minced fresh dill
1 bunch watercress, stemmed
3 green onions, including 1 inch of green

Place all the ingredients in a blender or food processor and blend until just evenly textured and almost smooth. Store in a covered container in the refrigerator until serving, for up to 5 days.

Champagne-Herb Mustard

Try this on Ham in Rye Buns, page 87.

Yield: About 1¼ cups

2 tablespoons fresh parsley sprigs
1 tablespoon each fresh dill and tarragon
*   leaves*
1 teaspoon champagne vinegar
1 cup Dijon-style mustard

In a blender or food processor, combine the herbs, vinegar, and mustard. Blend until smooth. Store in a jar with a tight-fitting lid in the refrigerator for up to 2 weeks.

Tomato-Basil Sauce

This is an excellent all-purpose sauce for pizza. Please note that it is better to chop or crush the tomatoes or to push them through a sieve or food mill than to puree them, as a rather chunky texture is desirable.

Yield: 3 cups

One 28-ounce can plum tomatoes packed in
*   puree*
2 garlic cloves
¼ cup good olive oil
3 tablespoons red wine
2 tablespoons chopped fresh basil, or 2
*   teaspoons dried*
1 tablespoon chopped fresh oregano, or 1
*   teaspoon dried*
Fresh-ground black pepper

Coarsely chop or crush the tomatoes, or push them through a food mill or sieve. In a large skillet or sauté pan, sauté the garlic briefly in the oil. Add the tomatoes and wine. Bring to a boil and adjust heat to low. Simmer uncovered for 15 minutes. Add the herbs and pepper and cook 5 minutes longer. The sauce will keep in the refrigerator for 2 days and in the freezer for up to 1 month.

Maple Stewed Blueberries

A very special topping for waffles.

Yield: About 2½ cups

3 tablespoons unsalted butter
¼ cup pure maple syrup
2 cups (1 pint) fresh or frozen blueberries

In a medium saucepan, combine all the ingredients and bring to a boil. Immediately turn heat to low and simmer until thick and juicy, about 5 minutes. Take care not to break up the whole berries.

Spiced Honey

Yield: 1 pint

2 cups light-colored honey, local if possible
1 vanilla bean, split
One 4-inch cinnamon stick
2 whole star anise
2 whole cloves

In a small saucepan or a microwave, heat the honey until just warmed. Place the spices in the bottom of a decorative spring-top or canning jar. Pour the warm honey over the spices in the jar. Cover and let sit at room temperature for 1 week to meld flavors.

Spiked Maple Syrup

Tennessee whiskey is the most famous American spirit and has a light, sweet flavor that is a favorite addition to both sweet and savory sauces.

Yield: About 1¼ cups

1 cup pure maple syrup
2 tablespoons Jack Daniel's whiskey or to taste
2 tablespoons unsalted butter

In a small saucepan, combine all the ingredients and simmer over low heat until the butter is melted, stirring occasionally. Pour into a small pitcher and serve hot.

Orange Syrup

Serve warm or chilled on crisp waffles.

Yield: About 2 cups

1 cup granulated sugar
½ cup orange juice concentrate
½ cup water
½ cup (1 stick) unsalted butter

In a medium saucepan, combine all ingredients and bring to a boil, stirring with a whisk. Reduce for 1 to 2 minutes, or until thickened.

Maple-Nut Granola

The secret to making excellent granola is to use very fresh, high-quality rolled oats and brans. This combination is so delicious, you'll be glad to have made what seems like such a big batch.

Yield: About 16 cups

Dry Ingredients
6 cups (1 pound) rolled oats
1½ cups raw sunflower seeds
1 cup (4 ounces) wheat bran
1 cup (4 ounces) wheat germ
1 cup (4 ounces) oat bran
1 cup instant nonfat dry milk
1 cup raw almonds or other nuts, chopped or
  slivered
1 cup unsweetened shredded coconut
⅓ cup raw sesame seeds
1 tablespoon ground cinnamon

Wet Ingredients
⅓ cup pure maple syrup
½ cup local honey, warmed for easier pouring
1 cup sunflower seed oil or other
  cold-pressed oil
1 teaspoon pure vanilla extract
½ teaspoon pure almond extract

1 cup raisins, currants, or dried cherries
1 cup dried apricots, chopped (or other
  favorite dried fruit)

1. Preheat the oven to 250°. Line 2 large baking sheets with aluminum foil or parchment. Set aside.
2. In a large bowl, combine all the dry ingredients and stir well. In a medium bowl, combine the wet ingredients with a small whisk.
3. Combine the wet and dry ingredients and stir until evenly moistened. Spread evenly onto the baking sheets. Bake in the center of the preheated oven for about 1½ hours, stirring every 20 to 25 minutes with a spatula for even toasting, or until pale golden and dry. When done, the granola will slide off the spatula and be a very light color. Do not brown, as the granola continues to cook while cooling and will become too toasted and strong in flavor. While hot, stir in the raisins and apricots on the baking sheets and place the sheets on a rack to cool completely. The mixture will become crisp as it cools. Remove to a tightly covered container and store in the refrigerator.

SOURCE DIRECTORY

Although this book was written to utilize the ingredients widely available in ordinary supermarkets and natural foods stores, included here is a list of regional specialty mills; sources for exceptional grains, hard-to-find ingredients, and special equipment; and seed houses that feature grains.

Quality Flours and Grains

The best flours come from small gristmills that grind their own grains. These creaky wooden wheels resting on the banks of swift-rushing creeks and rivers produce flours that are the pride of their millers. Most small mills buy from local farmers growing open-pollinated corn and grains without chemicals. Some East Coast mills, such as the Kenyon Mill in Rhode Island, date back to the 1600s. West Coast mills were mostly built in the mid-1800s, after the Gold Rush. Every mill is a repository of colorful anecdotes and local history. In the days before agribusiness, when America was predominantly an agricultural community, each neighborhood had its own mill, which was the social center for the town. As long as a mill could support a family, it was passed down for generations. Many mills fell into a state of disrepair until being restored by people interested in renewing the tradition of pure flours and meals, such as the owners of Gray's Grist Mill in Rhode Island and the War Eagle Mill in Arkansas. Today, they are functioning mills that are also tourist attractions and sources of local pride.

Historic gristmills are great places to visit as well as to buy fresh grains and flours. Here grains are rubbed between two water-powered thousand-pound granite millstones (known as "buhrs") to create a variety of finely textured stone-ground flours and nutty meals. Unlike those for mass-produced flours, the grains used in gristmills have not been stripped of their germ, or heart, and bran, which contain the vitamins.

Many mills use organically grown grains, and none adds preservatives to the flours. Slow rolling speeds assure that no extra heat will destroy the precious nutrients. This technique utilizes the same principle as the grinding stones used by Native Americans centuries ago, and the small European rotary household quern.

The mammoth millstones for some mills were shipped from France, where some quarries produced a particularly dense granite. The mills of the Southwest, such as the Cortez Mill in Southern Colorado, tend to be gravity-fed and cater to Indian trading posts, although many farmers have their own small facilities. Some small commercial mills, such as Grain Millers and Guisto's on the West Coast, Arrowhead Mills in the Southwest, and Weisenberger's in the South, rely on electric rollers, but are known for their dedication to producing the highest grades of flours. These flours usually are sold mostly to local restaurants and small groceries, or by mail order.

Mail-order sources for flour and grains offer their own catalogs and take telephone orders. The prices are moderate, but shipping is extra, and the grains can be very heavy. All come in attractive paper or cloth sacks, many with individual touches such as twine closed with a miller's knot, hand drawings of the mill on the bags, or the mill's own collection of recipes. These are outstanding products for baking. Some local products are otherwise available only by mail order, such as the blue corn products from Casados Farms on the San Juan Pueblo of New Mexico, which buys blue corn exclusively from Indian pueblos such as Santo Domingo; and Gray's Grist Mill's Narragansett Indian flint corn, the original strain of Indian corn grown by the colonists in New England. Please note that all stone-ground products should be stored in the refrigerator or freezer on arrival.

EAST COAST

Brewster River Mill
Mill Street
Jeffersonville, VT 05464
802-644-2987

Organic stone-ground wheat, corn, rye, oat, and buckwheat flours

Burnt Cabins Grist Mill
Burnt Cabins, PA 17215
717-987-3244

Original 16-foot overshot wheel; water-ground wheat, corn, rye, buckwheat

Cabot Farmer Co-op Creamery
P.O. Box 128
Cabot, VT 05647
802-563-2231

Premium aged cheddars

Falling Waters Stone-ground Flours and Meals
1788 Tuthilltown Grist Mill
Albany Post Road
Gardiner, NY 12525
914-255-5695

Stone-ground wheat, corn, and buckwheat flours and meals

Gray's Grist Mill
P.O. Box 422
Adamsville, RI 02801
508-636-6075

Stone-ground cornmeal from local Narragansett Indian flint corn

Great Valley Mills
687 Mill Road
Telford, PA 18969
800-366-6268

Large selection of whole-grain flours; in operation since 1710 (supplied Washington's troops during the Revolution)

Johnny's Selected Seeds
Foss Hill Road
Albion, ME 04910

Roughrider winter wheat, rye, oats, and amaranth seeds

Kenyon Cornmeal Company
Usquepaugh
West Kingston, RI 02892
401-783-4054

Stone-ground grains and flours, johnnycake meal

King Arthur Flour & Bakers Catalog
R.R. #2, P.O. Box 56
Norwich, VT 05055
800-827-6836

Grains, flours, baking equipment

Morgan's Mills
R.D. #2, P.O. Box 115
Union, ME 04862
207-785-4900

Stone-ground red spring, soft and winter wheat; rye, oats, barley, rice, cornmeal; muffin and pancake mixes

New Hope Mills
R.D. #2, P.O. Box 269A
Moravia, NY 13118
315-497-0783

Bread flour, buckwheat, and cornmeal from the waterfalls of Bear Swamp Creek; fabulous pancake mixes

Shelbourne Farms
Harbor Road
Shelbourne, VT 05482
802-985-8686

Exceptional aged cheddars

Walnut Acres
Penns Creek, PA 17862
717-837-3874

Catalog of whole grains, flours, amaranth, and quinoa

Wood Prairie Farm
R.F.D. #1, P.O. Box 164
Bridgewater, ME 04735
207-429-9765

Organic heirloom potatoes

MIDWEST

American Spoon Foods
411 East Lake Street
Petoskey, MI 49770
800-222-5886

Dried cherries and blueberries, mushrooms, fruit preserves

Brumwell Flour Mill
328 East Second Street
Sumner, IA 50674
319-578-8106

Stone-ground flours and grains

The Grain Exchange
Garden Grains
2440 East Water Well Road
Salina, KS 67401

Catalog of grains suitable for home gardening

Great Grains Milling Company
P.O. Box 427
Scobey, MT 59263
406-783-5588

Whole-wheat flours

Hodgson Mill
P.O. Box 430
Teutopolis, IL 62467

Grains, flours, pancake mixes

SOUTH

Maskal Teff
P.O. Box A
Caldwell, ID 83606
208-454-3330

Teff flour and grain

Nu-World Amaranth, Inc.
P.O. Box 2202
Naperville, IL 60540
312-369-6819

Amaranth flour, puffed and multi-grain amaranth flour blends

Ojibwe Foods
Leech Lake Reservation
Rt. 3, P.O. Box 100
Cass Lake, MN 56633
218-335-6341

Premium wild rice products; high-bush cranberry and chokecherry syrups and jam

St. Marie's Wild Rice
P.O. Box 293
St. Marie's, ID 83861
800-225-9453

Very mild-flavored wild rice

Teals Super Valu
P.O. Box 660
Cass Lake, MN 56633
218-335-2249

Top-grade hand-harvested wild rice

Adams Milling Company
Rt. 6, P.O. Box 148A
Napier Field Station
Dolthan, AL 36303

French millstone–ground Whole Heart grits and cornmeal

Della Gourmet Rices
P.O. Box 880
Brinkley, AK 72021
501-734-1233

Scented white and organic brown rices from Asian basmati strains

Falls Mill and Country Store
Rt. 1, P.O. Box 44
Belvedere, TN 37306
615-469-7161

Hand-quarried millstone-ground grits, cornmeal, and flours

Ledford Mill and Museum
R.R. #2, P.O. Box 152
Wartrace, TN 37183
615-455-1935/2546

Water-ground wheat, grits, and cornmeal; near the Jack Daniels Distillery

Old Mill of Guilford
1340 NC 68 North
Oak Ridge, NC 27310
919-643-4783

Water-ground and stone-ground flours, cornmeal, and grits

Shiloh Farms Flour
P.O. Box 97
Sulphur Springs, AR 72768
501-298-3297

Organic flours, meals, nuts, and beans

War Eagle Mill
Rt. 5, P.O. Box 411
Rogers, AR 72738
501-789-5343

Free catalog for stone-buhr ground cornmeal, wheat, and other grains

Weisenberger's Flour Mills
P.O. Box 215
Midway, KY 40347
606-254-5282

Small commercial mill specializing in Kentucky-grown wheat and corn; unbleached soft-wheat flour

White Lily Foods Company
P.O. Box 871
Knoxville, TN 37901
615-546-5511

The flour of the South; self-rising and pastry flour for biscuits

Woodson's Mill
P.O. Box 11005
Norfolk, VA 23517
800-446-8555

Nelson County white cornmeal for grits; johnnycake mix, three-grain pancake mix

SOUTHWEST

Arrowhead Mills, Inc.
P.O. Box 2059
Hereford, TX 79045
806-364-0730

Fine blue cornmeal, quinoa, amaranth, teff, and garbanzo flour; hearty organic grains

Blue Corn Connection
8812 Fourth Street NW
Alameda, NM 87144
505-897-2412

Blue corn and other corn products, earthenware, chilies

Casado Farms
P.O. Box 852
San Juan Pueblo, NM 87566
505-852-2433

Cornmeals and hominy from local pueblo corn

Coonridge Goat Cheese
Star Route
Pietown, NM 87827
505-842-5555

Goat cheeses in oil

Cortez Milling Company
P.O. Box 1030
Cortez, CO 81321
303-565-3119

Local hard red wheat from Utah and Colorado; Navajo maize

WEST COAST

Los Chileros
P.O. Box 6215
Santa Fe, NM 87501
505-471-6967

Blue corn products, *harinilla* (blue corn flour), coarse blue meal, dried chilies

Magic Mill
1911 South 3850 West
Salt Lake City, UT 84014
801-972-0707

Superior electric grain mills for household use

Mozzarella Cheese
2944 Elm Street
Dallas, TX 75226
214-741-4072

Fresh cow and goat cheeses with Italian and Southwest flavors

My Santa Fe Connection
P.O. Box 1863
Corrales, NM 87048
505-842-9564

Ristras, blue corn products, pine nuts

Quinoa Corporation
2300 Central Avenue, Ste. G
Boulder, CO 80301
800-237-2304

Bulk quinoa

Sierra Farms
P.O. Box 790
Tiejeras, NM 87059

Natural soft goat cheese

Butte Creek Mill
P.O. Box 561
Eagle Point, OR 97524
503-826-3531

Stone-ground flours since 1872, including graham, buckwheat, rye, corn, sesame, and soy meals; outstanding ten-grain cereal and muffin mix

Chukar Cherries
306 Wine Country Road
Prosser, WA 99350
800-624-9544

Dried cranberries and blueberries; sweet and tart dried cherries

DAK Industries
8200 Remment Avenue
Canoga Park, CA 91304
800-888-7808

Electronic breadmakers

Fall River Wild Rice
HC-01 Osprey Drive
Fall River Mills, CA 96028
916-336-5222

Wild rice

Gibbs Wild Rice
10400 Billings Road
Live Oak, CA 95053
916-695-1612

Excellent wild rice, and mixed brown and wild rice

Grain Millers
11100 NE Eighth, Ste. 710
Bellevue, WA 98009
800-443-8972

Organic oats from mills in Oregon and Iowa

Guisto's Specialty Foods
241 East Harris Avenue
S. San Francisco, CA 94080
415-873-6566

Fresh-ground organic grains and flours

Lundberg Family Farms
5370 Church Street
Richvale, CA 95974
916-882-4551

Organically grown aromatic rices

Mariani Nut Company
P.O. Box 808
Winters, CA 95694
916-795-3311

Gourmet nuts and dried fruits

McFadden Farm
Potter Valley, CA 95469
800-544-8230

Wild rice and organic herbs

Moore's Flour Mill
1605 Shasta Street
Redding, CA 96001

1550 South State Street
Ukiah, CA 95482
707-462-6550

Fresh-ground grains and flours from water-powered millstones

Nichols Garden Nursery
1190 North Pacific Highway
Albany, OR 97321

Specialty seeds

Olson Cherry Orchard
Rt. 1, P.O. Box 140,
El Camino Real
Sunnyvale, CA 94087
408-736-3726

Fresh and dried sweet cherries; cherry honey

Oregon Apiaries
P.O. Box 1078
Newberg, OR 97132
503-538-8546

Gourmet honeys

Oven Crafters
P.O. Box 24
Tomales, CA 94971

Plans for backyard brick ovens

Planned Pottery
294 Portland Street
Eugene, OR 97405
503-345-2471

Hand-crafted clay bread pans

**Redwood City Seed
Company**
P.O. Box 361
Redwood City, CA 94064

Early Stone Age wheat and amaranth
seeds

Seaside Banana Garden
6823 Santa Barbara Avenue
La Conchita, CA 93001
805-643-4061

The only West Coast organic banana
plantation

S.E. Rykoff & Co.
761 Terminal Street
Los Angeles, CA 90021
213-622-4131

Gourmet specialty foods catalog

Timbercrest Farms
4791 Dry Creek Road
Healdsburg, CA 95448
707-433-8251

Oil-packed sun-dried tomatoes

INDEX

*This book was
composed in Galliard types by
On Line Typography,
San Francisco*

*It was printed
and bound by
Dai Nippon Printing Co. Ltd.
Tokyo, Japan*

*Design & Production by
Ingalls + Associates
San Francisco*

mixture through the feed tube. Process until a ball is formed, about 30 seconds. Scrape the dough from the bowl.

3. Turn the dough out onto a lightly floured surface and vigorously knead to form a springy ball, adding flour 1 tablespoon at a time as necessary to prevent sticking, about 3 minutes. The dough should be quite soft, smooth, and very springy. Form into a flattened ball. Place in a greased deep container, turn once to coat the top, and cover with plastic wrap. Let rise at room temperature until tripled in bulk, about 1½ hours. The dough may be refrigerated overnight at this point and left to stand at room temperature for 45 minutes before proceeding. Prepare the toppings at this time and set them aside at room temperature or in the refrigerator, as necessary.

4. Preheat the oven to 500° or its highest setting. To simulate the intense, even heat of wood-burning brick ovens, place an unglazed baking stone or quarry tiles on the lowest rack of your oven at least 20 minutes before baking. If using power pans for the first time, season them by brushing with olive oil and baking them empty in a hot oven for 15 minutes. Remove, using insulated mitts, and cool before filling.

Shaping Dough with Rolling Pin or Hands

Rolling Pin: Flatten the dough into a disc. On a very lightly floured work surface, roll the dough from the center out, rotating it as you go. Lift the dough edges and flap them to relax them as you work. Place the dough round directly on a cornmeal- or semolina-sprinkled baker's paddle or pizza pan. This method is important for very thin and hard-to-stretch crusts such as semolina and whole wheat.

Stretching by Hand: Flour your hands and make two fists. Fit your fists under the center of the dough, forming a flat place for the dough to rest on. Gradually pull your fists apart, turning them at the same time to stretch the dough. Flour your hands when the dough becomes sticky. As the center becomes thin, move your fists farther apart. Work the dough to the desired diameter. Adjust the edges with your thumb and first finger to a thickness of ¼ to ½ inch. Place the dough round directly on a cornmeal- or semolina-sprinkled baker's paddle or pizza pan.

Pressing: Use the same technique as in rolling, but use your fingers to press and flatten from the center out in the pizza pan, taking care not to tear the dough, until it is evenly distributed.

Shaping Dough by Tossing:

Flour your hands lightly. Make two fists and cross your wrists under the center of the dough. In a smooth motion, stretch the dough by pulling it outward and uncrossing your wrists with a twisting motion to give the dough a spin and a toss at the same time. Cross your wrists farther down the sides of your arms to place your fists farther apart. The dough will be stretched in 2 to 3 tosses. Practice is the key here. Feel free to shape pizza as desired, in rectangular, round, or individual sizes. Immediately after shaping, assemble the toppings on the dough.

Tips for Great Pizza

- Limit yourself to 3 to 5 topping ingredients. Think of pizza as a starch plus a topping, like a sandwich.
- Include either a meat or a vegetable, an herb, and a cheese to balance the flavors.
- Always coat the dough with a layer of sauce or olive oil before assembling.
- Leave a full 1-inch margin around the edges to form a crust.
- Distribute the topping ingredients evenly, so that every bite will contain all flavors.

5. If using a baker's paddle, heavily sprinkle it with cornmeal or flour. The longer the dough sits on the paddle, especially if laden with too many topping ingredients, the softer it gets, and the greater the possibility that it will stick, creating a misshapen round. With a quick wrist motion, immediately slide the pizza onto the pan or shake directly onto a hot baking stone. Place pizza pans directly on the baking stone. Wipe and dry the paddle immediately after putting pizza into the oven.

6. Bake at the highest preheated temperature until the dough is crisp, the topping is hot, and the cheese is melted. Pizza cooked directly on a baking stone will take 8 to 10 minutes; pans can take 10 to 15 minutes. Always check the bottom of the crust with a large spatula during the baking time to assure a browned, crisp crust. The crust will soften as it sits after baking. Transfer the pizza to a cutting board and cut into wedges with a pizza wheel or a serrated bread knife.

Whole-Wheat Pizza Dough

For a rich, nutty flavor, substitute ½ cup whole-wheat flour and ¼ cup bran for an equal amount of unbleached flour. The more whole-wheat flour, the harder the dough will be to roll out, so be prepared to patch up holes if you use more.

Cornmeal Pizza Dough

Substitute ½ cup polenta or yellow, white, or blue cornmeal for ½ cup of unbleached flour.

Herbed Pizza Dough

Add 2 to 6 tablespoons of mixed chopped fresh herbs (or 1 to 3 tablespoons dried herbs), such as basil, tarragon, sage, rosemary, chervil, oregano, parsley, or marjoram, to the dough during mixing.

Garlic Pizza Dough

Add 2 cloves sautéed chopped or pureed roasted garlic to the dough during mixing.

Semolina Pizza Dough

For a flavorful, grainy texture, substitute ½ cup semolina flour for ½ cup unbleached flour.

Saffron Pizza Dough

Add ¼ teaspoon saffron threads to 1 cup boiling water. Let cool to 105° to 115°, then substitute for plain warm water.

Suggested Pizza Toppings

Oils: Virgin, extra-virgin, and pure olive oil; walnut oil; corn oil
Tomatoes: Fresh and canned Italian; sun-dried tomatoes; tomato paste
Cheese: Buffalo milk, cow's milk, smoked, and low-moisture mozzarella; fontina; provolone; Pecorino Romano; Parmesan; ricotta; Montrachet goat cheese; soft and dry jack; cheddar; Bel Paese; Gorgonzola
Olives: Black, purple, green, oil-cured, Italian, Greek, French, California
Peppers: Roasted or sautéed green, yellow, or red bells; dried or fresh chilies
Meats: Cooked pancetta, sweet or hot sausage, bacon, salami, pepperoni, prosciutto
Herbs and Spices: Onions, shallots, chives, green onions, garlic, fresh and dried herbs
And: Capers; fresh vegetables such as spinach, eggplant, and artichokes; anchovies and shrimp; wild and cultivated mushrooms.

Pane al Pizza con Formaggio (Pizza Pie with Cheese)

This is a layered pizza and cheese pie that is served in wedges hot from the oven with a glass of mellow red zinfandel. Use the combination of Italian cheeses suggested or three different kinds of mozzarella for variety.

Yield: One 9-inch torta

One recipe Pizza Dough, page 54

1 cup (4 ounces) each shredded mozzarella, Italian fontina, and smoked provolone
¾ cup (3 ounces) crumbled soft goat cheese such as Montrachet
1 cup (4 ounces) grated Parmesan
Cornmeal for dusting
Fresh-ground black pepper to taste

Egg Glaze, page 155

1. Prepare the pizza dough and let rise. Twenty minutes before baking, preheat the oven to 375° with a baking stone, if you like.
2. Combine the cheeses, reserving ⅓ cup of the Parmesan. Turn the dough out onto a lightly floured work surface and divide into 3 equal portions. With a rolling pin, roll the dough out to very thin 10-inch rounds. Place 1 round carefully in a greased and cornmeal-dusted 9-inch springform pan. Sprinkle with one half of the cheeses and fresh-ground pepper, leaving a 1-inch border all around. Brush the edge with egg glaze. Add a second layer of the rolled dough and sprinkle evenly with the remaining cheese and a little pepper. Brush the edge with egg glaze. Place the last layer on top. Roll the edges together in sections to form a rope pattern. Brush the top with egg glaze and sprinkle with the reserved Parmesan.
3. Place the pan immediately on a baking stone or an oven rack in the preheated oven until throughly browned, about 25 to 30 minutes. Remove from the oven and remove the springform sides. Slide the torta onto a cutting board and cut it while hot with a serrated knife.

Herbed Foccacia

The difference between pizza and focaccia is the thickness. Instead of being baked immediately after shaping to form a thin crisp crust, the dough is left to rise a second time before baking. Top with a simple com-

creature near Piltdown Common, Sussex County, England, after finding some flint tools on a casual stroll down a country lane. Over the next three years, he found flint tools and several other human and animal bones, including prehistoric mastodon, horse, and beaver. This seemed to prove the humanlike bones were very old, as old as those of the ancient animals. Dawson believed the pieces of jaw, teeth, eye socket, and other bones were from the same creature. When a famous anatomist pieced together the fragments of the skull, the result was a creature that looked human, except for its very apelike jaw. Another odd thing about the fossil was that the brain was very large, about the same as a modern human's. Scientists were divided in their opinions of this newly named *Eoanthropus dawsoni*, or "Dawson's Dawn Man" in Latin. Some thought it was the "missing link" between the apes and modern humans. Others were uncertain that the bits of bone even belonged to the same species of creature.

For more than 35 years, the Piltdown Mystery was unsolved. Many people spent a lot of time researching and writing about Piltdown Man, trying to prove their theories. Then, in 1949, new tests showed that the Eoanthropus bones were only about 50,000 years old, while the other animal bones were much older. A few years later, another test was done on the jaw and on the rest of the skull showing they were of different ages and could not be part of the same animal. In fact, the jaw was probably that of an orangutan!

Who was responsible for the Piltdown Hoax? No one is quite sure. Charles Dawson died suddenly in 1916, and there is still debate about who was to blame. Was Dawson just a bored lawyer who thought he could become famous as an archaeologist? Or was it an innocent mistake, maybe planted for him to find by someone else?

Modern Human Relatives

◆ Unlike the disappointment of Piltdown, most of the other bones that were being found were real. Once technology allowed scientists to compare the ages of the rest of the ancient tools and skulls that had been found, and they decided that Peking Man, Java Man, and many of the other recently found remains belonged to one ancestor of modern humans that they called *Homo erectus*.

Since the 1950s, there has been another change in the classification of *Homo erectus*. Scientists have now separated the African, Asian, and European *Homo erectus* back into different species. The earliest *Homo erectus*, the one that

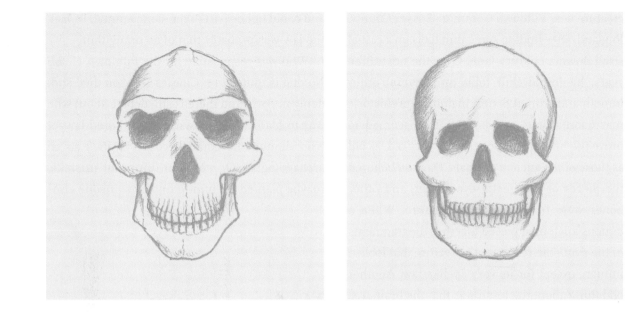

▲ *A Homo erectus skull (left) and a modern human skull (right).*

these discoveries were necessary for *Homo erectus* to survive in the cold climate of Northern Europe and Northern Asia.

Finding Remains

◆ At first, archaeologists did not believe that the skeletons and tools they were finding in Asia, Europe, and Africa were part of the same species. The first *Homo erectus* remains were found on the Indonesian island of Java by Eugene Dubois in 1890, but at the time Dubois referred to them scientifically as *Pithecanthropus erectus*, though most people called them Java Man. Similar remains found in China during the 1920s were called *Sinanthropus pekinensis*, or Peking Man. A German *Homo erectus* (found in 1907) was called *Homo heidelbergensis*, after the city of Heidelberg, which was six miles from where the remains were found in a commercial sand pit.

In 1908, an English lawyer and amateur archaeologist named Charles Dawson found some bits of bones from the skull of a humanlike